THE WHIG WORLD

The Whig World
1760–1837

Leslie Mitchell

Hambledon and London

London and New York

Hambledon and London

102 Gloucester Avenue, London N W 1 8H X

175 Fifth Avenue
New York, N Y 10010
USA

First Published 2005

ISBN 1 85285 456 1

A description of this book is available from the
British Library and from the Library of Congress.

Typeset by Carnegie Publishing Ltd, Lancaster
and printed in Great Britain by Cambridge University Press.

Distributed in the United States and Canada
exclusively by Palgrave Macmillan,
a division of St Martin's Press.

Contents

Illustrations

For Herrattis

Introduction

One of the strangest facts in British history, and one which had the most lasting consequences, was that Parliament was six hundred years old before universal suffrage emerged in 1918. In most European states, parliamentary life only began at the same time, or shortly before, the arrival of full democracy. In Britain, it was possible to be parliamentary without being democratic, which in the rest of Europe was largely impossible. Whigs were parliamentarians but not democrats. They passionately defended all the liberties associated with regular debate, the rule of law and a respect for majorities, but thought that universal suffrage might well put all this in jeopardy. Europe had no Whiggery because Europe had no parliamentary life before democracy. It was an exclusively British experience.

Today, of course, the link between parliamentary life and universal suffrage is thought to be unbreakable. It is a formula that America seems intent on exporting around the whole world. It has come to be regarded, with a certain lack of imagination, as the only acceptable system. Even so, criticisms are made of it and appear to be growing louder. If Parliament is controlled by public opinion, and that public opinion is moulded by an international media, who then effectively governs? Should it be a matter of concern that the bulk of public opinion may be neither educated, interested or informed? Why, having achieved universal suffrage, are fewer and fewer people inclined to vote? Perhaps the linking of parliamentary life with democracy is unsafe. The Whigs would certainly have thought so.

Whigs could only operate in a system where parliamentary life was firmly separated from most democratic considerations. It was a world with parties and elections, but, before the 1832 Reform Bill, only 14 per cent of adult males voted; and only 18 per cent could do so even after the Bill had passed. Politicians in London were under few of the pressures that complicate the careers of their modern counterparts. To be sure, some account had to be taken of the occasional mob, for otherwise windows would be broken and limbs endangered. Similarly, in the period 1780–1850, newspapers and reviews were founded, and their voices became more and more querulous. But for most of the time, for politicians living in the great west London squares, these were noises off. As a result, politics may have been more or less moral or more or less efficient. It was certainly different.

Far removed from democratic constraints, Whigs enjoyed a freedom of action and behaviour that modern politicians would find heady. Great aristocrats by wealth and birth, they did not so much despise public opinion as ignore it (unless a mob, like a bad winter, occasionally had to be noticed). Even if their morals and ideas were adversely dissected in cartoons and pamphlets, this had no consequences. Their position in politics was assured. Newspaper campaigns, which today routinely destroy political careers, had no purchase in their world. Whigs were free to think, speak and behave as they thought fit. It was a power which they often used reasonably and sometimes abused. In government, they had the option of leading opinion, along the path of religious toleration for example, being more knowing than their fellow men. In opposition, they had the privilege of being troublemakers, articulating views that governments did not wish to hear.

Whigs had another claim to status in this parliamentary, pre-democratic world. Quite simply, parliamentary life was Whig, in the sense that the Whigs had guaranteed its existence. In 1642, when Charles I had tried to destroy Parliament, Whig families had challenged him on the battlefield. In 1688, Parliament, for the first time, acquired an assured place in the country's political life, because Whigs had forced the despotic James II into exile in France. After 1688, Parliament had to be summoned every year. Whigs regarded these events as their victories. If Britain was odd because Parliament survived the dangers of the seventeenth century, the Whigs, as the patrons of Parliament, were for a time the national party.

It is therefore scarcely surprising that, from 1688 to 1760, the accession of George III, the Whigs were almost always in power. They were the party of government. The horrors of the seventeenth century gave way to a remarkable stability. Sir Robert Walpole was Prime Minister for twenty-one years (1721–42). Englishmen enjoyed trial by jury, Habeas Corpus and an increasingly free press. Their European cousins had none of these things. In a way, the Whigs were owed a debt of gratitude. A grateful country should have absorbed sharp lessons.

To be out of office for most of the period 1760–1830 therefore came, in contrast, as something of a shock. It needed explanation. Perhaps it was owing to George III's ambition to achieve what his Stuart ancestors had failed to achieve. No sooner, however, was the problem of an overmighty executive dealt with by the 1832 Reform Act than people began to talk about the advantages of universal suffrage. With would-be autocrats defeated, democrats appeared. Neither offered any future for the Whigs. As very specialised animals, they needed a parliamentary environment free of democratic constraints. There was a moment in the eighteenth and nineteenth centuries between autocracy and democracy that might be called the parliamentary period. It alone provided the oxygen which Whigs could breathe freely.

Living with the Whigs for the whole of a professional career has been very congenial. I count myself very fortunate. Expounding their way of life and habits of thinking has always been a great pleasure. Lecture audiences and pupils in tutorials have patiently listened to the stories, often laughed in the right places, and have exercised a sobering restraint on undue enthusiasm. I hope this book gives them the opportunity to reacquaint themselves with a tale to which they have indirectly contributed so much. I also hope that it will amuse many people to whom the mysteries of Whiggery are at present unknown. Special thanks must go to Alicia Black, Crofton Black, David Graham and Martin Sheppard for so professionally turning a manuscript into a book.

1

The Whigs

Who or what was a Whig? Between 1760 and 1837, many people claimed the title and just as many disavowed it. There was a political party of that name, but it was one of the most unsuccessful in British history. During the reign of George III and his sons, a period of seventy-seven years, the party enjoyed power for barely ten. Men with serious political ambitions, who wanted to sit in governments and do things, very sensibly avoided the Whigs. In 1830, few people living could remember a Whig government of any consequence, and what could be called to mind was unedifying. The so-called Whig administrations of 1765, 1782, 1783–84 and 1806–7, all of which were in fact coalitions with mongrel features, had been ugly experiences. Whigs seemed to have an unlimited talent to subdivide and bicker. In the 1780s, the Lansdowne Whigs fought the Rockingham Whigs. Ten years later, the Portland Whigs separated from the Foxites. Their taste for self-destruction was so marked that, from time to time, their political opponents were driven to beg them to pull themselves together, as their disagreements disqualified them both as a potential government or as a useful opposition. Quite literally, they seemed to offer the country nothing of value.

Whigs seemed to hold no common ground. Every issue engendered new disagreements. Every Whig seemed to be a party in his own right and, what was worse, to glory in the fact. They differed about the merits of Lord North, the Grenvilles and George Canning as coalition partners. There was no common view about the French Revolution or Bonaparte. Radicals were to be cosseted or shunned. Queen Caroline was either the rightful Queen of England or a harlot. Some Whigs were happy to receive the wife of Charles James Fox, while others thought that an ex-courtesan should know her place. On issues of national importance, and on the detail of social life, Whigs polished their differences. Their lack of party discipline was almost a matter of pride.

Party managers like William Adam had a thankless task. Whigs could never be counted on to attend Parliament or to vote the right way if they did. There was a childish wilfulness about so much of what they said and did.

Not surprisingly, many contemporaries abandoned the effort to define a Whig, They might admit that it had had a certain coherence before 1760. Whigs had done good work in opposing the wicked schemes of Stuart kings and in effecting the Glorious Revolution of 1688. But once parliamentary government had been assured, they seemed to have lost their way. The word Whig had become so diffuse as to be meaningless. They were exasperating. As a letter to the editor of the *Anti-Jacobin* put it, in March 1798:

> I will tell you in confidence ... that at present, when I am asked, what is it to be a Whig? 'J'y perds mon Latin', as our pleasant French neighbours so happily express it – I am asked, Is a man *born* a Whig, or is he *made* a Whig? and by what process?
> Is he once a Whig, and a Whig for ever?
> Does it go in Families?
> Can it be in *abeyance* – or lost? – or surrendered – or forfeited?
> Can a Whig be divested of the name by other *Whigs* who are more numerous or better united, and give *the ton*?
> Is it in the power of Clubs to monopolize it by a sort of Patent?
> Can a *Minister* be a Whig – and what makes a Ministerial Whig?[1]

These are all good questions, but none of them admitted of an easy answer. Not surprisingly, many people gave up the struggle and stopped taking the Whigs seriously.

One way out of the dilemma was to argue that the term had become obsolete. George IV in old age thought that 'the names Whigs and Tories meant something a hundred years ago, but are mere nonsense nowadays'.[2] But then he was at the same time fantasising about riding the winner of the Cheltenham Gold Cup and leading a cavalry charge at the battle of Talavera. Other witnesses are needed and they are not hard to find. In February 1830, *Fraser's Magazine*, a serious mouthpiece of the political Right, told its readers that 'we do not at present discern even the elements of what were once the so strongly marked distinctions of Whig and Tory'.[3] The word Whig carried historical resonance, but was void of all contemporary relevance. People who claimed it were either stuck in the past or happy to wave it as a kind of flag of convenience.

Some contemporaries thought that politicians were very much in need of one or two vague labels to cover up the unpalatable fact that party life was dead in England, and that politics had been reduced to an unsavoury scramble for jobs, pensions and sinecures. In this respect, the word Whig would do very nicely. It was indeed very convenient. In 1831, John Doyle produced a devastating cartoon entitled *Tommy Grey with the Tail of his Order!! or Look What a Long Tail our Cat Has Got*. It showed a cat with the face of the Prime Minister, Charles Grey. His self-satisfied smile in unmistakable. Equally clear was what was giving him pleasure. The cat's tail is divided up into sections, each of which gives the name of one of Grey's relations who had benefited at the public expense from his arrival in office. Now, Grey called himself a Whig and made a habit of appealing to Whig principles, but, since such principles were always disputed and cloudy, many people thought the word no more than a fig-leaf that barely covered flagrant corruption. The Russian Princess Lieven, who knew English politicians well, not least through sleeping with a number of them, was very clear on this point:

> It is ridiculous to say that there are political parties in England – it isn't true. There are only men who wish to keep their places, and others who wish to occupy them. These two parties only have a real existence. They adapt their principles to circumstances ... The place, not the thing, makes the man.[4]

For witnesses such as these, the label Whig was nothing more than a device which allowed a public man to be as capricious and corrupt as he wished.

To make matters worse, the experience, rare though it was, of actually being in government failed to produce any clearer definition of what the word meant. Commonly the governments headed by first Grey and then Melbourne between 1830 and 1841 are called Whig. But this was disputed, not least by Cabinet Ministers. People like Grey, Holland and Lord John Russell were comfortable with the label. It fitted them. On the other hand, Henry Brougham always regarded himself as a Radical, and the Duke of Richmond saw himself as an Ultra-Tory. Lord Althorp had Grenvillite antecedents, while Melbourne and Palmerston sometimes called themselves Canningites.[5] Cabinets of this period were in fact

political stews containing left-overs from several earlier political traditions. To call them all Whig was, on the face of it, as misleading as giving
them any other single denomination. Quite simply, they had been
brought together by the peculiar circumstances of 1830, and would
probably disintegrate once those circumstances changed. Sydney Smith,
allegedly a Whig, saw no reason not to take a good dinner off a Tory.
With splendid gastronomic cynicism, he insisted that

> Tory and Whig in turn shall be my host,
> I taste no politics in boiled or roast.[6]

Niceties of party life should never be allowed to interfere with the
digestive processes.

The hybrid nature of government in the 1830s merely followed an
established pattern. Apparently, Whig principles were so flexible that
they could be accommodated within the most surprising liaisons. For
most of the American War of Independence, Whigs had vilified Lord
North as someone who wanted to establish a tyranny over the colonies.
The Whig party colours of buff and blue were copied from the uniforms
of Washington's soldiers. To parade around London dressed as American rebels was designed to irritate North and his master, George III. In
this, they succeeded. But, in 1783, North and the Whigs became allies in
coalition. So notorious was this union of recent enemies that it was ever
after referred to as *the* Coalition. It was the unparalleled example of
political opportunism. In the general election of 1784, a pamphlet was
circulated entitled *The Beauties and Deformities of Fox, North and Burke*.
It was coruscating in its simplicity. It set out in parallel columns what
each of these gentlemen had said about the others over the previous
decade. How could Whiggery be taken seriously when it demonstrated
so little self-respect?

Worse was to come. Entering coalitions with detested opponents was
habit-forming. The Younger Pitt was a particular object of Whig distaste. Even though Pitt himself always, confusingly, called himself 'an
Independent Whig', party rhymesters and cartoonists had endless fun in
commenting on his private and public life. The 'Pitt of Hell' and the
'Bottomless Pitt' were just two of the more salubrious epithets that were
coined. Yet none of this was any impediment to serious attempts to
enter government as Pitt's partners in 1792 and 1804. Then the same

thing happened with George Grenville. He was first demonised as one of the main proponents of what Whigs saw as disastrous attitudes adopted towards the French Revolution and Bonaparte but then cheerfully embraced as a partner in the Talents Ministry of 1806–7. With respect to the possibility of a Canning government, in 1827, the Whigs excelled themselves. Some joined the administration, some opposed it, and some stood neuter. Here was a record of political promiscuity that led many to conclude that to discuss the question of Whig principles was simply to waste time. As a writer in *Blackwood's Magazine* observed:

> The nation actually thought, that a party which had made so many unnatural changes of side – which had been the common home of men of the most opposite opinions – had no principles whatsoever.[7]

Of course it followed that, if North, Pitt, Grenville and Canning were prepared to countenance, or solemnise, a coalition with Whigs, their principles must also have been somewhat elastic. But for some reason they were never called to account so regularly or so bitterly for their activities. Rather it was always the Whigs who were denounced as the ultimate political mongrels. Pitt was virtuous, Fox unprincipled. To explain this discrepancy is not easy, but it must have its origins in perceptions of Whig indiscipline. In private and public life, there was a randomness about their behaviour that could not inspire trust. At no level and on no subject could they take a common line. They appeared to be congenital nonconformists. The moral chaos which marked the private lives of many Whigs inevitably made them untrustworthy and unprincipled politicians. It was a common view, between 1760 and 1837, that the glorious Whiggery of the late seventeenth and early eighteenth centuries had become irrevocably tarnished. The word Whig no longer meant anything definable or of substance in politics.

A defence of Whiggery clearly has to go beyond politics. If Whig politics is to be explained, let alone justified, it is to understand that Whigs, as public men, were moulded by a whole range of factors. These included upbringing and marriage, a particular reading of the past, and the views of those who were your social equals, your 'acquaintance'. At its most basic, it was a question of instinct, of a preference for change over the status quo, of a belief that things could be done better.

Compared to these primeval forces, the actual detail of a political creed mattered little. As a political commentator of 1832 put it:

> This man is a fierce Whig or Tory, without knowing any thing of party creeds, because he was reared one, or became one early in life through accident, – that man devoutly believes in every thing Whigs or Tories utter, because he is a churchman and landowner, or a dissenter and manufacturer. Here a man outrageously lauds a measure because his neighbour abuses it; and there one execrates a principle because it strikes at his property ... Thus, if we analyse society, we can scarcely find one party man who has chosen his party from a careful examination of its creed, or who judges impartially of public measures as they come before him.[8]

To look to define Whiggery only or mainly in its political manifestations, in parliamentary speeches or coalition-making, is a mistake. It was most sure of itself in other contexts. It grew out of the psychology of individuals.

A political allegiance was therefore almost an inevitability. By instinct a man either had the caution of the conservative or the confidence of the reformer. This basic predisposition, reinforced by historical experience, family pressures and social contacts, determined political affiliations. John Wilson Croker called himself a Tory and dubbed his literary sparring-partner Henry Brougham a Whig. Brougham may not have found this flattering, but Croker's argument is compelling:

> There are two great antagonistic principles at the root of all government – stability and experiment. The former is Tory, and the latter Whig; and the human mind divides itself into these classes as naturally and as inconsiderately, as to personal objects, as it does into indolence and activity, obstinacy and indecision, temerity and versatility, or any other of the various different or contradictory moods of the mind ... I don't believe that any circumstances could have made you a Tory or me a Whig. We might very easily have been thrown into those parties. You might have attached yourself to Pitt, and I might have been a humble follower of Fox, but amongst our more homogeneous associates, we should have been considered as 'crotchety, troublesome fellows'.[9]

Palmerston took the same view. It was all a matter of contrasting 'those who hold liberal opinions and are friendly to improvement; and those whose prejudices are opposed to all innovation'.[10] Whigs were made by nature and confirmed by nurture.

Walter Bagehot took up this point in an essay in the great Whig journal, the *Edinburgh Review*. There was nothing to be gained by trying to
pin Whiggery down to a set of specific formulas. Whigs started with a
cool, informed nod towards the possibility of change, and everything
followed from that:

> In this defence of the principle of innovation ... the *Edinburgh Review* was
> but the doctrinal organ of the Whigs. A great deal of philosophy has been
> expended in endeavouring to fix and express theoretically the creed of that
> party: various forms of abstract doctrine have been drawn out, in which elab-
> orate sentence follows hard on elaborate sentence, to be set aside, or at least
> vigorously questioned by the next or succeeding enquirers. In truth Whig-
> gism is not a creed, it is a character. Perhaps as long as there has been a
> political history in this country there have been certain men of a cool, mod-
> erate, resolute firmness, not gifted with high imagination, little prone to
> enthusiastic sentiment, heedless of large theories and speculations, careless of
> dreamy scepticism; with a clear view of the next step, and a wise intention
> to act on it; with a strong conviction that the elements of knowledge are true,
> and a steady belief that the present world can, and should be, quietly
> improved. These are the Whigs.[11]

Alexis de Tocqueville was fascinated by the phenomenon of Whiggery,
not least because it had no equivalent in France, much to his regret. He
agreed with Bagehot about Whigs being defined by 'instincts' rather
than 'definite opinions', and that they were progressive. But he worried
that they were not always aware of where they were going; 'they let
themselves be carried without resistance by the spirit of the age which
goes that way. Those are the Whigs; they keep marching day by day
without knowing too much about where the road they follow will
end.'[12]

Both Bagehot and Tocqueville thought it futile to look for definitions
of Whiggery in party programmes, and two more credible witnesses
could hardly be produced. Both men agreed that a Whig was formed
instinctively in accepting and adapting to change, though one thought
he marched forward clear-eyed while the other pitied him as only half-
focused. Their perception on this point helps to explain why the problem
of Whigs forming coalitions with erstwhile opponents is not as damning
as many contemporaries found it. Quite simply, if Lord North or George
Grenville or George Canning was constrained by unusual political

circumstances to join Whigs on their progressive jaunt, they would be welcome. If party affiliation is determined by inflexible creeds, finding new allies is difficult if not impossible. If it is a matter of instinct, however, fellow travellers might easily be accommodated for part of the journey. For a Whig, a coalition was always a compliment to their values rather than an appreciation of their new partners.

Of course those with an instinct for change are always likely to be in a minority for most of the time, or at least the Whigs thought so. Inertia, habit, the comforting warmth of tradition and custom all worked against Whig claims. They were acutely aware of not being in the majority in most years. Promising careers were wasted in decades of fruitless opposition. The whiff of martyrdom hung over many of them. In the darkest years of the 1790s, Whig doctors had no patients, Whig lawyers had no clients, and Whig politicians had no prospects. There were real penalties to be paid. But then there is perhaps nothing better to engender a sense of common feeling than a sense of shared persecution. The trials and sacrifices of former generations became part of the oral tradition of Whiggery. Being endlessly out of office came as no surprise to anyone. Between 1760 and 1830, Whiggery learnt to become an oppositional creed.

At times, the situation was so bad that political opponents of the Whigs gleefully predicted their imminent extinction. After the split of 1794, Fox led perhaps only fifty members of the House of Commons and a dozen or so in the Lords. The same sad figures could be recorded in the years following Waterloo:

> The Whig body was reduced until it consisted only of the old Whig families, their dependants, the adventurers who had got inextricably tangled with them, the religious sects who make Whiggism a part of their religious creed, and a few crack-brained political fanatics.[13]

But mere numbers never mattered to Whigs. As will be seen, they believed themselves to be richer, cleverer and more informed than their fellow men. Majority opinion was, almost by definition, less informed and easily manipulated. For example, popular irrational attitudes to the French Revolution and Bonaparte pushed the Whigs into limbo for over two decades. The Whigs believed, however, that sooner or later their own views would be vindicated, because they were right and in tune with the times. The Whigs shared many of the characteristics attributed to minorities, including feelings of isolation and persecution, but there was one great point of reassurance. They knew that they would not be in a minority forever, and they knew that they would win in the end.

In order to understand the vitality of Whig self-confidence, even self-satisfaction, in the long years of political failure, it is crucial to see them as more than politicians. Most parties are mere conveniences for men to act together in the public sphere. Whiggery was more than that. It was based on a sense of caste that carried assumptions about almost every aspect of daily life. Politics after all was only a matter of a few hours a day for a few months of the year. Although managing the consequences of the Industrial Revolution and the great wars against France after 1789 steadily added to the burden of parliamentary business and the length of the parliamentary day, for much of the eighteenth century politics had to be over by two or three in the afternoon when dinner was served. Whig women regularly complained if politics made their menfolk late. For nearly all women and many men the day really began when politics had been concluded.

As the dinner bell sounded, Whigs moved from political failure to social success. Whigs dominated the activities that filled the leisure hours of London's social elite. In the early eighteenth century, 'the Town', or West End, had defined itself against 'the City'. The latter was occupied by the men of trade and finance, the former by anyone who really mattered. An elaborate round of entertainments had been developed in 'the Town' for its amusement and instruction. Dinners, balls, drums, routs, lectures and assemblies punctuated the day. In all of these Whigs were pre-eminent. In terms of wealth, birth and intellect they had few competitors. Whig entertainments were more elaborate and Whig dinners more entertaining than any provided by political opponents, including those put on at the Court of George III, which was generally reckoned one of the dullest in Europe. For every political reverse suffered in the morning there would be some compensating social victory later in the day. Unlike many minorities, Whigs could never be ignored. Their social ascendancy guaranteed them headlines.

Wealth and position gave the Whigs an assurance that opponents found insufferable. However frequently the electorate rejected them at general elections, the ownership of pocket boroughs and inherited seats in the House of Lords gave them a political base that was unassailable. In addition, that same wealth brought social control. Even when most ineffective in Parliament, Whigs could actually look down on and pity Prime Ministers who led great majorities. William Pitt was a sad creature and Lord Liverpool was worse. These were quite literally lordly views, and those to whom they were addressed resented them deeply. Whigs seemed to be irrepressible. Every new failure seemed to breed more arrogance. If Whiggery is narrowed to a political term only, this uppityness would be hard to explain. Only by broadening the concept into many other areas can the phenomenon be understood. To understand the Whigs, it is therefore necessary to spend as much time on discussing lives lived outside politics as is devoted to the vagaries of parliamentary life.

If Whiggery is seen only as a political force, the dismissive remarks of George IV and Princess Lieven quoted earlier have value. If, however, Whiggery is also seen as instinct, and as a social force, then its vitality was far greater than those two witnesses would allow. Richard Watson certainly thought so and paid a heavy price for doing so. He was bishop of Llandaff, a diocese many muddy miles from London and containing more sheep than Anglicans. Normally, Llandaff was merely a stepping-stone to a more congenial diocese. But Watson voted with the Whigs on a controversial Bill in 1783, and his action so irritated George III that he was still only the Bishop of Llandaff when he died in 1816. Few man ever suffered more for his views. Yet Watson was clear that espousing Whiggery was embracing something positive:

> Let the pensioners and placemen say what they will, *Whig* and *Tory* are as opposite each other, as *Mr Locke* and *Sir Robert Filmer*, as the soundest sense, and the profoundest nonsense, and I must always conclude, that a man has lost his honesty, or his intellect, when he attempts to confound the ideas.[14]

To understand what these 'ideas' were invites a very wide enquiry.

It was more than that Whigs drank port after dinner while Tories preferred claret, although this was alleged by some diarists.[15] Every aspect of daily life could be given a political allegiance. Party discipline may have been less than perfect in Parliament, but common feeling could be confirmed in many other ways. The Russell family, Dukes of Bedford, were at the heart of the Whig world. One of them memorably described late Georgian politics as follows:

So the great battle between Whig and Tory was fairly joined; and its varying fortunes make the history of England from 1760–1832. In passionate earnestness, in fanatical faith, in close comradeship between allies, in complete unscrupulousness as to methods of defeating the foe, the strife bore all the characteristics of actual warfare; and the area of its operations covered all social as well as political life. The whole world was divided into Whigs and Tories. There were Whig families and Tory families, Whig houses and Tory houses, Whig schools and Tory schools, Whig universities and Tory universities. Thus the Duke of Norfolk and his clan were Whigs, the Duke of Beaufort and his clan were Tories; and the cleavage ran right down, through all ranks of the peerage into the untitled gentry. In London, Holland House was a Whig House; Northumberland House was a Tory house. In the country, Woburn was a centre of popular movements; Stowe, thirty miles off, the headquarters of Prerogative. Eton was supposed to cherish some sentimental affection for her former neighbours, the exiled Stuarts; so good little Whigs were sent to Harrow. Oxford had always borne a Jacobite character; so adolescent Whigs went to Cambridge. There were Tory poets, like Scott, and Whig poets, like Byron. There were Tory publishers, such as Murray,[16] and Whig publishers, such as Longman; Tory actors, like Kemble, and Whig actors, like Kean. There were even Tory prayers and Whig prayers, for of the two Collects for the King, which stand at the beginning of the Communion Service, the first was supposed to teach the Divine Right of kings, and the second the limitations of royal authority.

Members of the two great parties regarded one another with a genuine ill-favour and suspicion ... The first Earl of Leicester [Thomas Coke, 1752–1842], whose life spanned the most stormy age of English politics, used to say that his grandfather took him on his knee, and said, 'Now, Tom, mind that, whatever you do in life, you never trust a Tory.' And he used to add: 'I never have, and by God, I never will!' When a scion of a great Whig house married a Tory Lord Chamberlain, the head of the house, exclaimed in prophetic agony: 'That woman will undo all that we have been doing for two hundred years, and will make the next generation Tory.' It was said that a Whig child, who from her earliest hours had heard nothing but abuse of the Tories, said to her mother: 'Mamma, are Tories born wicked? Or do they grow wicked afterwards?' And I myself knew an ancient lady, who had been brought up in the innermost circles of Whiggery, and who never entered a hackney cab until she had ascertained from the driver that he was not a Tory.

Meanwhile Tories were by no means backward in reciprocating these amenities, and little Tories were trained to believe that Whiggery meant treason to kings, and impiety to God, and that all the frequenters of Whig houses were in their secret hearts atheists and revolutionaries. The high-water mark of this polemical intemperance was reached when the Tory ladies of society, infuriated by Queen Victoria's Whiggish proclivities, hissed their young sovereign at Ascot Races.[17]

Russell was not alone in playing the game of defining party by extra-political attributes. Lots of people who struggled to see clearly defined political programmes had no inhibitions about describing allegiances in other ways. Bulwer Lytton thought a Whig had probably lived in Paris too long, was half an atheist, gambled and womanised to excess, and prided himself on being in tune with the spirit of the age.[18] In 1822, schoolboys at Eton produced a magazine, the *Etonian*, which was devoted entirely to this theme. Two fictional Etonians are conjured up, Martin Stirling, a Tory, and Frank Wentworth, a Whig. Their rooms are described, including the contents of their bookshelves. Stirling's are dominated by volumes of Bampton sermons. Wentworth's, on the other hand, contain Adam Smith, Jeremy Bentham and, most compelling of all, a complete run of the *Edinburgh Review*, which was the Whigs' holy book.[19] Simply to have the famous Nollekens bust of Charles James Fox prominently on display in a drawing-room might be enough to establish a family's credentials.

Any study of Whiggery in the round therefore has to go beyond politics. It is perfectly reasonable to talk of a Whig state of mind and of a Whig lifestyle. Such a person probably lived in London rather than the country, had more sympathetic views about France and Frenchmen, had doubts about revealed religion and what passed for conventional morality, and behaved in a way that his fellow Englishmen would regard as too clever by half. To be a Whig was a matter of whom you dined with, whom you borrowed money from and whom you slept with. It was about preferences in reading and architecture, and therefore about whom you patronised. Whigs were likely to have had the same educational experiences, even the same tutors. They of course married each other. Long before a young Whig entered Parliament, he already had had innumerable points of contact with those men who were now to be his political allies. As has been said, none of this translated neatly into disciplined voting, and none of this prevented a Whig tendency to break ranks. But extra-political aspects of Whiggery did mean that the party was never quite so dilapidated as some contemporaries thought. Quite simply, when political prospects were grim, Whigs turned to other things.

Above all, the word Whig mattered. Disputes would arise about who had a claim to that title and about what its historical legacy actually was, but all those engaging in the debate were intent on defending something they thought important. Thomas Coke, first Earl of Leicester, has already been mentioned. As the owner of the Holkham estate in Norfolk, he was a man of the first consequence. Born in the Whig reign of George II, he lived long enough to vote for the Great Reform Bill of 1832. For him the word Whig comfortably described his political views for ninety years. When canvassing in Norfolk, not only his postillions but also the very carriage horses would be decked out in the party colours of buff and blue.[20] Sometimes, it is true, he would dine with a neighbour who was a Tory. But, on those occasions, politics was never discussed, and his host 'with great delicacy of feeling, used to turn with its face to the wall a picture of William Pitt which hung in his dining room'.[21]

2

Circles of Acquaintance

Before the passing of the great Reform Bill in 1832, the political world was incredibly small. Only fourteen per cent of adult males voted, and far fewer took the policy decisions that mattered. This exclusiveness reflected the harsh reality that, in 1760, four hundred people owned nearly a quarter of the land surface of England. Most of these sat in the House of Lords. Many more of their clients and relations filled the Commons. As a result, Henry Fielding could confidently define the word nobody as 'all the People in Great Britain except about 1200'. Byron agreed. He thought that the fashionable world consisted of 'the 1500 fillers of hot rooms' in West London. More generously, Lord Melbourne deferred to the opinions of the few thousand people who read the *Morning Chronicle,* and Edmund Burke defined 'the people of England' as approximately thirty-five thousand individuals.[1] All these witnesses agreed that most people had no established role to play in politics. They might occasionally influence events by rioting or other violence, but this merely confirmed Lord Chesterfield's popular aphorism that, where two or three were gathered together, there was mob.

Predictably, not much physical space was needed for the work of politicians to be done. A few drawing-rooms, a few clubs and a few coffee-houses would almost suffice. Symbolically, the dimensions of Parliament itself were in miniature. Before it was providentially burned down in 1834, the House of Commons was only fifty-seven feet six inches long and thirty-two feet ten inches wide. There was no seating for nearly half the Members. To rise and vote by walking through one of the lobbies was to run the risk of standing for the rest of the day. This situation was only made tolerable by the fact that attendance by many Members was spasmodic and occasional. Only at moments of national drama and crisis was overcrowding difficult to bear. For an elite whose members dominated the world of politics there were many other ways of passing the time. So a lack of space was not necessarily a problem. It merely reflected how few people were involved in the process. To understand the Whig mind, it is first crucial to accept the intimacy of the world in which they worked.

Having introduced the idea of smallness, the refining process must now go further. The elite itself was subdivided into groups which saw themselves as distinct from other people and better or worse than other people. These were called 'circles of acquaintance'. Who you admitted to knowing or who you condescended to recognise as an acquaintance were matters of extreme importance, and the rules which governed this behaviour were very complicated. There were families with whom cards might be left or visits conducted, but whose members could never be invited to dine. There were people who could be acknowledged socially but who could never be seen as partners in marriage. Context might be all important. Individuals who might be known in the country or a provincial spa might have to be snubbed in a great London house. A character in Congreve's *Way of the World*, embarrassed by the possession of country cousins, offered the opinion that 'it ain't modish' to recognize relations in London.

When 'circles of acquaintance' overlapped or collided, social embarrassment could be acute. What should have been kept separate had instead become promiscuous. A passage from Jane Austen's *Persuasion* illustrates the difficulty. Sir Walter Elliot and his daughter are in Bath, a city fraught with social danger for it brought together people from different worlds. The problem for Sir Walter is that his London cousin, Lady Dalrymple, has arrived in the spa, but so has a self-made sailor, Admiral Croft, who is currently the tenant of the Elliot country estate. Could these two acquaintances, each acceptable in the particular context of London or a Hampshire estate, now be introduced? Circles of acquaintance were touching. Miss Elliot is very firm on the question:

Oh! No, I think not. Situated as we are with Lady Dalrymple, cousins, we ought to be very careful not to embarrass her with acquaintance she might not approve. If we were not related, it would not signify; but as cousins, she would feel scrupulous as to any proposal of ours. We had better leave the Crofts to find their own level. There are several odd-looking men walking about here, who, I am told, are sailors. The Crofts will associate with them![2]

One London lady solved the problem by receiving members of the aristocracy on any day except Sunday, when her house was open to everyone else, 'by which smuggling of her small Acquaintance she keeps this nice Division between Lords and Gentlemen unjumbled together'.[3]

To cope with practices such as these, knowing your place in society was vital if solecisms were to be avoided. Above all, this involved recognizing how you stood in relation to other people. Clues were not hard to find. Dress, accent, style of living and manners were just a few of the things that decided social gradations. Everyone was taught to defer to their 'betters'. They were not 'better' morally or in the sight of God, although one duchess found it hard to believe that her maid would inherit the same heaven as herself, but 'better' according to the rules that society had erected. The eighteenth century accepted the importance of such rules and refined them lovingly. Many English and foreign commentators noted the apparent openness of society. No one was actually rude or unpleasant to anyone else. But they also noted codes of deference and condescension that sustained oligarchy in its most ruthless form.

If some people were better than others, the Whigs were best of all. This was certainly their own view of the matter, and it was sometimes grudgingly conceded by even some of their most violent critics. First of all, their sense of caste was unbeatable. The cliché that Whigs were born and not made is of the greatest importance. It was almost impossible to achieve Whiggery and only rarely was it thrust upon someone. To be born into certain families and to carry certain surnames marked an individual for life. Their Brahmin quality was clearly exposed in any family tree. They married within their own circles and therefore 'they're all cousins'. Ancestors held in common led the Whigs to be called 'the Great Grandmotherhood'.[4] Admittedly, cousins do not always agree or act in concert, but, in a society in which blood counted for so much, these people always knew their own kind. It gave them an unbreakable team spirit. According to a Tory historian, the trouble with Radicals was that 'they had none of the *esprit de corps* of the Whigs. They had none of the social and private links by which that party is bound together. See the Russells and Cavendishes, the Greys, the Lambtons, the Ponsonbys, the Foxes, the Lansdowns [sic] etc., how they are all interlaced together by ancient recollections, by early friendships, by habitual intercourse, by family alliances.'[5]

As members of a small world within a small world, Whigs gave no credit to mere numbers. It was infinitely better to be in a distinguished minority than to be part of a gross and ignorant majority. Being in opposition so often was almost a matter of pride, suggesting that they were indeed right. At the heart of Whiggery, numbers were so small that they were treated as an endangered species. Commentators wondered whether a particular virus or an unusually severe winter might produce a total extinction: 'really ... if any sudden pestilence, or other visitation of Providence, had taken away about eight or ten peers, and some two dozen members of the lower house who might be named, we should have looked round upon each other, a week afterwards, and asked "Whither has vanished the Whig Party?"'[6] Being popular was never a Whig priority. Cocooned in their own society and assured of their own importance, they had no need of a wider approbation.

Two factors underpinned their ascendancy, money and history. For the whole of the eighteenth century, and much of the nineteenth, the ownership of property was thought to be the main qualification that fitted a man for political life. It gave you what contemporaries called 'a stake in the country', something to lose if governments failed. It probably guaranteed a level of education and leisure that made the study of politics comprehensible and possible. Above all, it was believed that a man resisted would-be tyrants principally to defend his property from harm. On rules such as these, Whig families had an assured role. Many of them were of fabulous wealth. The Duke of Devonshire owned so much of Derbyshire that he was inclined to refer to the county as 'my little kingdom'.[7] A cousin was said to live 'with the idea that Derbyshire' was 'an heirloom in the family of Cavendish'.[8] Much the same could be suggested of the Russell Dukes of Bedford's control of Bedfordshire and tracts of Devon. Great palaces were built to emphasise such control. The remodelling of Chatsworth by the fourth Duke of Devonshire cost £40,000. The Marquess of Rockingham poured £83,000 into Wentworth Woodhouse.[9] These were not homes in which families expected to live.

Whigs were too metropolitan for country life. Rather, they were power statements in stone that bespoke indisputable pre-eminence.

Critics of the Whigs affected to be unimpressed by great possessions. They created 'an aristocracy, not of talent, or of virtue ... but of rank and station',[10] and it was true that great wealth was no guarantee of either ability or goodness. But, for good or evil, British politics worked on the principle that property was king. Its ownership entitled a man to a vote, to consideration, to influence, to respect. It was no doubt galling for enemies of the Whigs to see them in possession of so much of what was thought valuable, but there was nothing to be done about it. Whigs might often find themselves in a minority, but their place within politics was assured. Secure of their place and possessions, Whigs could entertain total confidence in their own values, without troubling themselves too much about what the rest of the country thought or said.

Allied to great property was great history. English people were acutely conscious that they were the only nation in Europe to have enjoyed six hundred years of parliamentary government. Lesser breeds on the Continent had fallen back on tyrannies of one sort or another. Despotisms had been attempted in England too, but on each occasion had been defeated by valiant defenders of the representative tradition. In each crisis, men with Whig surnames had been highly visible and courageous. The owners of Chatsworth and Woburn Abbey and Castle Howard had had ancestors who had taken on potential tyrants, Charles I and James II, in Parliament and on the battlefield. At determining moments in English history, in 1642 and 1688, the Whigs believed that they, and they alone, had saved the parliamentary process, and they knew that the cost had been high. There were Whig martyrs among their ancestors. Lord William Russell was beheaded in 1683 for resisting the despotic intentions of Charles II, and his sacrifice was cushioned in family memory ever after. Whigs claimed a central role in the parliamentary life of their time because, in their view, their grandfathers and great-grandfathers had saved and defined this invaluable gift to the English. History gave them a proprietorial attitude to Parliament. At Holkham, the Norfolk home of the Earls of Leicester, a frieze of panels illustrating the triumph of liberty over despotism decorates the central lobby. Inevitably, one panel shows King John signing Magna Carta. He is surrounded by parliamentary-minded barons, each of whom has the face of a member of the Whig government of 1830. Whiggery was an apostolic succession in liberty.

If Whig houses were in some sense history lessons in stone, and if the possession of great wealth guaranteed position, it is easy to understand why Whigs were born, not made. The fifth Duke of Bedford explained that he was a Whig because he simply could not be anything else.[11] Even if a man was by nature of a rather conservative disposition, to be dignified or cursed with a particular surname left him no choice. Anthony Trollope created a character who was 'no liberal at heart', but 'he was born on that side of the question, and has been receiving Whig wages all his life. That is the history of his politics.'[12] In these circumstances, to rat on the Whig tradition and turn Tory was the most heinous treason. It was to avert the eyes from the still fresh blood of martyrs. One Whig warned his wife that, 'If my sons turn Tories I shall break my heart'.[13] When the eldest sons of Rosalind, Countess of Carlisle, broke ranks over Irish Home Rule in 1886, she took the only course open to her and persuaded her husband to disinherit them. Whigs lived among ancestral portraits, and every figure so represented admonished each new generation that they must use the privileges that great wealth afforded them to fulfil the obligations for which their forebears had suffered and bled.

A Whig's pride of family therefore knew no bounds. Even the Royal Family could not offer a worthwhile comparison. After all, when the Hanoverian dynasty arrived in England in 1714, they owed their claim to the throne to an astonishing, genealogical fluke. At least thirty people then living had a better claim. Further, the Whigs believed that they had themselves secured George I his crown, and that thereafter the Hanoverians were in some sense their protégés. Continued supervision might be necessary. Coming from north Germany, the new dynasty was bound to be politically schizophrenic. Its members were despots in Hanover but only constitutional kings in England. Throughout the eighteenth century, Whigs had no compunction about lecturing monarchs on their duties and the limitations of their powers. History gave them the right to do this and so did a feeling of equal worth. When George III commissioned Henry Bone to produce portraits of the entire Royal Family in enamels, the sixth Duke of Bedford immediately did the same for his own family.[14] The House of Russell and the House of Hanover both had a glorious past. Indeed, in terms of taste and education, some Whigs might see the Russells as superior.

Whig hauteur, maddening to those outside the charmed circle, was a resource for the novelist well into the nineteenth century. Trollope's Duke of Omnium (Duke of Everything) exemplifies his kind, and never more so than when his attitude to Queen Victoria was examined:

> He rarely went near the presence of majesty, and when he did do so, he did it merely as a disagreeable duty incident to his position. He was very willing that the Queen should be queen as long as he was allowed to be Duke of Omnium. Nor had he begrudged Prince Albert any of his honours till he was called Prince Consort. Then, indeed, he had, to his own intimate friends, made some remark in three words, not flattering to the discretion of the Prime Minister. The Queen might be queen as long as he was the Duke of Omnium. Their revenues were about the same, with the exception, that the Duke's were his own, and he could do what he liked with them. This remembrance did not infrequently present itself to the Duke's mind. In person, he was a plain, thin man, tall, but undistinguished in appearance, except that there was a gleam of pride in his eye which seemed every moment to be saying 'I am the Duke of Omnium'.[15]

This passage is justly regarded as one of the best descriptions of Whiggery in literature. Omnium sets off waves of condescension in all directions, even towards the monarchy. He could do so because his personal and monetary resources were the same. Even today, several aristocratic families are listed as enjoying a greater personal wealth than Elizabeth II.

A profound sense of caste gave the Whigs many advantages, not least of which was an entire indifference to the opinions of people who were not of their company. Some newspapers thundered against them, and cartoonists regularly pilloried them, but none of these attacks influenced their views. They could quite literally afford to ignore them. As Lady Bessborough explained:

> If I made use of the word *world*, it was as most people generally use it, I believe, as a short way of expressing that set of people they usually live with. My world, of course, is a very contracted one ... it is the people I live with constantly whose opinions I mind, whether from fearing to give

pain to those I love amongst them, or from hating being teaz'd and
plagued ... *Propriety of conduct* was never my forte.[16]

In democratic politics, the power of opinion expressed in the media is
something that all politicians must take seriously. Whig politics was
differently constructed. Their political and moral behaviour was medi-
ated only by people like themselves.

Only on very rare occasions did comment from outside their ranks
succeed in stinging. In 1805, the same Lady Bessborough, her sister and
niece were the victims of a writer of poison-pen letters. She frankly
admitted to 'hating being in the power of a person who could write
thus'.[17] But such moments of sensitivity were few. More typical was the
Whig response to Charles Pigott, who, after having an address rejected
by Charles James Fox, set out to make a career in vilifying the Whig
leader and his friends. Unfortunately, Pigott's complexion when a
schoolboy at Eton had been less than perfect, earning him the nickname
of 'the Louse'. His attacks on the Whigs were rebuffed with spirit:

> Who shall expect the country's friend,
> The darling of the House,
> Should for a moment condescend
> To crack a Prison Louse?
>
> For servile meanness to the great
> Let none hold Pigot [sic] cheap
> Who can resist his destined fate?
> A Louse must always creep.[18]

In fact, Fox collected cartoons against himself. They were bound in
folios for the amusement and edification of visitors. Whigs could ignore
the views of both kings and commoners.

One group in particular, however, invoked the greatest Whig wrath.
Like all castes, they had a virulent distaste for any social pretension that
dared to seek acceptance by people like themselves. Throughout this
period, they complained loudly and vigorously against attempts to
dilute the exclusiveness of the House of Lords. In truth, the figures
were alarming. Between 1727 and 1760, only thirty-two new peerages had
been created, barely keeping pace with extinctions. By contrast, the
twenty years from 1780 to 1800 saw the membership of the Lords jump

from 189 to 267. People with surnames like Smith, Robinson and Atkinson were being ennobled, and Whigs were in no doubt that George III and his crony William Pitt were demeaning aristocratic titles on purpose. Lady Spencer thought that the latter's 'whole object was to raise Commercial men and to lower landowners and old families; and he had time and opportunity afforded to him to accomplish that vile project'.[19] The idea that this new peerage could be considered in any way the equivalent of the old was absurd and constitutionally dangerous.

It was also comical. In 1785, the Whigs founded the Esto Perpetua Club in the Strand. Here down-at-heel writers could earn money by writing scandal and satire about the Whigs' opponents. The deficiencies of the new Pittite peerage were an endless source of amusement. One piece of satire involved drawing up imaginary instructions for the door-keepers of 10 Downing Street on how the new peers were to be received:

> Atkinson to be shown into the ante-chamber – he will find amusement in reading Lazarrello de Tornez, or the *complete* Rogue. If Lord Apsley and Mr Percival come from the Admiralty, they may be ushered into the room where the large *looking* glasses are fixed – in that case they will not regret waiting – Don't let Lord Mahon be denied an instant at the door, the pregnant young lady opposite having been sufficiently frightened already!!! Jack Robinson to be shewn into the study, as the private papers were all removed this morning – Let Lord Lonsdale have *my Lord*, and *your Lordship*, repeated in his ear as often as possible ... The other new Peers to be greeted plain *Sir*! That they may remember their late *ignobility*. You may, as if upon recollection, address some of the last list, *My Lord*! – and ask their names – it will be pleasing to them to sound out their own titles ... Don't blunder a second time, and question Lord Mountnorris as to the life of a *hackney coachman* – it is wrong to judge by appearances! – Lord Graham may be admitted to the library – he can't read, and therefore won't damage the books.[20]

Another device for exposing aristocrats with no name was to place advertisements in major newspapers asking for information about any forbears they may have had. A reward of one guinea was offered for any genuine grandmother or grandfather so unearthed, 'and no questions shall be asked'.[21]

Such people could not be invited to dinner tables or be seen as partners in marriage contracts. In fact, Whigs chose to talk of there being two peerages in George III's reign, a 'proper' and an 'improper'. Some contemporaries, like Bulwer Lytton in 1833, bewailed this division, believing that it impaired the overall effectiveness of the aristocracy: 'A line has been drawn between the upper and middle aristocracy which, until then, had been united. The high nobility has set a tone and convention of its own; it has flaunted the superiority of convention, treated the middle aristocracy with arrogance and alienated it.'[22] But Whigs were unmoved. In their view, titles could be created but not the attitudes that should support them. These could only mature over time. Defeated over and over again in the House of Lords, the Whigs consoled themselves with the thought that in many divisions they had had a majority of 'proper' peers with them. As the Duchess of Devonshire observed:

> When a Peerage they give to some son of the earth,
> Yet he still is the same as before;
> 'Tis an honour if gained as the premium of worth,
> But exposes a blockhead the more.[23]

Confronted with unfounded pretension, the Whigs took the only possible course. They reordered their defences by paying out yards and yards of social barbed wire. The rules by which their approval and recognition were to be won simply became more complicated. The most obvious example of this in everyday life was accent. Whigs developed a private language. They pronounced English words in ways that set them apart: 'Gold was goold, lilac laylock, bracelet brasslet, yellow was ialo or yaller, china cheyney, balcony balcony, sovereign suvereign; envelope was pronounced as in French, the h was dropped in hotel. Coffee was inexorably cawfee, governess was governess (the o as in of); a carriage was quite often a chariot.'[24] Even a change of politics brought no change in accent. When the French Revolution frightened Walter Spencer Stanhope into Pittism, he continued to pronounce London Lunnon, cucumber cowcumber, and woman 'ouman.[25] Oddly enough, the contemporary pronunciation of Derby is the last example of Whig influence on language. Just to make matters even more intimate, the Devonshire House circle at the heart of Whiggery were reputed to have variations of their own.

If accent betrayed a man as soon as he opened his mouth, what he said could be just as undermining as how he said it. James Harris's

Hermes: or A Philosophical Inquiry Concerning Universal Grammar of 1751 and Dr Johnson's famous *Dictionary* of 1755 had established the grammatical rules and vocabulary of polite language. It stood in stark contrast to what Johnson called 'the fugitive cant' of 'the laborious and mercantile part of the people'.[26] Henceforth, the way a letter was set out and punctuated, and the choice of words employed, was potentially incriminating. To make matters worse, Whigs employed a private code of nicknames as a further weapon in the linguistic armoury. Outsiders would be left baffled by Whig conversation and letters unless they had been provided with a check-list along the following lines:

Silence	Lady Jersey	*The Racoon*	Lady Elizabeth Foster
Vraiment	Madame Lieven	*Canis*	The Duke of Devonshire
The Eyebrow	Charles James Fox	*Ego*	Lord Erskine
The Bear	Edward Ellice	*Doodle*	Lord Granville
The Brush	Henry Brougham	*Harum*	Lord Bessborough
Mr Third	Adolphe Thiers	*Tybald*	Harriet Cavendish
Mr Mantalini	Lord Normanby	*Loo*	Duke of Bedford
The Bravo	Lord Aberdeen	*Mr Black*	Charles Grey
The Rat	The Duchess of Devonshire	*Pug*	Frederick Howard

The three Miss Berrys were predictably Elderberry, Blackberry and Gooseberry.[27] In sum, Whigs under siege contrived to use all the possibilities of language as weapons for repelling boarders.

Even more socially lethal was the question of marriage. To ally with a family in marriage was to give public recognition of their worth. As a result, the Whigs were extremely cautious in such matters, and most people were beyond consideration. Generally, Whigs preferred to marry each other. Otherwise there were real risks to be run. Lady Bessborough was appalled to hear that her son was enamoured of a lady from the Tory family of the Earls of Westmorland. She admitted that there were financial advantages in the match, but insisted that she 'was not very partial to all the Fane family'.[28] Mercifully, the marriage went ahead without compromising the purity of anyone's politics. Similarly, when the Duchess of Devonshire heard rumours that the fifth Duke of Bedford might marry a Tory, she feared that his brain would soften in a life spent farming, smoking, and watching children 'jump over the backs of chairs'.[29] To her great relief the Duke remained a bachelor. There could be no hint of compromise in such matters. If a lady with Tory antecedents married into a Whig family, she was expected to switch allegiances immediately,[30] and, indeed to sever social links with her former circle of acquaintance. When a member of Lady Salisbury's family married the Whig John Foster Barham, she philosophically confided to her diary that 'he is a Whig, and will probably avoid associating with us as much as possible'.[31]

It was not mere snobbery that demanded that blood lines be kept pure. Much more fundamental things were at stake. For two hundred years at least, certain families with certain names had guaranteed parliamentary government against the attacks of despotic kings. Since the Hanoverians could not be trusted to act decently, that historical mission still had substance. To admit an unrepentant Tory into the family might poison the next generation and make them reluctant to carry on the crusade. This danger was best avoided by so arranging marriages that points of political divergence simply never arose. Whigs had no doubt that when they married cousins they were fulfilling a great public duty. What looked like arrogance and exclusiveness was in fact self-sacrifice for the national good.

It followed naturally that the children of such marriages should be educated according to a syllabus that would instruct them on the duties that they had inherited at birth. Such 'Whiglings' were not as other children. Their careers and opinions were predestined by uncontestable forces. When Thomas Coke received a letter from the headmaster of Eton extolling the school's conservative ethos, he was compelled to clarify matters about what he expected for his own boy: 'I am sure you will allow me to say that I ... must feel very anxious ... that, as regards my own son, the feelings which he may derive from home may be those and those *only* which will guide him in the future conduct of his life.'[32] For reasons such as these Harrow was usually thought to be a safer bet.

Similar caution had to be exercised about the choice of a private tutor. Infant ears could only be allowed to hear Whig songs. In 1775 the Marquess of Granby wrote to thank his old tutor, Richard Watson, 'for making me study Locke; while I exist, those tenets, which are so attentive to the natural rights of mankind, shall ever be the guide and direction of my actions'. He went on, half apologetically, to say that he had married a woman with Tory affiliations, but he assured his tutor that 'Whig principles are too firmly riveted in me ever to be removed'. Watson's reply was both sympathetic and firm: 'I heartily wish you well in the new mode of life you are entering into; much depends upon your setting out properly; be a Whig in domestic as well as political life, and the best part of Whiggism is, that it will neither suffer nor exact domination.'[33] At every stage of private and public education, Whig children were trained for particular roles in politics. In particular, this involved reading history books that related the story of how English Parliaments have defeated tyrants. In such accounts, the surnames of the principal actors would have been their own.

If such an upbringing could be questioned as unduly prescriptive, it also carried great warmth and sense of purpose. Whigs applauded every production of their children and protégés. No group of people ever indulged in such mutual admiration and congratulation. The puffing, or praising, of each others' books and speeches encouraged real talent and even gave a certain confidence to the less endowed. It also greatly irritated political opponents. As a contributor to the Tory journal *Blackwood's* put it:

> When a Whig wit – and there are a few such characters among that dull party – produces a political pasquinade, a most uncommon ferment ensues over the land. Good heavens! What a noise of trumpets! At the corner of every street stands a young man of that persuasion, with his tiny bugle at his lips, puffing away with a pair of cheeks that might set Boreas at defiance ... It is a pity the Whigs should be such charlatans. This eternal puffing blows nobody good.[34]

Another critic complained that the Whigs had turned themselves into 'a sort of oligarchy, from whose judgements there was no appeal'.[35] Every time a young Whig wrote a book of some quality or made a promising speech, prophecy would be fulfilled. Such productions indisputably proved that they had inherited the talents and responsibilities of their forbears. They were educated to this end and were lauded to the skies when they achieved it.

Accordingly, the aristocratic temperament coloured every aspect of their lives. Living differently from other men and cultivating different tastes was not exclusively for the sake of being exclusive. Rather, having preferences in common that were not those of most men reinforced the values of aristocracy and the obligations that went with it. Questions of taste therefore came to be of considerable importance. Whigs tended to live in houses built in a particular style and were inclined to commission the same architects over and over again. Equally, Whig bookshelves and dedications to Whig patrons were strong indications of decided preferences in literature. Of course it was ultimately impossible to arrogate certain tastes to themselves. Art and literature could never run neatly on party lines. But certain tastes were undoubtedly more Whig than non-Whig. As has been observed: 'Taste, however capricious, always depends on more than taste. Any aesthetic system, however loosely held together, is inextricably bound up with a whole series of forces, religious, political, nationalist, economic, intellectual.'[36] The Whigs would have agreed. The house in which a man lived, and the objects with which he surrounded himself, were windows into the mind and soul.

In architecture, neo-classicism was what Lord Spencer called 'the aristocratic style'. Colonnades, columns with appropriate capitals, galleries full of statuary and gardens full of temples all evoked fifth-century Greece or the glorious days of the Roman Republic. The idealised politics of these centuries sat easily on Whig shoulders. Representative government had been jealously guarded by statesmen who kept tyrants at bay. Both Socrates and Brutus had been Whigs. The serious excavation of first Rome and then Herculaneum and Pompeii from the middle of the eighteenth century reactivated an interest in such matters that the Whigs took to heart. Their self-identification with the past rarely wanted too much prompting. In his lowest moments, Charles James Fox liked to call himself the English Brutus, the last of the Romans, in mortal combat with the Younger Pitt, who was often labelled Augustus as the bringer of a new despotism. So Henry Holland was the Whigs' preferred architect. His masterpiece, Carlton House, was commissioned by the Prince Regent to dwarf Buckingham Palace, the home of his parents, and to entrench aristocratic values in the very centre of London. Just as often, John Flaxman would be called in to mould reliefs.[37]

The building or rebuilding of houses like Woburn, Holkham and Wentworth reinforced the identification of Whiggery and neo-classicism. Exteriors spoke of the stern, public virtues of aristocratic centuries in the past, and interiors, crammed with busts of contemporary politicians in classical dress, reaffirmed connections between the living and the dead. Further, preferences also involved antipathies. If Whigs admired the classical, they detested the gothic. Anything that carried memories of the middle ages was to be deplored. Medievalism was nothing but religious superstition and tyrannical kings. Whigs who lived into the middle of the nineteenth century found it very odd that the gothic should be prized. Lord Palmerston, for example, loathed the Albert Memorial. He had wanted 'an open Grecian Temple ... with a statue of the Prince Consort of Heroic Size in the centre upon a suitable pedestal'.[38] Almost certainly, Palmerston was indulging a well-honed talent for irony in making this remark, but it struck a chord. Whigs would have preferred the Prince to be represented as a Roman senator rather than as a rather clammy knight errant.

There was a preferred classicism in literature too. Whigs tended to the view that a peak of achievement in English literature had been found in the early eighteenth century. Augustan writers like Swift and Pope modelled themselves on the writers of Greece and Rome with profit. Since their time all was decline. At the turn of the nineteenth century, Whigs believed that most contemporary literature was debased. For Byron, 'a proper appreciation of Pope' was the 'touchstone of taste' and 'the present question is not only whether Pope is or is not in the first rank of our literature – but whether that literature shall or shall not relapse into the Barbarism from which it has scarcely emerged for above a century and a half'.[39] Francis Jeffrey, editor of the *Edinburgh Review*, wholeheartedly agreed: 'if we must abjure all our classical prejudices, and cease to admire Virgil, and Pope, and Racine, before we can relish the beauties of Mr Southey, it is easy to perceive that Mr Southey's beauties are in some hazard of being neglected'.[40] There was a harmony and consistency in reading Pope in a neo-classical house.

In contrast, there could be no truck with the Romantics. Wordsworth, Coleridge and their friends were chased through the Whig reviews with whips and scorpions. Such writers trampled all over Whig sensibilities in almost every way, but two crimes deserved particular and insistent mention. The first concerned a perverse tendency in Romantics to give feeling primacy over reason. Whigs found this dangerous and childish. Unrestrained emotion rarely helped to improve a

situation. Even the very idea of love was doubtful. Swift had likened it
to a disease of the mind, and Sydney Smith agreed that it was best
avoided:

> I read several beautiful sonnets upon love, which paint with great fidelity
> some of the worst symptoms of that terrible disorder, than which none
> destroys more completely the happiness of common existence, and substi-
> tutes, for the activity which life demands, a long and sickly dream with
> moments of pleasure and days of intolerable pain. The Poets are full of false
> views: they make mankind believe that happiness consists in falling in love,
> and living in the country – I say: live in London; like many people; fall in
> love with nobody.[41]

Whigs believed that the intellectual triumph of their own time had been
to substitute reason for superstition. The Romantics seemed to be
unaware of this.

Worse still, Wordsworth and his allies not only thought emotions of
interest, they were also inclined to give them unrestricted play. They
were too wild and unregulated. Whereas progress came about through
science and system, the Romantics always seemed to be standing in a
gale. Typically, Sydney Smith disliked a novel by Madame de Staël, for
it not only seemed to justify 'adultery, murder, and a great number of
other vices, which have been somehow or other neglected in this country', but was also filled with 'screams innumerable'. In Smith's view, 'the
passions want not accelerating, but retarding machinery'.[42] This is the
authentic voice of Whiggery in literature. Indeed, Edmund Burke had
seen the French Revolution as a political corollary of the sort of unrestrained emotions that the Romantics valued. In his famous *Reflections*
on that event, he reminded his readers of the story about the Roman
poet who, unfortunate in love, leapt into a volcano. In Burke's view, this
was nothing more than 'a frolic', rather silly, and 'an unjustifiable poetic
licence'.[43]

The second crime perpetrated by Romantic writers concerned the
subject matter of their productions. For some inexplicable reason they
chose to write about the lower orders, peopling novels and poems with
shepherds and cottagers of a philosophical disposition. Whigs were
unsympathetic to 'the charitable endeavours of Messrs Wordsworth and
co. to accommodate' the common people 'with an appropriate vein of

poetry'.[44] There was something unpleasantly democratic about the enterprise, for, if shepherds could be philosophers, why should they not vote? On top of this, there was the question of taste. Every class in society experienced love, hatred, jealousy and self-sacrifice, but the higher the social strata the more refined the expression of these feelings. Poets should only follow the best models therefore and write about polite society. As Francis Jeffrey put it:

> Now, the different classes of society have each of them a distinct character, as well as a separate idiom; and the names of the various passions to which they are subject respectively have a signification that varies essentially, according to the condition of the persons to whom they are applied. The love, or grief, or indignation of an enlightened and refined character is not only expressed in a different language, but is in itself a different emotion from the love, or grief, or anger of a clown, a tradesman, or a market wench.

Writers should not 'take their models from what is ordinary, but from what is excellent'.[45]

Certain authors were therefore unlikely to find themselves at Whig dinner tables or on Whig bookshelves. Charles James Fox returned a presentation copy of *Lyrical Ballads* to Wordsworth with the ungracious comment that it was not his kind of thing. His niece, Lady Holland, tried dining the poet, but then decided that no more time or food should be wasted on a 'man who writes about caps and pinafores and that sort of thing'.[46] The same lady had difficulty in understanding Dickens's obsession with London's low life, a category which for her included all Americans.[47] Coleridge's productions were out of the question as well. His foggy pronouncements were proof that he had 'withdrawn altogether from the correction of equal minds'.[48] Worst of all was Sir Walter Scott. His novels united a love of the Middle Ages with tales of cottagers and cobblers, an altogether lethal brew in Whig minds. Francis Jeffrey regretted that Scott had been 'corrupted by the wicked tales of knight-errantry and enchantment'.[49] Less charitably, Lady Rosslyn would not have any of Scott's works in the house, calling him 'the Beast', and expressing the hope that he might be hanged.[50]

Whig patronage therefore flowed in other directions. To act as discriminating patrons of the arts was considered a vital aspect of aristocratic society. Indeed, the sixth Duke of Devonshire believed himself to be more munificent in this respect than the whole Royal Family, and to show infinitely greater taste.[51] Though convinced that they lived in degenerate times, one or two writers were still thought worthy of help. These included Thomas Campbell, George Crabbe and Leigh Hunt.[52] Radical politics were no impediment to assistance, though Whig loyalties would have been preferable. The crucial thing was to accept the conventions of Augustan poetry, and to confront the nineteenth century and its possibilities with openness and hope. The writer, the poet and the artist would dine at Whig tables as of right, but all had to subscribe to its aristocratic ethos and the history that had fashioned it. In this way Whig exclusivity was further strengthened by being given artistic approbation.

So self-sufficient was the Whig world that its only deficiency was the more glaring. Contemporaries called it the problem of 'the talented man'. Quite simply great birth and great wealth did not guarantee great ability, or enough of it, with the result that the Whigs always had to co-opt talent. Charles James Fox never finished *The Wealth of Nations* and found *Le Contrat Social* unreadable. To name a racehorse Jean-Jacques Rousseau hardly made up for this lapse. On the bullion question, he frankly admitted to Charles Grey: 'You know, Grey, you and I don't mind these things.'[53] Someone else would be needed to advise on such matters. Such people were particularly needed in the House of Commons, for too many Whigs of necessity found themselves in the other House. Accordingly, Whigs patronized talent in both meanings of the word, seeking it out, dining it and paying good wages. As Lady Melbourne observed, much could be done with a rough diamond if it was constantly smoothed by attrition in good society.

Accordingly, promising young men would find themselves with invitations to great Whig houses. The process of entrapment would then begin:

> Many a time has the successful debutant in parliament, or the author just rising into note, repaired to Berkeley Square or Kensington with unsettled views and wavering expectations, fixed in nothing but to attach himself for a time to no party. He is received with that cordial smile which ... warms more than dinner or wine: he is presented to a host of literary, social and political celebrities, with whom it has been for years his fondest ambition to be associated; it is gently insinuated that he may become an actual member of that

brilliant society by willing it, or his acquiescence is tacitly and imperceptibly assumed; till, thrown off his guard in the intoxication of the moment, he finds or thinks himself irrecoverably committed, and suppressing any lurking inclination towards Toryism, becomes deeply and definitely Whig.[54]

Tories were advised to confront 'a furious bull' or 'a mad dog' rather than someone who passed for 'an interesting young man' in Whig circles,[55] but they bemoaned the fact that they had no comparable network. They had 'nothing of the sort'.[56] Equally, James Mill for the Radicals made the same point. Confirming that the Whigs were 'a coterie, not a party', he described the system of inveiglement, which had, in his view, swallowed the talents of people like Francis Horner, Sir Samuel Romilly and Henry Brougham.[57] Whig salons and their owners simply charmed talent into the party.

This system of recruitment was formidable but carried dangers that exposed the Whigs' Achilles heel. At its best, it bolstered exclusivity with talent. At its worst, it exposed the fact that the Whigs were for once forced to look outside their own ranks. The career of Edmund Burke showed the system working well. For nearly all his life, he was paid to put his formidable intellect at the service of the Whigs. But he was never invited into a Whig Cabinet and never expected to be. He knew his place as a talented man. In his opinion, 'the road to eminence and power, from obscure condition, ought not to be made too easy, nor a thing too much of course. If rare merit be the rarest of all things, it ought to pass through some sort of probation.'[58] Thackeray too in a later generation, suggesting that it was easier to become a Jew than a Whig, admitted that Whigs were 'our superiors'.[59] Samuel Rogers and Sir James Mackintosh rehearsed their conversation and epigrams before dining out at a great Whig house, that they might impress the more.[60] Such men never claimed that mere talent could be considered the equal of the wealth and birth that gave the Whigs their primacy. So all was smooth and rounded.

Not all men of talent were so accommodating. Richard Brinsley Sheridan was literally moved to tears by the thought that he wanted high office badly and that the Whigs would never give it to him.[61] Mocking them as The School for Scandal barely made up for his distress. Even Sydney Smith was once heard by an American visitor to say that he found his Whig patrons 'oppressive'.[62] Most tiresome of all was George Canning. Although his mother had been an actress, he had 'a passion for distinction' that his background could not justify.[63] With only formidable talent to commend himself, he had the temerity to aspire to be Prime Minister. When he actually became Prime Minister in 1827, Whigs were simply baffled. To support him would be to recognize the claims of mere talent. Not to support him would fatally impair the prospects of major reform. As Sydney Smith observed, Canning was 'a fly in amber, nobody cares about the fly; the only question is, how the devil did he get there'.[64] Sheridan and Canning personified the Whig dilemma. They needed such men, but on their terms only. The Whig attributes of birth and wealth must always overbear simple talent. Anthony Trollope was quite right, in describing Mrs Proudie as 'a pure Whig', to conclude that 'no one is so hostile to lowly born pretenders to high station'.[65] William Mackworth Praed's poem *The Talented Man* ends with the couplet

> I've promised mamma to remember
> He's *only* a talented man.[66]

Whigs never needed to be reminded of this fact.

With the important exception of the talented man, Whigs had no needs that could not be met from within their own circle of acquaintance. The confined nature of their world seemed perfectly natural in a society in which the ownership of property meant everything and in which great property was concentrated in few hands. To be born into these families guaranteed a place in public life, and demanded that the duties that such positions involved should be done whatever the personal sacrifice. To outsiders and political opponents to their Right and Left, Whigs could seem arrogant, self-satisfied, blinkered. Their reluctance to bow to either monarchy or democracy was resented. Yet it was this very self-sufficiency that gave Whiggery its real character and power. Whigs could quite literally afford to be themselves. Their views were their own. History had made them special, as guardians of the parliamentary tradition. Wealth made them special in every other sense. They could set their own rules for living, whether they lived up to them or not.

Just how closely these rules moulded the life of an individual may be illustrated in the career of William Lamb, second Viscount Melbourne. Living between 1779 and 1848, he knew the world before the French Revolution and survived to hear of socialism in Europe. He came from what might be called a usual Whig family. His mother and father had entered into an arranged marriage, in which everything turned on convenience rather than affection. The first Viscount was dull and heavy, while the first Viscountess proved to be one of the most entertaining women in London. Inevitably they led separate lives. He found solace with the actresses of Covent Garden and Drury Lane; she in a succession of aristocratic lovers. Of the five children of the marriage, only the eldest boy was the product of husband and wife, and he died young.

William Lamb was therefore illegitimate and never made any great secret of the fact. He rather enjoyed discussing the question with other Whigs in a similar situation. Having only a mother in common with most of his siblings in no way prevented him from being on the best of terms with his brothers and sisters. One brother was comfortably provided for as soon as William achieved high office. One sister married Lord Palmerston, who, as Foreign Secretary, often disagreed with Melbourne when Prime Minister, but never about family matters. An extended sense of family was more powerful than concern about mere biological niceties.

In due course, Lamb's own marriage was arranged. His mother and her great friend Lady Bessborough simply united a son and daughter. The young people concerned barely knew each before vows were exchanged. Unfortunately, the new bride was Lady Caroline Ponsonby. As a girl she had already given some evidence of mental instability, and, after marriage, this increasingly took the form of lechery and alcoholism. From 1812 to 1825, William Lamb was compelled to retreat from public life in order to monitor his wife's behaviour. Today, such a retreat would destroy the career prospects of a public figure. In the Whig world, by contrast, these years were only an embarrassing interlude. Lamb family property and influence in Hertfordshire and Derbyshire meant that he could resume his political life whenever he wanted.

Like his parents, William Lamb, as a partner in an arranged marriage, exercised his right to find emotional outlets elsewhere. He took mistresses as a matter of course. There was nothing unusual about this. What was controversial was his choice of women. Lady Brandon and Caroline Norton were both women of excitable character with querulous husbands. In 1836, London society hugely enjoyed the spectacle of the Prime Minister being prosecuted for adultery. When the case was thrown out, even the Lamb family admitted that he had had a lucky escape. Not for a moment, however, did they think that this episode compromised his standing as a public man. In the Whig world, private life and public action were very different things.

In education, too, Lamb's instruction ran on predetermined Whig lines. It is true that he passed a few years at Eton, not the most Whiggish of establishments, but any intellectual damage incurred there was easily remedied by trips to France and an extended stay at Glasgow University. Here the pupils of Adam Smith allowed no deviation from the belief in progress and the bettering of the human condition that would come from free trade and industrialisation. Nor did this course of instruction allow much space for religion. Melbourne lived through the enthusiasm associated with the Evangelical Revival and the Oxford Movement, but, like his family and friends, was untouched by them. Indeed, he famously saw no place for religion as an influence in politics. Theology and church history were suitable to occupy hours spent in a library, but should not be invoked at the dinner table or in the bedroom. For this reason, Melbourne's influence with the young Queen Victoria from 1837 to 1841 was deeply suspect.

Above all, Melbourne exemplified the Whig approach to politics. Matters of state should fill only part of each day. With a serious interest in history, literature and philosophy, Melbourne had many other options. Equally, no one with a Scots training, aware of the general and inexorable movements in history, should ever feel too deeply about anything. Philosophy and fatalism precluded emotion. Melbourne was vaguely against parliamentary reform but was content to go along with the idea if its time seemed to have come. He had no interest in the detailed clauses of important measures, preferring to accept changes with a benevolent and knowing philosophy. Melbourne exemplified the Whig world in London as peopled by informed amateurs.

On all these points Melbourne attracted criticism. His private life was exposed to censorious scrutiny in newspapers, novels and cartoons. He was taken to be a notorious example of the shortcomings of the London world in which he lived. As Prime Minister from 1834 to 1841, his lethargy and prevarication in the conduct of business were frequently denounced. Epigram apparently took the place of policy. Yet, as with the rest of his kind, none of this compromised his claim to a great position in politics or dented his self-confidence. Wealth and birth conferred a status that public opinion could not yet seriously threaten. Within the tribal boundaries of West London, the life of William Lamb, distinctive as it was, passed with little or no acknowledgement of a wider audience.

3

London

By instinct and habit Whigs were metropolitan. London was their home for eight, nine, ten months in every year, or rather that section of the capital that was known as 'the Town'. There were Whigs who lived in the country, but such behaviour gave rise to gossip about ruined finances or unwanted pregnancies. Quite simply, as Sidney Smith put it, 'All lives out of London are mistakes, more or less grievous, but mistakes'. The reason was that 'the parallelogram between Oxford Street, Piccadilly, Regent Street and Hyde Park, encloses more intelligence and human ability, to say nothing of wealth, and beauty, than the world has ever collected in such a space before'.[1] This was 'the Town' as opposed to 'the City', and its inhabitants were a chosen race. The 'Ton' or society people lived in the first and 'cits' in the second. Foreign visitors often commented on the existence of at least two Londons, an East and a West End, overlapping when money was in question but socially distinct.[2] Further, all quarters of the capital were swelling. London's population was 200,000 in 1600 but 900,000 two hundred years later. In 1750, 11 per cent of the entire English population lived in the capital and one in six had done so at some stage of their lives.[3] London was the centre of politics, money and society. For significant sectors of this sprawling conurbation to be nothing more than miniature Whig kingdoms was a matter of importance.

Crucially, the West End was built by the Whigs. The squares and terraces that give it character were constructed between 1680 and 1780 as Whig speculations. In many cases their ownership remains intact today. Bloomsbury and Covent Garden were the fiefs of the Dukes of Bedford, who are commemorated in Russell Square (the family surname), Tavistock Square (the heir's courtesy title), Woburn Square (the family house) and Bedford Square itself. North of Oxford Street, the Cavendishes and their cousins, the Bentincks, lorded it over Devonshire

Square, Cavendish Square and Manchester Square. Greatest of all was the Grosvenor family, which owned the square that bears its name and much of Belgravia. Smaller baronies also existed, and it is almost impossible to find any public space or thoroughfare which does not proclaim a Whig connection. Tories could not compete and complained bitterly about the fact. Lord Randolph Churchill protested about 'the great Whig dukes who covered London with their bloated estates'.[4] His colleague Drummond Wolffe gloomily reflected that 'we are in London the vassals of Whig Dukes who rule us through a lot of solicitors and surveyors'.[5] The enemies of the Whigs usually controlled the Houses of Parliament and Buckingham Palace, but these buildings were always under a kind of siege, surrounded as they were by talismanic Whig names in every street and square.

The West End had been built for a purpose. It was to house families coming to London to take part in the Season. Roughly coterminous with the parliamentary session and therefore running from October to May or June each year, the Season compounded money, politics and amusement in an irresistible brew. Nearly every family of standing took part in it, and to choose not to do so was thought eccentric. For to miss the Season was to involve the family in loss. Girls who were denied the Season, and a well-appointed 'coming out', lost the opportunities of the vigorous marriage market that was such an important aspect of the arrangement, and might have to settle for a curate. Wilde's Lady Bracknell and her type had been hunting up suitable sons- and daughters-in-law for decades. Equally, heads of families lost investment opportunities by not knowing the City, and chances for family advances in the line of jobs, pensions and sinecures by not knowing politicians. Worst of all, the whole family suffered the deprivation of not attending the theatre, gambling at Almack's or dining in Vauxhall Gardens. No one of sound mind would opt out of any of this.

Importantly, much of West End life depended on display, and public and private spaces in which this was possible proliferated. To live in a square was more convenient than to live in a street, because it allowed an unrestricted view of all one's neighbours. Equally, parks, theatres, balls and clubs were parade grounds where calling attention to oneself was a positive virtue. As a character in Samuel Foote's play *The Lyar* instructed a newcomer to London, the methods employed to this end were numerous,

> such as encoring a song at an opera, hallooing to a pretty fellow 'cross the Mall as loud as if you were calling a coach. Why, do you know, my dear, that by a lucky stroke in dress, and a few high airs of my own making, I have had the good fortune to be gazed at and followed by as great a crowd, on a Sunday, as if I was the Turkish ambassador.[6]

Such advice was salutary, for, in a world in which a family's worth was computed by the way it presented itself to the rest of society, display was everything. West End society endlessly made comparisons. It talked of the number of servants attending a family, the scale of entertaining, how a family dressed – this year's fashions or last year's – where the Season was kept and for how long. Each of these attributes gave a clue to a family's financial health, and in turn rendered it more or less acceptable as dinner companions or marriage partners.

Inevitably, success in the games played in the West End demanded access to money. Those who could not afford London tried to compensate themselves by recreating its social round on a smaller scale in the spas that sprang up all over eighteenth-century England. But no one was fooled. Bath, and later Brighton, might have acquired real social status, but there was no point in claiming that the marriage market at Droitwich or Malvern had the same magnetism as London's, or that the entertainments put on in Buxton or Bury St Edmunds could be compared to those in the capital. Whether or not a family regularly expected to keep the London Season was one of the major fault lines running through eighteenth-century society. The fact that the Whigs were so closely associated with London therefore carried real consequences for their party. It was the more respected or feared because of its associations with the capital. The Season was played out on Whig-owned territory. In its most extravagant displays it was sustained by Whig wealth. Whigs dominated society in a way that they never dominated politics. To aspire to the Season was Whiggish; to suspect it was also to suspect those who were its celebrities.

In fact the phenomenon of London and its pre-eminence in national life was much resented. Many English people saw the capital as the home of things foreign, things irreligious and things vicious.

Degradation and degeneracy were thought to be so rampant that societies were formed with the hopeful ambition of extirpating vice. Evidence of moral decay was found in the loss of America, the spread of a Frenchified effeminacy, and in the luxurious lifestyles adopted in London. It was sincerely lamented that those who should have set an example were in fact the most forward in publicizing vice. The aristocracy were 'the fountain-head of luxurious Ostentation, and vicious indulgence ... Some years ago, there was a Toast in vogue among the fashionable World, to this purpose, "May elegant Vice prevail over dull Virtue"'.[7]

These concerns were real and widespread. It was 'a melancholy reflection that infidelities are much more frequent among people of elevated rank, than those of a less exalted station'.[8] It was sad that 'we certainly live in times of universal depravity ... A shameless, daring effrontery, a carelessness of reputation, an inattention to the good opinion of the world, are the notorious and very reproachful characteristics of the present age'.[9] This last remark was addressed to the Duchess of Devonshire. The writer would have been distressed, but not surprised, to know that the lady's favourite novel was the notorious *Les Liaisons Dangereuses*. She had found it 'very instructive'.[10] Many people believed that a reformation of manners was urgently required, and that missionary work should be undertaken in the West End.

If London living was contaminating, the Whigs were inevitably believed to be the most contaminated. Stories proliferated about how differently Whigs and non-Whigs approached moral problems. In 1815, a committee of Tory ladies erected the statue of Achilles that stands on Hyde Park Corner to celebrate Wellington's victory at Waterloo. On only one issue were the ladies divided. Should the statue carry a fig leaf or not? A majority thought that it should. Lady Holland, the great Whig proprietress of Holland House, impishly set out to cause trouble by trying to secure a list of those who had voted in the minority. But what else could be expected of a woman who had married, at fifteen, a man of forty-nine. A quite different attitude to nudity was shown by Lady Brownlow and two other Tory ladies on a visit to the studio of the French painter David. Confronted by a picture of Leonidas at Thermopylae, they were told that his nakedness was vital because 'heroes and demigods could not be put into the trammels of dress like

common mortals'. Lady Brownlow was unimpressed, sniffily commenting: 'Surely never was there such absurd sentiment, such sentiment on
stilts. And as I looked at the picture, and listened to the artist's expla-
nations, I could not help thinking, if this was the production of one of
the best French painters, how little they had profited by the possession
for so many years of the *chefs d'oeuvre* [sic] now taken from them.'[11]
Whigs and non-Whigs seemed to inhabit different moral spheres.

As the leaders of London decadence, the Whigs were always good
copy for the cartoonist, the moralist and the pamphleteer. They seemed
to live in 'unsubstantial Temples of Pleasure, where Syrens warble forth
the notes of Delusion, to charm the unwary into those flowery paths
which lead to the caverns of Dishonour'.[12] In 1777, the Duchess of
Devonshire successfully demanded that society adopt hairpieces composed of ostrich feathers several feet long. For this, she was vilified: 'that
preposterous Plumage was at once, the ornament of your head, and the
emblem of yourself ... for the ostrich is remarkable for being a foolish
bird'.[13] In the 1790s, pamphlets entitled *The Whig Club*, *The Jockey Club*
and *The Female Jockey Club* brought their author, Charles Pigott, a certain income and notoriety. The verb 'to jockey' could mean to cheat,
and prominent Whigs were described as practitioners of the art. Sheridan's landlord was forced to untile the roof to rid himself of a difficult
tenant; the Duke of Norfolk was illiterate, a lover of bagpipes, only five
foot six inches in height yet the owner of a mistress ten inches taller; Sir
Charles Bunbury 'ever beguiled the moments, between Newmarket
meetings, in an amorous intercourse with farmers' daughters, milliners'
prentices, and servant maids; Lord Robert Spencer was so embarrassed
by debts earned in vice that he was forced to act as croupier in Brooks's
Club for five shillings an hour. Female reputations fared no better.
Gertrude, Duchess of Bedford was so mean that she toured Woburn
Abbey collecting up candle ends for recycling, while the list of Lady
Elizabeth Foster's lovers reputedly included the Duke of Dorset, the
Duke of Cumberland, Gustavus III of Sweden and Cardinal Bernis.[14]

It mattered little whether these accusations were true. Some were and
many were not. Crucially all were believable, and all of them therefore
contributed to the way Whig society in London was perceived. Cartoonists endlessly showed Whig figures in brothels, at race-courses and in
gambling dens. They were the most adept jockeys in a world that lived

by jockeying. They were accused of having little regard for morality in this world or little hope of salvation in the next. As leaders of the London Season they infected its whole operation. Whigs acquired a reputation for being unclean and untrustworthy. Reformers with Christian consciences like William Wilberforce and Christopher Wyvill, who badly wanted Whig help in the attack on slavery or the promotion of parliamentary reform, found it difficult to be in the same room as the often unwashed and unshaven Charles James Fox. Such encounters were like touching pitch. Worse still, Fox seemed to find their discomfort moderately diverting.[15] Without any doubt at all, however, the effectiveness of Whigs as politicians was undermined by their performance as leaders of Society.

A particular point of controversy concerned Whig sexuality inside marriage and outside it. Historians largely agree that, as the eighteenth century passed into the nineteenth, more and more people inclined to the belief that affection should play some part in the choice of a husband or wife. But Whigs acted differently. They liked to marry their cousins. Quite simply, too much was at stake to do anything else. Marriage was regarded as the union of great fortunes. Its purpose was to produce an undisputed heir to the joint property. Once that task had been accomplished, the marriage was counted a success in Whig eyes, and husband and wife could then do as they pleased. To marry into the lower orders was immorality according to Whig law. When the Earl of Derby married an actress, Lady Bessborough sarcastically noted that the new Countess was 'always acting the part of a dignified Lady of Fashion – *toujours Reine de Carthage*'.[16] Even someone with the immense stature of Charles James Fox hid the fact of his marriage to a former courtesan for seven years. By contrast, heiresses from good families were escorted around London by crowds of admirers 'as the Guards do about ... Kings'.[17]

To talk of marrying for affection was irrelevant, and something best left to Romantic poets. Jonathan Swift, at the beginning of the eighteenth century, had denounced love as 'a ridiculous passion which hath no being but in plays and romances'.[18] A hundred years later, Lord John Russell agreed. He defined love as 'that violent, unjust, irritating, magnifying passion'.[19] When a Whig wife by chance actually loved her husband, she opened herself up to endless teasing. Lady Harriet

Granville complained that 'they all think it a good joke my loving him just as they might if I was *amourachée* of some snuffy old Frenchman'.[20] Such couples were a social menace. They became so fond of each other that they withdrew from polite society altogether. Such a fate befell Lord Aberdeen, who quite 'vanished'.[21] Parents who allowed children to marry for any other reason than the enlargement of a family's property and status were a rarity and worthy of comment. When Lord and Lady Harrowby consented to the union of their Tory daughter to the Whig Lord Ebrington, because the girl though 'not desperately in love' was 'quite enough so for happiness', tongues wagged. Such behaviour '*n'est pas de ce monde*'.[22]

Since marriage was seen as merely the agency for safely transferring great property from one generation to another, with no nonsense about love involved, not much could be expected of the institution and it certainly forfeited claims to much reverence. Whigs were fashionably cynical about the whole enterprise. When marriages proved unhappy, that was only to be expected. As Lord Melbourne explained to the young Victoria: 'Why, you see, a gentleman hardly knows a girl till he has proposed, and then when he has an unrestrained intercourse with her, he sees something and says, "This I don't quite like".'[23] For Richard Payne Knight, admittedly a bachelor, marriage was a battle between cruelty and tedium:

> But when in bounds indissoluble join'd,
> Securely torpid sleeps the sated mind;
> No anxious hopes or fears arise, to move
> The flagging wings, or stir the fires of love:
> Benumb'd, the soul's best energies repose,
> And life in dull unvaried torpor flows;
> Or only shakes off lethargy, to teaze
> Whom once its only pleasure was to please.[24]

Mercifully, once heirs had been produced, husband and wife could lead separate lives. Whig marriage in this sense was infinitely elastic. In Frederick Reynolds's play *Life*, Mrs Decoy explained to her fiancé, Gabriel Lackbrain, that 'a husband musn't sit next to his wife at table, nor hand her out of the room, nor dance with her', for, 'we can't quarrel if we don't meet you know'.[25] This advice was hardly romantic but it had a certain practicality.

If affection was absolutely demanded, Whigs saw nothing wrong in finding it outside marriage. It was an option open to both genders. The taking of a lover or a mistress was called 'gallantry', and it was regulated by certain rules. A mistress might be passed from hand to hand like a good book. Mrs Armistead had been the companion of Lord George Cavendish, the Earl of Derby and George IV before ending her career with Charles James Fox, and it was frowned upon to marry such women. But courtesans were received in Whig society and had to be properly provided for. Fox thought it a particularly redeeming aspect of Charles II's character that on his deathbed he should have been so preoccupied with promoting the financial security of his mistresses.[26] Equally the Duchess of Devonshire was determined to remain the friend of George IV's mistress, Mrs Fitzherbert, explaining to her mother that, 'an unmarried woman suffering the visits of an unmarried man, is no reason for not being civil to her'.[27]

Normally, though, lovers and mistresses would be found within their own world. Horace Walpole noted that 'a quarter of our peeresses will have been wives of half our peers'.[28] As a result, some truly remarkable ménages were established, to the delight of the cartoonist and scandal monger. At Devonshire House in the late eighteenth century, the fifth Duke lived with his wife and mistress, Lady Elizabeth Foster, à trois. The two ladies were in fact the greatest of friends. At one point, they went to France together, with Lady Elizabeth carrying the Duke's child while the Duchess was pregnant with the daughter of Charles Grey, the future Prime Minister. None of the participants could understand that anything was amiss. When doubts were expressed, 'The Duke ... could not help thinking it a most extraordinary circumstance that when a man and his wife both agree in living with a person, that you should be persuaded to imagine that there was a cause of complaint'.[29] In Melbourne House at the same period, the first Viscount lived with his wife and five children. The heir was undoubtedly his son, but another son was accredited to the Prince of Wales, a son and a daughter to Lord Egremont, and one daughter to serendipity. Matters remained harmonious because Lord Melbourne himself was more interested in the chorus at Covent Garden and Drury Lane.

If the non-Whig world found all this difficult to accept, Whig promiscuity also caused them problems. Whigs had no monopoly in this activity. Indeed they enjoyed comparing notes with political opponents like Wellington. But they seemed to throw up the most glaring examples of a total disregard to what many Englishmen would call morality. Palmerston, for example, famously kept notebooks, like Don Giovanni, in which his conquests would be recorded, with general comments on the quality of the evening. All women seemed to be fair game. Canning jealously observed that 'Palmerston always put him in mind of a Footman who thought his mistress was in love with him; but *who was mistaken*'.[30] None of this disturbed Palmerston's personal and political relationship with his brother-in-law Lord Melbourne, or with his wife, who was happy to have adventures of her own. Many people took mistresses and lovers, but Whigs did it on a scale and in a manner that invited criticism. For them, all their behaviour flowed from defining marriage in a particular way. For their critics this was a deceitful rationalization of vice.

Inevitably, illegitimacy held no stigma in the Whig world. Nurseries would be full of children of uncertain parentage, who were called 'Children of the Mist'. Contemporaries were only too aware 'that vices are wonderfully prolific among the Whigs. There are countless illegitimates among them, such a tribe of Children of the Mist'.[31] It was the height of bad manners to enquire too closely into a child's parentage. A visitor to the home of Lord Robert Spencer and his mistress, Mrs Bouverie, 'saw several children playing about, but thought it most prudent not to inquire minutely into their birth and parentage, for fear of getting into some scrape'.[32] Again, Whigs held no monopoly in this area. Wellington and Melbourne disagreed about much in politics but hugely enjoyed talking about their own bastard status.[33] Whigs, however, were more open and brazen about biological mishaps. Illegitimates were brought up and educated in the same nurseries as male heirs and heiresses. They were found dowries, married off appropriately, and launched into genteel careers. Caroline St Jules, the daughter of the Duke of Devonshire and Lady Elizabeth Foster, was married to Melbourne's brother, while Harriet Stewart, the offspring of Lady Bessborough and Granville Leveson Gower, became Duchess of Leeds. For many contemporaries, this was carrying a pride in bastardy too far.

To Whigs, however, vulgarity lay in another direction. Divorce was thought troublesome and in doubtful taste. After all, if marriages could be conducted on such liberal terms, it was perverse to look for a divorce, which required an Act of Parliament, considerable expenditure and public scrutiny. If husbands or wives were intolerable, separate lives could be lived as long as a proper inheritance of family title and property was assured. Those who did divorce could expect criticism, not only from society in general but also from other Whigs. Lady Holland, for example, was never received at Court and that was to be expected, but she also suffered to some extent in Whig eyes for having had recourse to the law. Being a woman of character, she simply retaliated by establishing at Holland House a court of her own, that in terms of intellect and distinction rivalled any gathering at Buckingham Palace. But she still felt the injury and its social consequences for the whole of her life.[34] Whig marriages were so loosely regulated that it was hard to understand why anyone should find the rules intolerable.

To many of their contemporaries the Whig definition of what marriage entailed was anathema. Even those who were not labouring under the dictates of a Nonconformist, Methodistical or Anglo-Catholic conscience found their conduct often hard to take. Society at large began to prepare a charge-sheet against the Whigs, and if marital eccentricity was the first article, drunkenness was the second. Many people drank immoderately, Whig and Tory, Londoner and provincial. William Pitt the Younger was often the worse for drink, and allegedly declared war on France in February 1793 while inebriated. But, again, it was the Whigs who paid the penalty in cartoons and moralizing tracts. Fox's sottish forays around London at the head of bands of drunken young men were notorious. The sound of Tory windows being smashed reverberated for years. Critics endlessly deplored the dissolution of many talents in alcohol.

The personification of the baleful consequences of bringing Whiggery and drink together was Richard Brinsley Sheridan. A brilliant playwright and orator, he abandoned writing for Whig politics in 1780. As a result, his abilities liquefied. Known everywhere as 'Sherry', he was represented in cartoons, with tankard or bottle in hand, rubbing the bulbous and glowing nose of the alcoholic. Byron often saw him to bed when he himself was hardly in a condition to do so: 'Poor fellow! he got drunk very thoroughly and very soon. It occasionally fell to my lot to convey him home – no sinecure – for he was so tipsy that I was obliged to put on his cock'd hat for him – to be sure it tumbled off again and I was not myself so sober as to be able to pick it up again.'[35] True, a Whig drunk was wittier than a Tory one. When a night watchman found Sheridan lying in a gutter and demanded his name, the answer he gave was 'Wilberforce', the teetotal and very Evangelical member of the Clapham set.[36] Tales such as these provoked laughter in London clubs, but for many people they showed Whiggery and the metropolis at their most vicious and untrustworthy. On one occasion, a drunken Sheridan crawled across a ballroom floor and bit his lover, Lady Bessborough, on the ankle.

Then there was gambling. Losing money on a heroic scale often produced the strange spectacle of wealthy men and women short of ready cash and in hock to bankers. The great Whig Clubs of St James's were admittedly centres for discussing politics and male socializing, but they were also gambling dens. Members of the public passing the windows of Brooks's could see eminent politicians losing fortunes. It was believed that the aristocracy in general and the Whigs in particular had contracted the disease as Grand Tourists in Paris. Most of the new card games introduced into England in the late eighteenth century had French names. It was well known that a young man who refused to gamble in Paris was dismissed as '*inutile*'.[37] As a result, it became almost fashionable to lose money, and to do so in a manner that became a gentleman. Certainly it was a serious business. Often gambling parties would go on all night, and participants would wear special clothes. Coats would be discarded, leather aprons and cuffs protected ruffles on shirtfronts and sleeves, visors would protect the eyes. Beside each player specially designed tables were placed, which held food, drink and counters. Little wonder that a pamphleteer of 1780 described the Whig Club as distinguished 'for the congregated talents of its members' but also 'for the strange *mélange* of morals, of which it is composed'.[38]

In fact, in the last three decades of the eighteenth century, gambling reached epidemic proportions. At the race-course and in the London clubs huge sums of money changed hands. The betting book at Brooks's Club proves that Whigs would bet on anything. Wagers were contracted about the outcome of a war or an election, but also about whether the Marquess of Cholmondeley could successfully have sex with a courtesan in the basket of a balloon suspended several hundred feet above the ground. He did. Not surprisingly, some mothers pleaded with their children not to take up the gambling habit. Lady Stafford reminded her son that:

> You know Gaming is, in his [father's] Eyes, an inexcusable Fault, because it leads to ruin, not only by hurting the Fortune, but it erases every good Affection, it destroys Health, it brings into the worst Company, and destroys all good Principles. He says it is by Degrees that Men and Women learn this destructive Vice ... therefore the surest and the only prudent resolution upon that subject is never to play at Games of Chance.[39]

But, significantly, Lady Stafford was a Tory, and she saw gambling as one indication that her son was drifting into Whig ways.

The losses suffered and the debts incurred were colossal. In the winter of 1774–75, Fox's gambling losses were reputedly £140,000, the equivalent of millions in modern money.[40] He was sold up for debt in 1781 and again in 1783. People walking down Clarges Street could have enjoyed the spectacle of the great statesman sitting in his one remaining armchair reading a Greek historian as the bailiffs cleared his house. Voters might wonder if this was a man to whom the nation's fortunes could be safely committed. Similarly, Georgiana, Duchess of Devonshire was in debt for most of her life, leaving £40,000 of gambling debts at her death.[41] Inevitably the banker and the money-lender were never far away, and nor was the contracting of desperate, but doubtful, obligations. To be in the power of Thomas Coutts was one thing. He merely required the Duchess to promote society marriages for his daughters. But the 'Mr Hutchinsons' and 'J.D.'s who also figure as creditors of the Whigs were more dangerous. At one point, Fox was paid by a marriage broker-cum-brothel keeper to leave his carriage outside her door, to give her establishment more tone. Little wonder that contemporaries should marvel at 'great folks' putting themselves 'under such disgraceful obligations'.[42]

There was a penalty to be paid for this addiction. Public images of the Whigs often recorded the vices associated with gambling. In Cruikshank's cartoon The Imposter Unmasked of 1806, Sheridan is shown addressing a group of voters. He talks of giving the oppressors of Englishmen a check. The voters reply that his cheques are worthless. In Rowlandson's The Gaming Table at Devonshire House, the Duchess is shown acting as hostess and the bank to a motley assortment of Whigs and demi-reps.[43] These images carried a harsh message. Many electors were of the opinion that the Whigs were simply irresponsible in money matters. Their performance in London proved that they were incapable of managing their own finances, and that they therefore should never be entrusted with the nation's. As ever, the Whigs were able to ignore this advice in the conduct of their private lives but not in its political consequences.

In debates on marital infidelity, excessive drinking and addictive gambling, there were gender problems as well. Whig women drank and gambled alongside their male relations. They even claimed the same sexual licence. In 1724, Lady Mary Wortley Montagu opined that 'the appellation of rake is as genteel in a woman as in a man of quality'.[44] A generation later, Lady Bessborough complained that it was 'very hard that men should always have *beau jeu* on all occasions, and that all pain, *Moral et Physique*, should be reserv'd for us'.[45] She remedied the situation in her own case by taking a lover twelve years her junior, bearing him two children, and passing him over to her niece as a husband when he bored her. This was questionable behaviour for a woman claiming respectability. Worse still, a few Whig women tiptoed into the male preserve of politics. Such ladies had always enjoyed roles that might be called political, as the promoters of talent, or as facilitators of politics in introducing one man to another or reconciling one man with another. Now they went a little further. They still played no part in decision-making, but they claimed a new visibility in political life.

Notoriously, in the Westminster elections of 1784 and 1819, first the Duchess of Devonshire and then her niece, Lady Caroline Lamb, openly canvassed for Whig candidates. This involved drinking in taverns and exchanging kisses for votes. Such behaviour was almost universally condemned. Tory ladies thought it 'a pity that any of our sex should ever forget what is due to female delicacy'.[46] Nearly all men resented these sallies into areas in which women were not fitted by nature to participate. Cartoonists showed these ladies wearing trousers, thereby giving expression to the common belief that they had become awful sexual hybrids. There seemed to be no rules that Whigs were not prepared to redefine for the use of their own circle. As ever, Whig ladies took no notice of what the world in general thought. Castigated for her misbehaviour in 1784, the Duchess only slightly modified her role in an election of 1788: 'Her Grace of Devonshire did not go about the streets, as she did in the last Election, but she wrote numberless Notes every Morning to solicit, and at Night the Heads of the Party met at Devonshire House to sup and settle matters – which the Dutchess [sic] liked exceedingly, as she said it was very Jolly.'[47] When a few Tory ladies tried the same thing, they were dismissed as

> Lady Lackpension and Dowager Thrifty
> And many a maiden the wrong side of fifty.[48]

At considerable cost to their public image, Whig women gently nudged gender barriers in ways that were at once outrageous and chic.

Covering all these activities was concern about the sheer expense of it. Living in the capital had never been cheap, but the scale of Whig expenditure raised the stakes in the game of financial respectability. Luxuriousness seemed to be overtaking so many aspects of life, and with luxury came vice of the kind that had destroyed Rome. In the first half of the eighteenth century, over four hundred and fifty books had been published on the awful consequences of luxury. It led people into debt and waste; it undermined the personal restraint that was the basis of the virtuous life; and, above all, it promoted the values of money and materialism over those of deference and paternalism. It was the solvent of the proper divisions in society. London took the lead in this terrible trade and the Whigs were the masters of London. Everything they did was done to excess and immorality followed. For those who thought in this way, Whigs threatened the very foundations of an ordered society.

Perhaps the most visible sign of this decadence could be seen in what people actually wore. Fashion was deliberately employed in social and political battles. For much of the eighteenth century, and particularly after 1750, fashion changed violently from one year to the next, and both genders were involved. Women would be committed to long trains and panniers one year and forced to discard them the next. Men's waistcoats and the reverses on men's jackets could be enormous or miniscule. Both genders wore shoes with heels that could be six inches high or flat on the ground. Hairpieces, in several colours, could be three feet high or virtually level with the scalp. The result was that it was very easy to distinguish between those wearing the latest fashion and those who were not. Unfortunately, the cost of endlessly renewing wardrobes of clothes made of expensive materials and even precious stones was prohibitive. But not to keep up in this ruinous competition was to invite speculation about the state of a family's finances. The flaunting of fashion suited the Whig propensity for social devices that excluded the unworthy, but the moralist only saw gross expenditure on trivialities. All agreed that it was a matter of great importance.

Contemporaries were only too aware of what was at stake. William Hazlitt described the furious changes in fashion as 'gentility running away from vulgarity and afraid of being overtaken'.[49] As a writer in *The World* noted, the polite world could only maintain its social distinction by endlessly accepting change: 'the nobility [have been] beaten out of all their resources for superior distinction; out of innumerable fashions in dress, every one of which they have been obliged to abandon as soon as occupied by their impertinent rivals'.[50] Established families changed the rules of fashion to catch out the social interloper, and the aspiring ran breathlessly towards a fashionable acceptability that would never be theirs. It was an accelerating madness for the improvident that every moralist deplored. George III unsuccessfully tried to provide an antidote by drastically simplifying dress worn at Court.

Inevitably the Whigs were recognized as the leading participants in this frenzy. For much of the 1780s, what the Duchess of Devonshire wore was fashion. When she became pregnant, many society ladies adopted clothes that simulated that condition. When she sat for a portrait to Gainsborough wearing a large straw hat, 'the Devonshire Hat' or a variation of it became a standard feature of London life.[51] Similarly, Charles James Fox's Macaronis in the early 1770s dictated that young men should wear blue wigs, red-heeled shoes, tight knee-breeches, *boutonnières* and miniature tricorn hats. Such bravos were the direct ancestors of Byronic dandies in the early nineteenth century. As ever, it seemed likely that Whigs took everything to excess. Most influential was the future George IV, who, when Prince of Wales, shared Whig company and vices, improving on most of them. As an arbiter of fashion he had no equal. In 1788, for example, he prescribed the wearing of leather pantaloons 'made so excessively tight, that the wearers need to be slung into them by pullies'.[52] As one of his obituaries recorded, 'Whatever his late Majesty did, was little short of wholesale'.[53] To critics such metropolitan extravagance was beyond all sense. There was nothing but expenditure without profit and the subversion of true values. To Whigs their control of high fashion in London allowed them to design the uniforms of social acceptability in terms that were unattainable by most of their countrymen.

Taken together, the charge-sheet against London and its principal inhabitants was a lengthy one. Contemporaries rightly complained of the Whigs' joy in exclusivity and a sense of separateness from their countrymen. In politics, they genuinely laboured for the people, but believed that they could only do so if ruthlessly confirmed as independent in wealth and status. The aristocratic code implied duty and obligation. It might involve the loss of your head if the government turned tyrannical. But none of this led them to think that most people would ever say or think anything of interest. The two 'worlds' were different and rightly so. London and its Season allowed Whiggery to parade. For every parliamentary defeat, there was a social victory in some club or salon. Quite properly Whigs viewed things in their own way. They called 'gallantry' what others called adultery; conviviality to them was drunkenness to others; gambling was not a vice but a gentleman's philosophical acceptance of what the Fates had waiting for him at the tables. Aristocrats who were the trustees of parliamentary liberties were not as other men, and could not be expected to live by their rules.

Impervious to criticism coming from outside their own ranks, Whigs dismissed it as motivated by malice or an unhealthy preoccupation with the salacious. When Sydney Smith was asked to write on the work of the Society for the Suppression of Vice, his conclusion was that: 'Beginning with the best intentions in the world, such societies must, in all probability, degenerate into a receptacle for every species of tittle-tattle, impertinence, and malice. Men, whose trade is rat-catching, love to catch rats; the bug-destroyer seizes on his bug with delight; and the suppressor is gratified in finding his vice.'[54] The moralist was sicker than the rake. Vicariously to enjoy vice by sniffing out its haunts and practitioners was more doubtful than wholeheartedly indulging in it. Rarely therefore were Whigs penitent or apologetic. Many aspects of religious systems were missing in the Whig make-up, and none more so than the idea of guilt purged by confession.

Instead they counter-attacked, using wit as a battering-ram.[55] To be known to have wit or *esprit* was in the eighteenth century to make a man or woman a social asset. The success of a dinner party or house party depended on such people, many of whom, like Richard Sharpe or Poodle Byng, exchanged epigrams for a free meal. Whatever else was in doubt in political life, no one questioned the Whig superiority in this respect. Quite simply, they were more intellectual than their opponents and funnier. So, faced with an avalanche of hostile comment about what they believed and how they lived, they established the Esto Perpetua Club in 1785. Situated just off the Strand, the club was open to any scribbler, hack or essayist prepared to take Whig wages. Often recruited by Sheridan through his extensive contacts in the press and the theatre, these men produced paragraphs for the daily newspapers that pilloried the Whigs' opponents by holding them up as objects of ridicule. Collected together as *The Rolliad, The Probationary Odes* and *Political Miscellanies*, they constitute one of the great landmarks in political satire. As contributors, leading politicians like Charles Grey and George Tierney rubbed shoulders with Grub Street inhabitants like Joseph Richardson, 'a remarkably fine, showy young man'.[56]

Humour is always irresistible but not always kind. It was particularly upsetting for moralists to have their own conduct come under scrutiny. Equally, Whigs particularly enjoyed pricking bubbles of pretension, both moral and social. To take one of the most glaring examples, Whigs endlessly publicized their belief that Pitt the Younger and George Canning were both homosexual, and that the former had promoted the career of the latter for this reason alone. No two men had inflicted more political irritation on the Whigs and both were therefore subjected to literary harassment. It is true that, late in life, Lord Holland denied that either man was homosexual, only saying that 'Pitt used to go to brotells [sic] – but was never known to touch a woman. Dundas said he would give a place of £500 a year to anyone who could prove that Pitt had done so.'[57]

Such moderated views were not, however, in evidence when Pitt and Canning were at the height of their careers. Pitt was always 'the Immaculate Boy', a virginal creature whose purity was suspect. Innuendo about his private life was therefore endlessly possible. There was a healthy trade in epigrams:

> Though Pitt has to women told some things, no doubt;
> Yet his private affairs they have never found out.

'Tis true, indeed, we oft abuse him,
Because he bends to no man;
But Slander's self does not accuse him
Of stiffness to a woman.

Who dares assert that virtuous Pitt
Partakes in female pleasures;
For know there ne'er was woman yet
Could e'er endure half measures.[58]

Pitt was the political hero of the sort of Englishman who found Whig behaviour offensive. To show that he and his principal associates had feet of clay made a useful point, for use both in Parliament and at the dinner table. In the Whig view, public men who position themselves on the high moral ground must always expect mirrors to be held up to their own lives.

Whigs were therefore largely unmoved by tabloid scandal-mongering. Their wealth and birth gave them a position in politics and society that was impregnable. Their excesses were visible and public because they had no concern for popularity. Indeed, in some cases, they enjoyed jokes against themselves almost as much as sallies against their opponents. In 1802, Fox was accorded an interview with Napoleon that went badly wrong. Bonaparte opened the conversation by complaining about his treatment by the English press. Fox answered that 'in England people don't mind being abused in the newspapers', whereupon the Emperor muttered '*c'est autre chose ici*'.[59] The thickness of a Whig skin when confronted by criticism was in direct correlation with the scale of their bank-balances and the quality of their ancestry.

Yet there can be no doubt that the Whigs suffered harsh penalties for their association with London and their leadership of its Season. Too many of their contemporaries found the capital a problem. It seemed to be a city with a new function. True, its commercial and financial aspects were intact. Also unchanged was its role as the epicentre of politics. But these traditional and even honourable activities seemed to have been overlayed by something new and menacing. Some Londoners now lived a social round in which what many would call vice and immorality were the norm. If England was a country being undermined by decadence, the capital was the place where the vicious learnt their trade. Worse still, this was a gangrene that had an alien quality about it. London was full of foreigners who came as visitors, traders and refugees, and brought with them strange codes of behaviour. France could not defeat England in many wars, but Grand Tourists adopted French immorality in Paris and returned home to live it out in London. On all these fronts Whigs were perceived to be in the van. They lived in London most of the year and directed its revels. At every election many voters found this too compromising. How could Fox claim votes when he was often bankrupt, sometimes drunk and married to a prostitute? He and his friends and heirs inhabited a different world and voters turned away. None of this surprised the Whigs, and none of it led them for a moment to think of changing their ways.

4

The Country

If Whigs by preference and association were metropolitan, it follows that they put no store by country living. In fact they detested it. According to Joseph Jekyll, a day spent in the country was 'a day given to the grave before one's decease'.[1] As a result, families of consequence spent less and less time there. Great houses stood empty, towering over the English countryside as power statements in stone rather than family homes. Housekeepers and butlers would for a fee show the inquisitive around well-appointed rooms that were not in regular use. Their owners claimed local political and social leadership but were invisible for most of the year. Lady Elizabeth Foster frankly observed that 'she never wished to see more of the country than was comprised in the Parks in London'; that Chiswick even was too far removed from the metropolis; and that when people complained of the latter place being dull, she always replied, 'London is good enough for me at all times'.[2] Helpfully, one of the London parks was home to a model farm. Visitors could stroke perfumed animals and talk to well-scrubbed Arcadians, thereby securing contact with country values without any of the inconveniences.

The retreat of persons of quality into their London fortress had many consequences. For example, successful local government crucially depended on gentlemen undertaking the responsibilities of justice of the peace. By the end of the eighteenth century, such gentlemen were in such short supply as residents of counties such as Cumberland, Devon and Merioneth that local clergymen had to be drafted in to fill the vacancies. No one thought this satisfactory. But the magnetism of London life exercised an ever-increasing pull. Equally, actually to prefer country life was considered eccentric. Lady Sophia Fitzgerald's wish to remain out of London was overruled by her mother, who thought her decision 'very odd'. Her brother insisted that she should come to London, because her behaviour was tarnishing the family's name. There was talk of seditious politics and unwanted pregnancies.[3] As this change in the pattern of living was more and more confirmed, London became grander and grander, while country people increasingly felt isolated and at risk. The scramble to get to London and stay there discounted all rival values.

Whig diatribes against country living would constitute a book in themselves. When forced to spend time there their condition was piteous. Sydney Smith summed up the condition as being always twelve miles from a lemon. Joseph Jekyll was more expansive, cataloguing

> The Miseries of Life in the country ... as, blowing weather; no fish at the market; newspaper not arriving; window broke in bed-chamber, glazier five miles off; leg broke, surgeon eight miles off or gone a-hunting; family circle, opera eighty miles off; bores on a fortnight's visit, with a desire to be shown the lions of your neighbourhood; a rainy day, and the last volume of your favourite new novel in the paws of an old-lady checkmated by words of five syllables.[4]

Such suffering was exquisite and real. All in all the experience was best avoided.

At the root of the problem was the entire absence in the country of what was subsumed in the eighteenth-century use of the word 'company'. There was no conversation, nothing to divert or amuse, nothing to engage the intelligence. Even a provincial spa failed to meet these requirements. In 1820, William Lyttelton found himself marooned in Harrogate. Reporting the situation, he threw himself on his wife's sympathy:

> There is a scarcity of anything like real gentlemen, the company consisting chiefly of Yorkshire, Lancashire, and other squires, many of whom come here with their wives and daughters a-pleasuring, and there are many persons of yet inferior rank ... At one of the inns on the heath – the Granby – there is almost always ... a strong colony of Irish, sent here for their health ... Add to them a sprinkling of mere rival dandies, and you have a fairish notion of the society in this *hilligant* place. I think it is unaccountably bad upon the whole, and so it must have been for some time past, for I have looked over one or two lists, and have not seen a single name even that I knew ... I had rather much be alone than be involved in constant talk with the Lord knows who.[5]

True, he later found a Manchester industrialist who was not

uninteresting on the problems of his home town, but, if Yorkshire squires and all Irishmen were not 'real gentlemen', prospects were bleak.

Everything in the country was out of date. As the competition in London to keep up with every new fashion and invention became more and more frantic, the refusal of country people to enter the race at all was insupportable. It literally took years for a ray of London enlightenment to penetrate the minds of rustics, whose clothes were as behind the times as their ideas. Sydney Smith made a telling analogy between ideas and furniture to a brother cleric:

> If you go into a parsonage-house in the country, Mr Archdeacon, you see sometimes a style and fashion of furniture which does very well for us, but which has had its day in London. It is seen in London no more; it is banished to the provinces; from the gentlemen's houses of the provinces these pieces of furniture, as soon as they are discovered to be unfashionable, descend to the farm-houses, then to cottages, then to the faggot-heap, then to the dung-hill. As it is with furniture so it is with arguments. I hear at country meetings many arguments against the Catholics which are never heard in London; their London existence is over – they are only to be met with in the provinces, and they are fast hastening down, with clumsy chairs and ill-fashioned sofas, to another order of men.[6]

Quite literally discourse between London and the provinces operated on different levels. It was increasingly difficult for the two worlds to hold a dialogue or to feel sympathy for each other's problems.

Sydney Smith at one time held a benefice in Yorkshire and had to suffer the disadvantages of his position. He was so keenly aware of the antagonism between London and the provinces that he was uncertain whether metropolitan visitors should be encouraged or not. In 1813, he urged Lady Holland to 'take a ramble to the North', even though she would certainly 'alarm the village'. Ten years later, the advice was different. 'Never venture into the country, dear Lady Holland, it does not suit you.'[7] When the inhabitant of one world ventured into another, embarrassment could follow, which in turn could become the motor of comedy. In Goldsmith's *She Stoops to Conquer*, a young London man about town attempts to repair his damaged fortunes by travelling north to marry the daughter of a wealthy Yorkshire squire. His preoccupation with fashion nearly loses him the match. The squire's wife is wearing clothes that are five years out of date, and the wig on her husband's head is ageless. As a result, the young suitor concludes that they are an innkeeper and his wife and treats them accordingly. In the end, Mr and Mrs Hardcastle forgive his impertinence, but the young man has learnt the hard lesson that to award status on the basis of dress and accent might be the norm in London but other rules obtained in Yorkshire. They were quite literally alien societies, standing increasingly apart for fear of committing solecisms.

Predictably, most Whigs had no knowledge of, or interest in, plain agriculture. True, the odd individual like Coke of Holkham was renowned for his experiments in selective breeding, and he would don a smock to supervise the annual sheep-shearing. The parties held after this event were famous throughout the county, but they included as much politics as agriculture. On each occasion, a major London figure would be invited down to lecture the farmers on Whiggery. They were hardly qualified to talk of matters of more immediate interest to their audience. Thomas Erskine, a future Lord Chancellor, embarrassed his host, when passing a field of barley, by saying, 'Good God, Coke, what magnificent lavender!'[8] John, sixth Duke of Bedford, with the help of Joseph Paxton, experimented with grasses, and published a *Hortus Grammaticus Woburnensis*. A new species of ornamental willow was named after him as *salix Russelliana*.[9] But not much of this activity had anything to do with the nuts and bolts of the agricultural industry. Whigs were attracted to the exotic and the ornamental, but had little concern for country life. Theirs was a world of greenhouses rather than open fields. The same Duke of Bedford on a shooting party only managed to kill one of his host's lapdogs.[10]

Field sports in fact were not for Whigs. It was very unwise to place a gun in their hands. When Henry Brougham went on a shooting party, he only managed to set fire to the powder-horn and singe his eyebrows, leading his friend John Ward to suggest that 'we Edinburgh-bred gentlemen ought not to meddle with field sports'.[11] Harriet Granville thought her husband placed in a similar situation was a menace to the neighbours,[12] and Lord Holland never shot anything until he was forty, and was then overcome by remorse.[13] To the intense fury of Tories, Whigs, who cared little about shooting, also had no interest in defending the Game Laws, the totemic legislation on country life, or in pursuing poachers. Benches of JPs on which Whigs predominated had a quite different record in such cases from those on which Tories were in a majority.[14] After all, the Tory Marquess of Salisbury won a bet in 1829 that he could find four gentlemen able to kill a hundred brace of pheasants in an hour.[15]

Nor were many Whigs to be found in the hunting field. In spite of the fact that a fox was, for obvious reasons, quite often referred to as a 'charlie', Charles Fox himself never hunted. Lady Harriet Granville in the country complained about being surrounded by 'so *borné* a set of minds ... all the *élans* are kept for hedges and ditches'.[16] When a Whig like Lord Althorp showed an interest in the sport, it was simply distressful, as Lady Sarah Lyttelton explained to Lord Robert Spencer:

> God knows some people do love fox-hunting in rather an inconceivable way. Believe, if you can, Bob, that there exists a young man, calling himself a gentleman, and I dare say pretending to a liberal education and a polished mind, who lives now at a little ugly cottage in the little ugly village of Harbottle; never can see or speak to any living soul except the day-labourers of the said village; never does read, write, or anything in the said cottage, but put on his red coat to go out to hunt of a morning, take it off and go to bed at night, and probably sleeps on frosty days, spends the *whole* winter in the same profitable manner; and he calls himself a friend of Althorp's. I really longed to look at this man; and he dined here the other day. Of course his society is, in my opinion, not quite upon a par with that of a whipper-in; the latter follows his profession, does his duty, and probably understands his business, and is, in short, a respectable person; but t'other? Oh, what a being! Somebody said that in a chase, first in rank comes the fox, next the hound, next the horse, and last the man. Now tho' I do know and see that dear Althorp has in him much more than enough to put him high, very high, above all his fellow-sportsmen, yet when he covers all that with that muddy red coat, and does his best to forget it – oh, Bob, what a pity![17]

Hunting seemed to be the antithesis of the polite behaviour that marked the conduct of a gentleman. Famously, as has been noted, Lady Melbourne did not like young men she described as rough diamonds. She preferred them to be polished by attrition in good society.

In fact, life in the countryside was particularly challenging for Whig women. Even if men had no interest in country sports, they could inspect local militias, talk politics with the worthies of the neighbourhood, and had the right to be bored by hearing cases as JPs, 'and what was worse ... to dine with the judges'. Their wives, mothers and sisters were abandoned to the company of 'curates, land-surveyor-looking people with wives hanging on their arm'.[18] Letter-writing, charades and card games hardly filled the hours. The search for something *pour me distraire* was unending.[19] The contrast with life in the West End could hardly have been sharper. In 1797 Lady Bessborough found herself in St Albans. It was an awful experience, and she described her situation to her lover back in Piccadilly as though she had been exiled to Siberia:

> Nothing can be a greater contrast than my life here and that I usually lead. As the clock strikes eight I am down at Prayers, then breakfast, then I give Caroline her lessons as usual, read or write for a while till my mother sends for me to help her in teaching her School Girls. I acquit myself *tant bien que mal*, and often wonder what you, and still more Sol [Lord Morpeth], would say to see me stuck up in the midst of an old ruin'd Abbey teaching some little beggar Girls to spell and sing. We dine at three, are out all evening after tea, return generally to have some music, in which the Chaplain's wife principally shines. She has a very fine voice *d'un très gros Volume*; it makes the house echo again, and tho' I din the right note in her ears as loud as I can, she disdains such narrow limits, and with laudable perseverance keeps constantly a half note too high or too low the whole way thro! At nine ye bell rings for Prayers, then supper, and at ten not a mouse is stirring in the whole House. I hope you are edified with the length of my letter and the importance of its contents.[20]

For a London lady to be up by eight and abed by ten, and so prayerful in between, was astonishing and, for the lady, hard to bear.

Understandably, Whigs looked for revenge for their sufferings, and their recourse was to the theatre. The polarity between country living and London life was so marked that it became a stock comic mechanism for two hundred years. From Restoration comedy to Wilde and Pinero, playwrights could bring the capital and the countryside into collision with wonderfully humorous results. Of course, since such productions were overwhelmingly intended for London audiences, it was the country characters who came off worst in the encounter. The stage was peopled by rustics and bumpkins, sometimes well-meaning, but always ignorant, boorish and deficient in personal hygiene. A list of names given to country characters makes the point. Sheridan created Bob Acres of Clod Hall (*The Rivals*), Sir Lucius O'Trigger of Blunderbuss Hall (*The Rivals*) and Sir Tunbelly Clumsy of Muddy Moat Hall (*A Trip to Scarborough*). Samuel Foote in the same generation allowed London to laugh at Sir John Buck (*An Englishman in Paris*), Sir Toby Tallyhoe and Squire Racket (*An Englishman Returned from Paris*) and Sir Penurious Trifle of Gripe Hall (*The Knights*). They are all heirs of Sir Wilful Witwood in Congreve's *The Way of the World*. London characters like Lord Foppington could also be grotesques of course, but the balance was heavily weighted against the countrymen.

The joke was to bring the two worlds into abrasive contact with each other. In *A Trip to Scarborough*, Lord Foppington is taken into the country in search of a wife. After a series of humiliating and often muddy encounters, he is forced to ask his intended: 'For God's sake, madam, how has your ladyship been able to subsist thus long, under the fatigue of a country life?'[21] Even more comic potential lay in bringing a country cousin to London. In John Tobin's *The Faro Table*, Lady Wellgrove has tried to polish up her rustic relation, Sapling, but without success:

Lady Wellgrove	In spite of all my endeavours to make you a human creature, you don't make the least progress towards civilization.
Sapling	Why, you don't give me any encouragement.
Lady Wellgrove	Not give you any encouragement? – Didn't I carry you with me on Saturday night to the Opera? – and didn't you begin snoring in the middle of Cherubini's famous Bravura?
Sapling	I'd a nice nap, that's the truth on't: but you know I woke time enough to encore it; and ecod, I don't see but that's as much as many of your dili-what-d'ye-call-em?
Lady Wellgrove	Dillitanti?
Sapling	Aye, Dillitanti do.
Lady Wellgrove	What, I suppose you would rather have heard the roaring of a dozen fox-hunters in your father's great hall?
Sapling	No, no, I don't say that: but dash it if I wouldn't rather our Doll in the country call the bees together with a poker and warming pan.[22]

Successfully to transfer from one context to the other was, according to London dramatists, almost impossible. Perhaps this is most poignantly expressed in *The School for Scandal*. Sir Peter Teazle has brought his young country wife to London. Unsophisticated and impressionable, she falls in with a scandal-mongering circle that is a synonym for the Devonshire House set. Inevitably she gets into scrapes. At the end of the play, Sir Peter demands that they return home and Lady Teazle pronounces in an epilogue that she is once again to be buried alive:

> Must I then watch the early crowing cock,
> The melancholy ticking of a clock;
> In a lone rustic hall forever pounded,
> With dogs, cats, rats and squalling brats surrounded?[23]

To move the other way was just as difficult. In *Cheap Living*, a London couple descend on a country-living uncle in the hope of being named his heirs. Such is the tedium of life, however, that they begin to wonder if even the inheritance of a fortune could justify it, for, as the nephew complains, 'if he don't die soon, I certainly shall'.[24] Any audience watching such comedies, even as they laughed, could only have been confirmed in the conviction that it was unwise to cross such formidable social frontiers.

If Whigs suffered so much out of London, the question arises of why they visited the countryside at all. Yet for a period of weeks in the summer, great houses would finally see their owners. Obviously, no one thought that 'women of fashion left London to turn freckled shepherdesses'.[25] In fact they went because they had to. Politics demanded it. Whig power in London reflected to some extent the impact of their own votes in the House of Lords and the capacity to exercise influence in the House of Commons. Whig money and Whig property turned tenants and shopkeepers into potential Whig voters. Sometimes it was a matter of simple bribery. Voters would be 'treated' to drink or cash payments. Much more often it was a matter of what the eighteenth century called influence. It was right to vote for the landlord's candidate, just as it was right for the landlord to look after his people. Influence can therefore be defined as the harmonious exchange of deference for condescension. Whigs requested support from their clients, and they, as free men, were often happy to give it. For the system to work, however, the two worlds had occasionally to meet.

Keeping up a family's interest in a borough or county was an expensive and wearing business. All kinds of duties had to be carried out by both men and women, and if obligations were ignored influence was quickly lost. First and foremost, Whigs had to entertain lavishly. Mayors and corporations, voters and non-voters expected to be made much of. At Chatsworth, Dukes and Duchesses of Devonshire presided over 'open days', when seemingly all the inhabitants of Derbyshire were made welcome. Men who would have been happier in Piccadilly were forced to inspect country militias in their parks and sit as JPs at the Quarter Sessions. Their womenfolk would be expected to visit schools and almshouses, spending lavishly in the shops of local tradesmen. There were horse races to organize and charity work to be done. Whigs had to be visible and properly aristocratic in the communities whose votes underpinned their London pre-eminence.

None of this was particularly pleasant. Apart from the possibility of being killed by an over-excited militiaman,[26] bruising encounters of all sorts were hard to avoid. At Stafford Races, Harriet Granville was greeted by Lord Bradford's steward with the words, 'G. d–n you, how is Granville today?', and she had to admit that 'it is difficult to meet this sort of fire and spirit in conversation with any degree of success'.[27] At St Albans, which normally allowed the Bessboroughs to return its Members of Parliament, the family had to work hard for its privilege, as Lady Bessborough described:

My brother sent to me to beg I would come here to do civilities for him, but more to attend a morning ball and visit some freeholders' wives, whom he wanted to please. Conceive being dress'd out as fine as I could at eleven o'clock this morning, squeez'd into a hot assembly room at the Angel Inn, cramming fifty old Aldermen and their wives with hot rolls and butter, while John and Fred danced with the Misses, playing at fourpenny commerce and tradille [card games], and then visiting all about the gay town of St Albans. Can you boast of anything to surpass this? and to crown all, a mad Mr Cavendish who lives here *se fait jour parmi la foule*, in the midst of the ball-room, and after demanding silence, repeated, *à ma tête*, a long copy of verses, in which he compar'd me to Venus visiting her favourite Island, my children to Cupids, the old coach horses to doves, the tea to Nectar, and all the fat aldermen – my votaries.[28]

The costs were high, but the Bessboroughs' control of the politics of St Albans remained intact.

Whigs spoke often of 'the people' in speeches and books. They endlessly proclaimed themselves the guardians of the people's rights, and none of this language was insincere. Even when democratic ideas grew more prevalent in the nineteenth century, the Whig instinct was to accommodate rather than to resist. But meeting the people in the flesh was always a mixed blessing. Some, like Charles James Fox, seem genuinely to have enjoyed the rough and tumble of electioneering, joining in the back-slapping and toast-sharing with real enthusiasm. Many others bore it all with the resignation with which one approached the prospect of a bad winter. On one occasion, a neighbour of Sydney Smith's left an estate worth £4000 a year to a 'little linen draper' and his eight sons, 'all brought up to low professions, and they are coming to live here. What can this be but a visitation of providence to my Whig principles? This is indeed a severe dose of the People.'[29] The smooth running of society and politics demanded that London should from time to time rub shoulders with the rest of England, but for metropolitans it was more of a penance than a pleasure.

If visits to the country were unavoidable, the question arose of how to make these visits tolerable. Whigs became adept at fashioning the countryside to their own requirements. Their central ambition was to endow it with something of interest. It had none before London people set to work. There was no wit in a mountain range and no babbling brook ever coined an epigram. The answer was, as far as possible, to transplant the West End into a rural setting. The most obvious manifestation of this process were the rituals of the house party. If large numbers of friends could be persuaded to pay visits, some semblance of the daily round in London could be recreated and boredom kept at arm's length. In the 1770s, those living on the Chatsworth estate complained that the fifth Duke of Devonshire's 'grandfather used to spend nine months at Chatsworth, his father six months, and himself three months'. They also complained that, even when he was in residence, the great house was too often closed to locals, being full of 'London hours, London habits, London morals'.[30] Individuals and whole families undertook social pilgrimages around the country in the summer months, reinforcing London numbers where they were most needed.

In such company, country life took on something of a familiar pattern. Flirtations and liaisons could be supplemented by charades, pencil-and-paper games, gambling and private theatricals. Guests who were embarrassed by such pastimes were dismissed as *borné* or limited in mind. In one play, a duchess of Tory ancestry was given the part of a blousy pub landlady on the grounds that her limited acting ability would not thereby be too stretched. She could effectively play herself.[31] The revels frequently fell under the direction of bachelors known as lounge lizards, who entertained in return for board and keep. Men like Richard Sharpe and 'Poodle' Byng were prized for their wit and entertainment value. They could warm away the intellectual damp of country life. Predictably, many aspects of the house party upset local opinion. To import London ways into the country was provocative. For example, in the capital the word actress and the word prostitute were virtually synonymous. Great ladies who turned their homes into theatres and who acted themselves blurred moral lines and worried their neighbours.

In 1811, Harriet Granville found herself staying in a small country house called Lilleshall, 'so quiet, such thorough country'. Her feeling of isolation was so intense that she feared that she would become 'quite a misanthrope'. What sustained her was the thought that she was moving on to Chatsworth, and 'Chatsworth will make me worldly again'.[32] Her use of the word 'worldly' is of interest. For her, Chatsworth was not in the country at all, but was rather an extension of the London world transplanted into the wastes of Derbyshire. In a sense, when people like her perambulated around the house-party circuit, they never left the capital at all. Obligations were honoured to tenants and dependants and social bills were paid, but there was the minimum of real contact between the worlds of London and the countryside, and probably less and less as the century wore on. The house party was a very effective kind of social insulation.

Another way of polishing rural life was to turn the countryside into something interesting. The acres immediately surrounding Whig houses had very little to do with mere agriculture. Something more was needed. One Duke of Devonshire started a ménagerie of exotic animals at Chiswick House which included kangaroos, elks, emus 'and other pretty sportive death-dealers'.[33] There were unEnglish plants in the great glasshouses at Chatsworth and Woburn, and selective breeding of animals at Holkham. Whig estates might also contain model farms inhabited by perfumed animals, follies and grottos, some of which had

a resident hermit, Greek temples and statuary, and beautiful examples
of the disciplining of water into fountains and cascades. All of these
examples were aspects of landscaping the countryside to endow it with
interest. For Richard Payne Knight, even the sweeping lawns of Capa-
bility Brown were too bland. In his view, a garden had two functions: it
must set off the House and it must engage the mind. In other words,
the garden was an adjunct to the great house and subordinate to the
representation of its power.[34]

In 1808, the Duke of Bedford asked Humphry Repton to redesign the
gardens at Woburn. In response Repton produced what he called 'a
modern garden'. There were to be terraces and parterres around the
house itself, allowing uncluttered views of the stone grandeur of the Russells. Further off, there was planted a private garden for the family, an
American garden, a Chinese garden set out around an oriental pavilion,
a botanic garden, an 'animated' garden or ménagerie, an English garden
and 'a shrubbery walk' connecting all of them.[35] There was little correlation between Whiggery and the taking of exercise, but, for those of a
robust disposition, the Woburn gardens offered much that was of interest. Repton and Payne Knight, however, thought basically in terms of
imposing on the countryside something created by an artist and seen
through his eyes. Not for the first time therefore, Edmund Burke's belief
that there was nothing more sublime than raw nature put him at odds
with mainstream Whig thinking. As Payne Knight observed, if Burke

> had walked up St James's street without his breeches, it would have occa-
> sioned great and universal *astonishment*; and if he had, at the same time,
> carried a blunderbuss in his hands, the astonishment would have been mixed
> with no small portion of terror; but I do not believe that the united effects
> of these two powerful passions would have produced any sensation
> approaching the sublime.[36]

For Whigs, nature should be under control at all times, and should give
evidence of a regular and engaged mind.

Crafted gardens and the presence of familiar faces in house parties
mitigated the strains of country living, but Whigs never really solved the
problem. The London world and its values held them too tightly in its
grip. Sometimes desperation was brilliantly turned into humour. In the
1820s, country dwellers who subscribed to London lending libraries

could have books delivered by stagecoach. Joseph Jekyll puckishly suggested that this trade in providing the good things of London to rustics might be expanded to include guests. He therefore composed the following spoof advertisement for publication in London newspapers. It was entitled 'Interesting to Country Gentlemen':

> Mr Jekyll having witnessed with regret Country Gentlemen of the utmost respectability reduced in their Country Houses to the dullness of a Domestic Circle and thereby frequently induced to attempt suicide, in the fall of the year, or what is even still more melancholy, driven to invite to their Tables those ancient and well known families the Tags, the Rags, & the Bobtails, and having observed the facility with which the Public is supplied with Job Horses from London, and with Books from circulating Libraries, he has opened an office in London for the purpose of furnishing Country Houses with a regular succession of Company and Guests on the most moderate terms.
>
> An annual subscriber of 30 Guineas will be supplied with four Guests a week to be changed at the will of the Country Gentleman.
>
> An annual subscriber of 15 Guineas will be supplied with two Guests to be changed once a fortnight.
>
> Nonsubscribers within twenty-five miles of London may be furnished with Guests by the Day or the week upon being answerable for breakage on the road.
>
> Mr Jekyll's Catalogue contains an elegant assortment of 617 Guests, amongst whom may be found three Irish Peers – seven Scotch Ditto – thirteen Poor Baronets – six Yellow Admirals – nineteen Major Generals on half pay, who narrate the entire Spanish War – thirty-seven frogging [frowsty] Dowagers – 314 Old Maids on annuities – and several unbeneficed Clergymen who play the Fiddle – Deaf and Dumb people – Sportsmen and Gentlemen who describe Paris and Fonthill may be had at half price . . .
>
> If any Guest is disapproved of Mr Jekyll desires the Country Gentleman subscriber will mark 'Bore' against his name in the Catalogue or chalk it on his Back when he leaves the House and his place will be supplied by the return of the Stage Coach.[37]

London laughed at the deficiencies of the countryside and its inhabitants, and jokes always suggested the superiority of the capital over the provinces. But they also covered up several layers of unease. Whigs could not ignore the country completely. Political clout could not come from a London residence alone. Therefore the worlds of London society and rural England had to confront each other from time to time, but such encounters were often discomforting for both sides. Different value systems could not be easily brought into accommodation. Widespread suspicion of the Whigs was in part due to their identification as representatives of only a small section of the English population, and perhaps not the most salubrious section at that.

To compound the problem, there was a direct correlation in Whig minds between the limitations of country life and the gothic politics of the people who lived there. Toryism was the articulation of country values. Such a narrow correlation was a generalization only, and one with many exceptions, but Whigs delighted in calling their opponents 'the stupid party'. To Lord Holland, they were 'a large mass of fools'. For Lord John Russell, they were country clowns: 'In England the Tory party had always had the benefit of the weight and influence of the stupid part of the nation. The unlettered squires, with heads muddled by their own ale, embraced with cordiality the notion of the divine right of kings.' They were completely unfitted to 'pretend to the higher offices of state'.[38] Even Sir Robert Peel once famously surveyed his own backbenches, and wondered how men whose only interests were hunting, shooting and fishing could dare to claim the government of a great nation. Ignorance, too, was a kind of moral failing in Whig minds. When one of Lady Anne Keppel's children asked her whether 'Tories were born wicked, or grew up wicked', she replied 'that they are born wicked, and grow up worse'.[39]

Again, playwrights and novelists capitalized on this caricature of rural Tories. Their jokes at their expense amused audiences for decades. Typical was Gabriel Lackbrain, a character in a play by Frederick Reynolds. At one point, he ruminates on the use of classical and foreign languages: 'I know nothing of these Roman warriors, and I don't see why I should: Latin won't teach me to sow barley; or Greek to fatten a pig ... I am no foreigner; I can write and read my native language; and I wish, with all my soul, your great scholars could do the same.'[40] At a time when an education in the classics helped to define a gentleman, Lackbrain was effectively disqualifying himself from being seen as such. Fifty years later, the joke had still not run its course. Thomas Love Peacock's Sir Simon Steeltrap was lord of the manors of Spring-Gun and Treadmill. Unlettered, his only interest in life is field sports, in defence of which he fights an unending war with his tenantry: he 'committed many poachers, shot a few; convicted one third of the peasantry; suspected the rest; and passed nearly the whole of them through a wholesome course of prison discipline'.[41]

There was a reason why country-dwellers were generally ignorant of foreign and classical languages, other cultures, new discoveries and new lines of thinking, all fundamental aspects of polite living. They simply lacked the resources to remedy the situation. The income of many Tory squires could not sustain protracted stays in Paris or even London. Judged by income alone, the small landowner had a very lowly status. Henry Brougham thought that 'the regular country gentleman' was 'only one degree above a parson'.[42] Sometimes they were in such straitened circumstances that wives and daughters had to be left at home. In 1830, Joseph Jekyll uncharitably noted that 'the Squires will come sulky to Parliament, and leave wives at grass for the rents won't pay opera boxes. They deserve it, for they huzzaed Mr Pitt and his wars into a debt which has ruined the country.'[43] And this relative poverty had other consequences too. Tories often talked of operating in the national interest, but the state of their finances forced them to seek their own advantage. Tories also boasted of their independence of mind when voting at elections and in Parliament, when in fact they could not resist a bribe or a job. As far as Whigs were concerned, Tory claims to be the national or patriotic party were a mixture of ignorance and moralistic humbug.

Denied the means of travel and improvement, Tories were believed to be happy to substitute prejudice for reason. They clung to the past because they were unacquainted with the mechanisms of change. Sir John Walsh, a Tory essayist writing in 1836, complained that Whigs dismissed people like him as full of 'blindness, narrow-mindedness and an ignorance of the spirit of the age ... They impute to it [Toryism] every narrow prejudice, an obstinate adherence to every antiquated abuse, a stupid dullness of perception to all wants, desires, and sentiments which actuate a community of advanced civilization and growing intelligence'.[44] Walsh naturally thought this unfair. But Tories often behaved in ways that substantiated Whig claims. In 1819, for example, Lord Castlereagh still powdered his hair, at which the 'great unwashed began yelling'.[45] Such a style suggested a preference for long-dead days before the French Revolution. Similarly, at the Oxford degree ceremony in 1834, Tory dons and undergraduates booed references to Whig government, the reformed Parliament, the idea of Catholic Emancipation and relief for religious Dissenters. Such yahoos were quite literally at odds with the times, preferring to find refuge in 'the darkness of the Oxford monasteries'.[46] Confined in a rural context, Tories were untouched by industrial England, voyages of discovery, new sciences or polite living. They were as antique as Castlereagh's hair powder.

Such an unwillingness to engage with changing circumstances might have been seen as merely sad by Whigs, if it had not been for the fact that it was all subsumed in bile. Tories seemed to hate whole categories of people. Persecution and punishment appeared to be the essence of their creed, and of course Whigs were to be included in the general proscription. In 1831, *Fraser's Magazine* published the *Rumbling Murmurs of an Old Tory*. Its frank confessions merely confirmed the Whig stereotype of a Tory:

> Having all my life a particular hatred of humbug, quackery, lying, and deceit, it is quite needless to add that I hate, in politics, Whigs, i.e. Jacobins in a cloak – in religion, Socinians, i.e. Deists in a cloak – in philosophy, useful knowledgers, that is blockheads in a cloak – and in all branches of human concernment rats, that is to say, rascals, who, to do them justice, seldom wear any cloak, but walk forth stark naked in all the majesty of scoundrelism.[47]

To this list could be added antipathy towards every species of foreigner, suspicion of the Celtic fringe, and distaste for London and everything it contained. In Whig eyes, this was a caricature that was uncomfortably near the truth.

This being so, keeping the Tories out of government became a Whig duty as well as a pleasure. The sense of obligation was real. Thomas Coke was presented with a son at the age of sixty-eight. To have produced an heir to the earldom of Leicester was of course a matter for celebration, but he worried that the boy's politics might be wrong: 'It was extremely natural that he should wish for a son, but so firmly convinced was he that the ruin of the country had been the Tory system, that rather than his son should prove a Tory, he should wish not to have a son at all.'[48] His political career as MP for Norfolk was prompted by friends pointing out that, if he failed to offer himself as a candidate, the Tories might carry the county: 'At the mention of a Tory coming in, gentlemen, my blood chilled all over from head to foot, and I came forward. Educated as I had been in the belief that a Tory was not a friend to liberty and the Revolution [1688] ... I could not resist.'[49] Similar pangs of conscience assailed the fifth Earl of Darnley. Although he died an unusually rural death for a Whig, by contracting tetanus in a tree-cutting demonstration, he knew when he had failed in his political duty. By not exerting himself in the Kent election of 1830, a squire was allowed to carry the day. The man wore the country uniform of 'leathers and tops' which 'is all right for a country gentleman', but clearly indicated that he lacked the qualifications to deliberate at Westminster.[50]

In Whig eyes, the Tory party in Parliament was a strange sight. Its numerical majority crowded its backbenches and approximated closely to the image of countrified ignorance personified. On its front benches sat men of talent, deficient in pedigree and resources, who tried to keep their wild followers on a leash. Talented men like Pitt and Canning, who would not take Whig wages, found themselves in company that was not always congenial. Inevitably, there were moments when the backbenches became too uncontrolable and frisky. Catholic Emancipation in 1829 and the Corn Laws in 1846 were just two occasions on which the backwoodsmen claimed the Tory tradition as their own. Whigs were not surprised. For them, the Tory party was the party of the backwoods. Clever men on its front bench merely masked this reality for a time. 1829 and 1846 exposed a truth of which the Whigs had long been aware.

Most Whigs, therefore, suspected the country, its inhabitants and the politics it preferred. Their caricatures of its pattern of life were always unflattering. In return, they were smeared with the image of the Londoner and his vices. To prove the depth of this antipathy, the voice of William Mackworth Praed may be called in evidence. Praed was no Whig in politics, but he was one of the 'Talented Men' in the Tory ranks who looked askance at some of the people sitting on the backbenches behind him. To describe their quality, he wrote a poem called *The Country Member*, the reading of which would have had Whigs smiling and nodding in agreement:

Acutely doth he read the fate
Of deep intrigues and plans of state,
And if perchance some powdered peer
Hath gained or lost the Monarch's ear,
Foretells, without a shade of doubt,
The comings in and goings out.
When placemen of distinguished note,
Mistake, mislead, misname, misquote,
Confound the Papist and the Turk,
Or murder Sheridan and Burke
Or make a riddle of the laws,
Sir Paul grows hoarse in his applause:
But when in words of equal size
Some Oppositionist replies,
And talks of taxes and starvation
And Catholic Emancipation,
The Knight, in indolent repose,
Looks only to the Ayes and Noes.
Let youth say 'Grand'! – Sir Paul says 'Stuff'
Let youth take fire! – Sir Paul takes snuff.[51]

5

The French Connection

Whiggery cannot be understood in an English context alone. Travel, intellect and curiosity led them to admire other cultures and pre-eminently that of France. Francophilia was every Whig's opportunity and birthright. For many Paris was more of a second home than the country house. Their London houses were stocked with French furniture and porcelain, and peopled with French maids, valets and chefs. Quite rightly, cartoonists showed Whigs hobnobbing with the various rulers of France, obsequiously bowing before a superior culture. The traffic was interrupted by the experience of the Revolutionary and Napoleonic Wars, but was cheerfully resumed whenever an interval of peace made crossing the Channel a possibility. All the great French upheavals of the period were watched by an eager army of English visitors. The French Revolution itself and subsequent revolutions were tourist attractions of a magnetic quality. Whigs knew the French, thought they understood the French, and were always tempted to find excuses for the French.

None of this endeared them to their countrymen. In 1789, France was potentially the world's only superpower. With perhaps twenty-eight million people to Britain's eight million, France represented a military threat that was literally visible across the waters of the Channel. Real attempts at invasion in 1690, 1715, 1745, 1796 and 1803 were interspersed with rumours of invasion. Englishmen feared France and with good reason. Little wonder that Hogarth's pair of prints entitled *The Invasion*, showing preparations on both sides of the Channel for such an event, sold in thousands. Mercifully, only Bonaparte himself was able to realize France's potential. Regimes before and after him were never able to unite France in a common purpose or to tap the country's real wealth. But this was of little comfort to most Englishmen. The Bonapartist years proved what France could do. The only sensible response was to maintain an unbroken vigilance. With that and a certain amount of luck, 'the Ragamuffins' could be consigned to Hell where they belonged.[1]

In spite of these odds, England not only survived but actually notched up victory after victory over France. Every war was ultimately won, French attempts at Empire in India and Canada were undermined, and the stability of English institutions and finance became the admiration of the world. Whigs might fawn on France, but most of their country-men were convinced that the balance of superiority lay heavily in the other direction. The English parliamentary tradition was unbroken for six hundred years, while representative institutions across the Channel had disappeared in 1614. Their resurrection after 1789 was a series of amusing parodies on a serious theme. As a result, the English enjoyed personal liberties about which the French could only dream or, worse, theorize. The ubiquitous phrase 'the liberties of Englishmen' traced free-doms like Habeas Corpus and trial by jury back to the Magna Carta. There had been no liberty in France before the great Revolution and it was only abused thereafter. The French stupidly dismantled venerable institutions for the sake of innovation, and thereby destroyed all solid-ity in politics. Not surprisingly there was never a sense of common purpose. Rather the French murdered each other with determination and single-mindedness. Every change of regime was accompanied by a Terror from the right or left. French refugees were a permanent feature of London society and a permanent reminder of just how superior the English way of doing things was.

Inevitably, feelings of superiority at a popular level degenerated into mere racism. Debased accounts of the work of Lavater, Lamarck and others on the progression and regression of species led to the startling conclusion that the French were in fact regressing to a childlike or even a monkeylike condition. Cartoonists who gave their French characters simian noses and foreheads were only reflecting common references to 'the Monkey French'. Kings of the Bourbon dynasty were called 'Louis Baboon'.[2] During the Napoleonic War, a monkey was allegedly hanged in Hartlepool by a mob who took the creature for a French spy. 'Child-ish' and 'frivolous' were two of the most popular adjectives applied to the French. Such theories were popular because they explained so much. A degenerate or degenerating people obviously could not be expected to sustain mature parliamentary institutions; naturally they preferred the mummery of Roman Catholicism to the sensible option of Anglicanism; and of course they were prone to violence, whether directed against their neighbouring countries or each other. Their poverty-stricken lives in such a potentially wealthy country underlined these deficiencies. The French earned the soubriquet 'Frogs' because that is what they were forced to eat. Freeborn Englishmen had roast beef.

Such a standard and unflattering view of the French could only be sustained by widespread ignorance. Significant tourism began only after the end of the Seven Years' War in 1763, but even so most English people had no personal knowledge of France or its inhabitants. Indeed, throughout the late eighteenth and early nineteenth centuries, writer after writer condemned travelling as wasteful and pointless. In 1828, the Tory *Quarterly Review* regretted seeing

> the English gentleman, who at home would have been improving his estates, and aiding the public institutions of his country, abandoned to utter insignificance; his mind and resources running waste for want of employment, or perchance, turned to objects to which even idleness might be preferred ... The man we have known to be surrounded by respect and attachment at home, where life is honourable and useful within his proper sphere, we have seen with his family drudging along Continental roads, painfully disputing with postilions in bad French, insulted by the menials of inns, fretting his time and temper with the miserable creatures who inflict their tedious ignorance under the name of guides, and only happy in reaching any term to the journey which fashion or family intreaty have forced upon him.[3]

Gentlemen should stay at home and contribute to English stability and prosperity. Why see France, when everything at home was better? An English soldier or sailor was commonly thought to be the equal of four or five French equivalents. David Garrick pointed out that Dr Johnson had singlehandedly knocked his entire native language into shape in his famous *Dictionary*, whereas at least forty French Academicians laboured in the same task across the Channel.[4] But if contacts were disapproved of ignorance abounded. On one occasion, Jane Austen's father was approached by a prosperous Hampshire landowner and asked to settle a bet. The question was whether France was the capital of Paris or Paris the capital of France.[5]

When such a view of France was all-pervasive, the Whigs' affection for that country was at all times puzzling, and in moments of crisis synonymous with treason. It is true that, when invasion threatened, Whigs cheerfully put on Militia uniforms or even raised whole regiments at their own expense in defence of their country. In 1779, the Duchess of Devonshire raised eyebrows and hopes by joining her husband in a camp on the south coast. It is true, too, that the Whigs shared the view that France before 1789 was an unpleasant tyranny that threatened Britain's peace. Whig historians referred to Louis XIV as 'that old Beast'.[6] Yet having gone this far the qualifications began. Whigs seemed determined to find as many excuses for French behaviour as they could. If England was happy and France unfortunate, one country had simply been lucky in its history and the other had not. Determined historians as they were, Whigs believed that the lessons of the past could be learnt and mistakes corrected. Most obviously, the French would be wise to copy English models of government and society as quickly as possible. Whigs tended to treat the French as protégés in need of instruction.

The miseries of the French all lay in the victory of absolutist monarchy in the seventeenth and eighteenth centuries, which had snuffed out the memory and practice of representative institutions. The French aristocracy, critically unlike their English counterparts, had failed in its duty of resisting the Crown. As Sir James Mackintosh put it, 'the downfal [sic] of the feudal aristocracy happening in France before commerce had elevated any other class of citizens into importance, its power devolved to the Crown'.[7] When the French looked to the aristocracy to defend their liberties, no response was forthcoming: 'When the people, raised by commerce and agriculture to importance, asked for the blessing of a free government, they had no leaders among the great proprietors of the land, to whose honesty and wisdom they could confide their cause.'[8] These words of Lord John Russell effectively recorded the fact that all the miseries of France came about because that country had no Whig party. Walter Bagehot was more forthright: 'If France had more men of free will, quiet composure, with a suspicion of enormous principle, and a taste for moderate improvement; if a Whig party, in a word, were possible in France, France would be free.'[9]

It was terrible that any country's politics should lack a Whig dimension and men of Whig temperament. The suffering that overwhelmed France as a result of this deficiency was piteous. All the more reason then for the English Whigs to intervene in French politics with advice and counsel. From 1789 to 1848 this policy was followed, even when it led to accusations that it was compromising the official foreign policy of the British government. The meddling of Lord and Lady Holland in French politics was so embarrassing that they were threatened with the withdrawal of their passports. From generation to generation, Whigs identified certain groups or individuals, proudly enveloped them with the title of 'French Whig', and then did everything possible to promote their prospects. There was always a missionary element in Whiggery. They felt that their own values, which had served England so well, should be generously offered to less fortunate nations. So, however much certain French regimes were to be condemned and resisted, Whigs always made excuses for a people who had had an unfortunate history and were in need of a little instruction.

These views were the easier to hold because Whigs, unlike the vast majority of their contemporaries, cherished deep and abiding contacts with France. The Grand Tour was almost obligatory for a young aristo-crat just down from Oxford or Cambridge. Under the usually relaxed supervision of a clerical tutor, the Whigling arrived in Paris for what was for many a defining experience. In the salons of Madame de Geoffrin, Madame de Genlis and Madame de Deffand, reputations for erudition and gentlemanly address were made or blasted. New vices were con-tracted, new friendships made. In 1764, for example, Charles James Fox visited Paris for the first time at the age of fifteen. He lost his virginity, considerable sums of money at cards, and any respect for any fashion that was not French. No one doubted that French was the language of polite society across Europe, and Whigs regularly mocked those among their political opponents who had trouble with the language. The sour quality of French politics had to be set alongside the sweetness of its society. In a short essay entitled *An Agreeable Man*, Lord John Russell confessed that, 'France, perhaps, affords the best model of an agreeable man. In them we see the most refined politeness towards others, mixed with the most perfect confidence in themselves ... which to all other Europeans must seem quite unattainable.'[10]

Such early contacts were assiduously kept up by a traffic of visitors crossing the Channel in both directions. Until 1792, such travelling was unaffected by the chance occurrence that England and France might be at war. In the 1780s, what was described as an inundation of French visitors, led by Louis XVI's cousin the Duc d'Orléans, descended on England. Many of the same people reappeared a decade later as political refugees. In return, English Whigs returned to France as often as possible. Between 1789 and 1792, Fox was offered first-hand accounts of the great Revolution by Lord Holland, the Duchess of Devonshire, Sir James Mackintosh and many others who had thoroughly enjoyed witnessing the event. When France reopened to tourism after the peace of Amiens in 1802, Fox led his friends to Paris *en masse* to meet the new phenomenon of Bonaparte, behaving like alcoholics at the end of prohibition. Revolutions in 1830 and 1848 were just as exciting. Even without treating major political disturbances as cabaret, the round of parties, opera-boxes and love affairs was compelling enough. Whigs expected to be fêted by all the leading figures on the left of French politics, and returned the compliment at home. Indeed, critics sourly observed that they only went abroad to be given a respect that they were denied in England: 'the Whig patriots travel abroad for the support they cannot find at home, and make the republicans and infidels of France their great party for keeping them in office. The Whig alien who rules us has his head and hands in this country, but his body, and of course his heart, are in Paris.'[11]

It is not fanciful to describe the consequences of this traffic in family terms. Lord Edward Fitzgerald, son of Ireland's leading Whig, the Duke of Leinster, and nephew of Charles James Fox, married the daughter of the Duc d'Orléans and his mistress Madame de Genlis. Lord Elphinstone's daughter, Mercer, married the Comte de Flahault, who, after distinguished service in Bonaparte's army, went on to become a minister under Louis-Philippe, and was twice appointed ambassador to London. On a more irregular level, mistresses were shared by Orléans and the future George IV, and Anglo-French *affaires* were by no means uncommon. As this list of names suggests, and one should add those of Talleyrand, Lafayette and de Broglie, French Whigs were to be found principally among the followers of Louis-Philippe and in Orléanist politics. One or two Bonapartists might be accorded the title after demonstrating good behaviour. This Anglo-French family gossiped, looked after its own, and endlessly promoted what was thought to be Whiggery on both sides of the Channel. Volumes of letters passed between them. Quite often English Whigs could justifiably claim that they knew more about French politics than any official sources could divulge. Whigs responded to France with the advice and guidance of their friends and relations. Talleyrand assured Lord Holland that he was 'un des votres. C'est un titre que Mr Fox m'a permis de porter depuis longues années'. Lady Holland could plausibly boast that her husband 'was received quite *dans l'interieur en famille* with the Duke of Orléans'.[12]

Such contacts generated a psychological dependence on France. Whigs offered tuition to the French on politics, but they humbled themselves before French style and culture. Paris for them was 'emphatically the city of light, intelligence, society, and refined life'.[13] Lord Melbourne cheerfully acknowledged that 'the French are the first nation in the world; we ought to be eternally grateful to them'.[14] His remark was specifically addressed to French cuisine but it had a more general application. Whigs dressed French. Even Lady Holland, whose forays into politics suggested a masculine temperament, filled her letters to friends in Paris with gossip on current affairs but also with demands for scarves, fichus and dresses in the latest fashion. Purchases could be paid for by drawing on accounts held with the banker Perregaux, who was a central figure in Whig finance for thirty years.[15] Equally, Whig houses were full of French chefs, maids and valets. They were without rivals in their trades. In October 1803, in the middle of yet another invasion scare, Lady Elizabeth Foster was summoned to the Aliens Office, and rudely asked why she continued to employ two French maids. She was told that, 'It is for ladies of high rank and fashion, like you, Madam, not to protect foreigners who may be hostile to this country'. In reply, Lady Elizabeth pointed at that no woman of her rank could do without the services of French maids. No concessions were offered or made.[16] Whig ladies continued to look French even at the risk of being accused of treason.

Even more demonstrative and controversial was the Whig predilection for living French. When great houses were built their owners slavishly followed French models. The Prince of Wales's great palace at Carlton House in the Mall was begun in 1781. True, the principal architect was Henry Holland, but his clerk of works was Guillaume Gaubert, his assistant architect was Jean Trécourt, all the furniture was commissioned by Dominique Daguerre, and one of the major painters employed was Berlanger, on loan from the Duc d'Orléans. As if this were not a sufficient guarantee of fashionable acceptability, Holland was despatched to Paris, in 1785, to view alterations that Orléans was making to his own Palais Royal, so that they could be incorporated in Prinny's new home.[17] During the Napoleonic Wars, the Prince was bullied into accepting furniture in a Chinese rather than French style for Brighton Pavilion. He was 'afraid of his furniture being accused of Jacobinism'.[18] Many Whigs followed the Prince's lead. Holland built Southill for Samuel Whitbread on French models, and remodelled Althorp for Lord Spencer in line with 'Lord Spencer's finances, and, as a Whig, his French tastes'.[19]

Perhaps these superficial tastes in dress and building could be dismissed as unimportant, but they were rightly suspected as being the outward manifestations of a profound reverence for French thought. In France intellectuals were honoured, while in England the very word intellectual came close to being a term of abuse. To call an argument academic was to dismiss it. The French cultivated conversation and the English watched sport. As Hazlitt put it:

> If a Frenchman speaks of Scribe, the celebrated farce writer, a young Englishman present will suppose he means Cribb the boxer; and ten thousand people assembled at a prize fight will witness an exhibition of pugilism with the same breathless attention and delight as the audience at the Théâtre Français listen to a dialogue of Racine or Molière. Assuredly, we do not pay the same attention to Shakespeare: but at a boxing-match every Englishman feels his power to give and take blows increased by sympathy, as at a French theatre every spectator fancies that the actors on the stage talk, laugh, and make love as he would.[20]

The salon, in which conversation was precise and disciplined, was a rare form of social life in England. Those presided over by Lady Holland and the Duchess of Devonshire were very distinctive. In these assemblies foreign visitors and refugees would be disproportionately represented, for they flocked to join a form of social life that was familiar. There was no equivalent in English for the French word *esprit*.

Entry into this superior world depended on having proficiency in French. To be at ease with the language was to feel comfortable with concepts and ways of thinking that had no English counterpart. When

1. Charles James Fox. (1749–1806), the leading Whig parliamentarian after 1782. Portrait by Sir Joshua Reynolds.

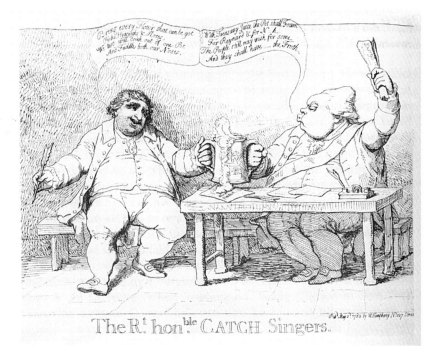

2. The Right Honourable Catch-Singers, May 1783. Sharing a two-handled tankard of beer, Charles James Fox and Lord North are spilling its froth on a petition from the Westminster Association, formed to press for parliamentary reform.

3. Holkham, Norfolk, the Hall.

4. Spencer House, north-east view. The London house of the Earls Spencer.

5. A Hint to the Ladies to Take Care of their Heads, cartoon by P. Dawe. A satire on the extravagant hairstyles of Whig ladies, typified by Georgiana, Duchess of Devonshire. (*British Museum*)

6. A Gaming Table at Devonshire House, by Thomas Rowlandson. Georgiana, Duchess of Devonshire (standing) holds the bank. Sheridan (second from the left) and other leading Whigs are shown as addicted to gambling and flirtation.

7. The Westminster Election, of 1788, in which Georgiana, Duchess of Devonshire, and her sister, Lady Bessborough, exchanged kisses for votes. (*Museum of London*)

8. Richard Brinsley Sheridan (1751–1816), by John Hoppner. Dramatist and politician, he was one of the 'talented men' in Whig politics.

9. William Lamb, second Viscount Melbourne, Prime Minister, 1834–41, by J. Partridge.

THE IN-"JUDICIOUS BOTTLE-HOLDER."

Gʜᴏsᴛ ᴏғ Pᴀᴍ. "AHA, DEAR BOY! WE MANAGED THINGS RATHER DIFFERENTLY WHEN *I* WAS BOTTLE-
HOLDER!"

10. The In-Judicious Bottle-Holder, a *Punch* cartoon of 1871. The ghost of
Palmerston addresses Gladstone observing the marked difference in their ways
of 'managing things'.

Tories proved inadequate in this skill, stories of their gaucheness abroad delighted Whig circles. Pitt stumbled along in French and Peel could barely manage a coherent sentence. A Whig ambassadress gleefully reported home that Sir Robert's dinner with the French Royal Family had not gone well: 'Sir Robert can hardly speak any French. The King talked English to him, but what was distressing, the Queen, under a natural *embrouillement* that being deaf to the language was being deaf to the sound, bawled out every word to him as if he was stone deaf, loud and distinct, *J'es–père que vous–vous–plai–sez–à–Paris.*'[21] Tories had to reply by accusing Whigs of lacking patriotism. As a contributor to *Fraser's Magazine* wailed:

> Oh, plague of plagues! Where'er I turn, French tricks
> French schemes, French morals, and French politics,
> Our clumsy statesmen, ape-like, imitate,
> Till a whole France obscenely daubs our state.
> The least French dirt I never could abide,
> And now I see our home-spun Frenchified.[22]

Such taunts had a certain sting, but Tories could not overcome the fact that they were excluded from experiences that fashionable Europe thought essential. The French connection gave the Whig world a dimension that the Tories could not challenge.

Publicly, by what they wore and how they lived, Whigs flaunted French sympathies. In March 1792, a performance at Drury Lane was delayed by a rather strange event. Half the audience wanted a rendition of 'God Save the King', while the Whig half yelled for the 'Ça ira', the unofficial anthem of the French Revolution. Order was only restored when the management apologetically pointed out that the 'Ça ira' was out of the question because 'l'orchestre n'avait pas la musique'.[23] The French monarchy would fall only five months later, yet, on this and on many other occasions, the Whigs fell over themselves to explain and excuse French behaviour. Arguing, probably rightly, that they were privy to better intelligence from France than their opponents, they felt fully justified in taking this line. Just because the French endlessly experienced 'the bad success of an attempt to make government perfect' did not mean that their intentions had not been honourable.[24]

As soon as the great Revolution of 1789 had broken out, the Whigs

begged understanding for France. The many Whig tourists to that country between 1789 and 1792 brought back glowing reports. A monarchical
tyranny had been destroyed and with it the power of superstitious
priests. Fox famously hailed the fall of the Bastille as the most wonder-
ful event in all history. As Wordsworth recalled, it was a moment to be
young in:

> Europe at that time was filled with joy,
> France standing on the top of golden hours,
> And human nature seeming born again.[25]

The constitution that was finalized in 1791 was to be uniformly admired.
Whigs could only cheer the emancipation of slaves, the granting of equal
rights to Jews and Protestants, and the establishment of a large, propertied electorate. The 'French Whigs' had more than done their duty. As
Richard Watson explained to the Duke of Grafton:

> I speak only of the general outline of their constitution; piddling objections
> may be made to particular parts, and experience will point out the necessity
> of reconsidering many things. But notwithstanding all the ridicule which
> apostate Whigs have attempted to throw on the rights of man, such rights
> are founded in nature ... and the French constitution is the only one in the
> world which has deliberately asserted these rights, and supported them in
> their full extent.[26]

Even when the Revolution turned violent, even when erstwhile
friends like the Duc d'Orléans and the Duc de Biron were guillotined,
Whigs remained its apologists. For them it was important to establish
why the whole project had ended in brutality. Was the Revolution
flawed from the start, or had it been undermined by the opponents of
freedom? Whigs took the latter view. Their arguments, though totally
out of step with the thinking of their contemporaries, had point. First,
the Revolution did not invent a tradition of political violence but rather
inherited it from the tyrannical regime it displaced. Unfortunately, it
never had time to establish better ways of doing things. 'We believe,'
pronounced the *Edinburgh Review*, 'it to be a rule without an exception,
that the violence of a revolution corresponds to the degree of misgov-
ernment which has produced that revolution.'[27] In the Whig view, the
awful shadow of monarchical brutality was extended in the persons of

Louis XVI and Marie-Antoinette. Neither ever gave the constitutional experiment full support. Indeed, both increasingly favoured its violent overthrow. Whigs mourned their deaths, but could only deplore the misguided politics that had brought them to the place of execution.

Secondly, and worse, the Revolution was attacked in 1792–93 by the armies of autocratic kings and empresses. It was never given time and space to establish itself peaceably. The new France could have become an orderly member of the European community on a reformed basis; but it was never given the opportunity. As a result, the war on France was unjustified:

> We are not convinced of the fact that the French government in the year 1791 was of such a nature as to be incapable of being so ripened and mitigated by a wise moderation in the surrounding Powers, that it might not become perfectly safe and inoffensive to the neighbouring states.[28]

Benjamin Vaughan, an eyewitness of much that had happened in the first two years of Revolution, was less circumspect in his language. The French descent into violence had been entirely the consequence of internal and external subversion. As he explained to Lord Lansdowne: 'With regard to the internal circumstances of France, when the *foul play* which their revolution has had is considered, they cannot be wondered at. If our own form of government had the same pains bestowed in confounding it, the same sums of money from *subjects* and *foreigners* spent in distracting it, we should not do much better.'[29]

When attacked, the French revolutionaries naturally had to defend themselves. The Terror, with its brutal system of summary justice, was a defensive measure made necessary by foreign invasion. Whigs were saddened by nearly everything that happened in France after 1792, but they thought they knew why it had happened. To excuse France in wartime was anything but popular, but Whigs continued to make the case inside and outside Parliament. As Lord Holland explained to his sister, the French

> are fighting to prevent the interference of other governments with their own, they are contending for the independence of their nation, fighting to prevent the dismemberment of their country and subversion of their rights as a people – I am willing to think it is this principle and not any affection for the bloody government they have that fills their navies and armies and warms

their heart with an enthusiasm which we have long imagined our times to be incapable of.[30]

Whigs knew that the great majority of people who were sentenced to death by the Revolutionary Tribunal were not aristocrats waiting for rescue by a Scarlet Pimpernel, but strike leaders in armaments establishments, black marketeers and food hoarders, and prostitutes who spread disease among soldiers. In short, they were people who one way or another disabled a war effort.

After England joined the war against France in the spring of 1793, Whigs had an unenviable choice to make. They could patriotically support George III and the other autocrats in their crusade, or they could continue to hope for representative government in France even if, for the moment, it had transmuted into the Terror. As Sir James Mackintosh bemoaned: 'The choice between two such dreadful evils is cruel and embarrassing.'[31] For two decades until Waterloo, Whigs writhed and wriggled on this particular hook. Yet their predilection for France was never really in doubt. Professional and public careers were destroyed in the public animosity that the Whigs provoked by endlessly construing French actions in the best light. In the 1790s, young Whigs abandoned powder, allowing hair to grow long and natural in the manner of revolutionary Paris. This identification with what was now republican France was made easier by the belief that they shared the dangers of the revolutionaries. If the Prussians, Austrians and Russians entered Paris, republicans could only expect the worst. Equally, after such an event, George III would move against the Whigs. After 1794, Fox enjoyed being likened to Brutus, the last of the Romans, and fully expected to end his days in the Tower, where some of his friends already resided. In such an apocalyptic situation, Whigs could only choose the French in the sure knowledge that the alternative was worse. It was inevitable, if not comfortable.

Nor were Whig options clarified by the arrival of Napoleon. From 1799 to 1815, they looked across the Channel to marvel and doubt in equal proportions. It was obvious that they were confronted by a genius. For Caroline Fox, Bonaparte was 'the most extraordinary man of the age'; for Lady Bessborough, he was 'the greatest man that ever liv'd'; for Charles James Fox, 'he certainly has surpassed ... Alexander and Caesar'.[32] In retrospect, he had been 'the most splendid of usurpers'.[33]

His energy and vision in remodelling the institutions of France were breathtaking. His creativity seemed to be on a par with the greatest artists. Even in territories he took by force of arms his attacks on superstition and privilege had long-lasting beneficial effects. Writing from Florence in 1814, Lord Holland was sure that it was 'difficult to imagine such power founded entirely on military superiority producing less evil than his did on the provinces subjected by his troops'.[34] In France and abroad, Bonaparte had brought a new world into being, which accorded in many respects with Whig ideals. They could only applaud. But such approval substantiated a widespread belief among their contemporaries that Holland and his friends were 'Bonaparte mad'.[35]

In fact, the Whigs were still choosing between evils. So much of what Napoleon achieved in educational, religious and administrative reforms was admirable. Yet so much else was dark and sinister. Neutralizing all representative government in France, he achieved what he achieved by the exercise of personal will. Whigs always suspected the corrupting nature of power and those who exercised it. Napoleon succumbed to its seductive nature. When they visited Paris in 1802–3, Whigs were shocked by his liking for titles and flattery, and by his distaste for a free press. Later, he silenced critics with exile or death. French friends of the Whigs like Madame de Staël appeared in England with all-too-believable tales of persecution. Further, after the breakdown of peace negotiations in 1806, Whigs had to accept that Napoleon was an inveterate warmonger. This realization, coming late in the day according to critics of the Whigs, led even Lord Holland to 'hate and detest Bonaparte'.[36] He was murderer as well as artist, a liberator and a plague.

Once again the Whigs had to weigh options. In 1815, Lord Holland went as far as to draw up a balance sheet for the whole Napoleonic experience. It was quite literally a case of opposing arguments for with arguments against. Sensibly, it opened with the caveat that 'the advantages enjoyed under Bonaparte's government are not to be exclusively ascribed to him. Many of them were due to the revolution and republic which preceded him.' Then the listing of points begins. On the positive side, there was the introduction of freedom of worship, the financial probity in public life, the magnificence of public works, and, above all, 'the easy access to office and distinction for all persons whose talents fitted them for the discharge of publick duties'. On the debit side, there was 'the enormous evil' of conscription, which turned the whole of France into a military machine, the persecution of critics and the curtailment of personal liberties.[37]

In the end, it came down to deciding whether, on balance, Bonaparte had been a force for good or evil, and whether he had been better than any possible alternative for France. On these questions Holland offered firm answers. First, the French had, for the most part, every reason to be grateful to their Emperor. Holland concluded his memorandum by reflecting that 'the traveller must be blind who in passing through France does not perceive that the division of property, the suppression of odious privileges and the real equality of condition have improved the face of the country and the state of its inhabitants and must ultimately exalt the moral and intellectual and political character of the people'. Secondly, any Whig would blench at replacing Bonaparte with another Bourbon king, thereby returning more or less to the nonsense of the Ancien Régime. In the same letter in which he expressed detestation of Bonaparte the warmonger, Holland confessed that 'it is difficult to know what to wish ... I am not sure if he were to fall that the *legitimate* sovereign would not be restored and that in my mind is the last of misfortunes – bad for France, for liberty and for Mankind and in a narrow view bad for England'.[38]

Unfortunately, the Whigs were not credited with nuanced views on Bonaparte by the world at large. Rather they were accused of wishing 'to linger about Napoleon'.[39] This was unjust, but Whig behaviour did little to dispel the illusion. Between Waterloo and the Emperor's death on St Helena, Whigs busied themselves in Bonapartist causes. Members of Napoleon's immediate family came to England and were dined in Whig houses. Campaigns were mounted to save Marshal Ney and General Lavalette from execution. Ministers were bullied into giving passports. Above all, attempts were made to mitigate the misery of the Emperor's imprisonment. Lady Holland, unsolicited, sent chests and parcels containing material for one hundred shirts, fourteen dozen stockings, five hundred pounds worth of wine, 'a machine for cooling water in hot climates', and fifty cases of eau de cologne.[40] In his will, a grateful Emperor rewarded these kindnesses by leaving her a snuffbox and a lock of his hair. To outsiders all this compromised the Whigs forever. Only those within their own ranks knew how doubting they had been. There was for them no simple or easy response to Bonapartism, but prolonged crisis and endless war made their hesitations criminal in the minds of their countrymen.

Whigs options became easier after 1814. The return of the old Royal Family in the persons of Louis XVIII and Charles X seemed to restore all that was objectionable in pre-revolutionary France. The royalists seemed intent on pretending that the French Revolution had never happened. Even when they were political refugees, their behaviour was condemned for what Harriet Cavendish called 'unsensitivity and frivolity'.[41] The sixth Duke of Devonshire recalled with horror that, as a little boy, he had been required out of politeness to kiss the refugees. As their royal faces and powdered heads approached, he only survived the ordeal by firmly closing his eyes. They were so much part of a long-dead society that 'one and all were called Madame de Pompadour'.[42] In Whig circles, a yo-yo was known as an 'emigrette'. Its exaggerated ups and downs mirrored the irrational politics of the royalist refugees. When George III ordered full Court mourning for Louis XVI and Marie-Antoinette, the only people to ignore this instruction were certain French aristocrats. Whigs saw the Bourbons and their supporters as congenitally out of touch with the times.

In 1814, however, these people were once again the government of France. Without ambiguity or hesitation, Whigs determined to oppose them. This was all the more a duty because Whigs believed that the Bourbons had only been restored by foreign armies, and that they enjoyed no support of any depth within France itself. As Holland informed the House of Lords: 'the restoration of that family in 1814 was a complete farce, and entirely owing to the presence of foreign bayonets'.[43] Disaster could be predicted. Charles X was 'a Hypocrite', or 'that old idiot', or 'a bigoted superstitious and wicked Ultra prince'. He and his brother were natural persecutors, who, left to their own devices, would have preferred a massacre of their liberal and Bonapartist opponents.[44] Between 1817 and 1830, the house of Mercer Elphinstone and her French husband, the Comte de Flahault, became an alternative British Embassy in Paris in the Whig interest. In spite of the fact that correspondence was regularly opened or intercepted, Whigs were kept informed of the details of French politics and of each new enormity perpetrated by the despotic kings. Indeed they often claimed to be better

informed about such things than the government of Lord Liverpool.[45]
As they recorded the blunders and vindictiveness of Charles X, they
were not surprised when he was removed by revolution in 1830, and it
was for them a matter of great rejoicing.

With the arrival of the Orléanist monarchy, in July 1830, the Whigs,
for the first time in a generation, were confronted with a French regime
which they could enthusiastically support without equivocation. Some
of them described the moment as rejuvenating. It made them feel
'young again'.[46] Louis-Philippe, the new king, was the son of the old
'French Whig' of the 1780s, the Duc d'Orléans. He wrote and spoke perfect English, testifying to an anglophilia of such depth that it was
suspicious in the eyes of many Frenchmen. As an exile, he had eaten his
first dinner in Holland House in 1802. When Whigs like Lord Holland
and the Duke of Sussex wrote to congratulate him on his accession to
power, they recorded that 'Contentment is the Order of the Day', and
that 'the Parisians have covered themselves with glory'.[47] By way of
reply, the new King modestly expressed the hope that by his actions
he 'would continue to merit the approbation of all honest men'.[48]
Mutual congratulations flowing between men believed to hold similar
principles were warming and cosy.

The same, comfortable familiarity could be enjoyed with nearly all the
leading figures of the new regime. A succession of French ambassadors
to London, Talleyrand, Sébastiani, Guizot, were old friends. The *Edinburgh Review* generously gave them the accolade of '*juste milieu*
Whigs'.[49] To see Lafayette once again at the head of the National Guard
reactivated pleasant memories of 1789. Charles James Fox had visited
him in 1802, planting a tree in the grounds of his estate, which still flour-
ished thirty years later as a symbol of common purpose. Lafayette's
return to prominence confirmed 'a spotless and distinguished career in
the cause of liberty'.[50] There were, it is true, other Orléanists who stood
outside these memories of shared persecution and liberal hopes. Thiers
and Molé had no special regard for England. But, particularly in the
1830s, they were the exceptions. Lady Holland had no compunction in
asking the staff at the French Embassy to supervise the safe arrival of
caps, scarves and muslins. A leading Whig visiting Paris could be sure
of a *tête-à-tête* with the French King.

For much of the period 1830 to 1848, Whigs and Orléanists saw

themselves as allies fighting for common purposes against common enemies. They egged each other on, cheered successes and offered
consolation in defeat. The dismissal of Grey's government in July 1834
was reportedly felt as keenly by Louis-Philippe 'as if he had been his own
minister'. The reinstatement of the Whigs under Lord Melbourne a few
months later gave 'great satisfaction' at Paris, and not least to the Prime
Minister, the Duc de Broglie, another venerable 'French Whig'. By royal
order, the news was posted up in the Bourse.[51] Long letters of a confes-
sional nature passed to and fro, setting out policy decisions in a context
that an English Whig and a French Orléanist would both find congenial. Admissions of failure were included, as were apologies for
misunderstandings. On one occasion, Louis-Philippe reflected that
being king of the French was very grand, but that it was also very wearing. How much better to be once again chatting in the library at Holland
House. He gloried in the fact that Whigs saw him 'toujours dans le juste
milieu, et j'en conviens volontiers'.[52] The royalist, republican and Bonapartist traditions in French politics had been for the Whigs more or less
menacing. Responding to them had presented difficulties. Mercifully,
Orléanism proved that the vein of liberty, first mined in 1789, had not
run out. Under the right circumstances, French Whiggery might yet
entrench stable, parliamentary government.

From these accumulated experiences Whigs could claim a special
knowledge about France. Indeed, on many issues, they would insist that
they were better informed than their political opponents. None of this
guaranteed that Whig prophecies would prove to be right, but at least
they would be wrong for very interesting reasons. Again and again, they
interfered directly in French affairs, because their interest gave them the
right to do so and their friendships gave them the means to do so. In
the early years of the Revolution, Fox and his allies in letters to Lafayette
and others mingled congratulations with suggestions about the forms
of the new constitution. He lobbied Barnave about the fate of the
monarchy after the flight to Varennes. The mere possession of a letter
from 'the great man' so impressed Vergniaud that he ordered the release
of an Englishman who would otherwise have been guillotined.[53] In the
next generation, Lord Spencer and Thomas Grenville begged Louis
XVIII to spare the life of Marshal Ney, and expressed the hope that the
King would eventually be hanged himself when he refused to do so.[54]

Under the July Monarchy the number of such incidents multiplied. Whigs identified so closely with certain French political traditions that promoting their interests was a matter of duty.

Normally, intervention took the form of offering advice and guidance, whether it had been asked for or not. The astonishing success of English constitutionalism gave its practitioners the right to lecture other nations. Some French people, particularly those with Whig friends, accepted this tuition gratefully. Madame de Boigne, who was a refugee in England for most of the period from 1789 to 1806, was one of these:

> The organization of political life in England has always seemed to me the most perfect in the world. On the one hand is the complete and real equality in the eyes of the law, which assures individual independence and therefore inspires the individual with self-respect; on the other hand are the great social distinctions, which create defenders for the public liberties, and make these patricians the natural leaders of the people, who return in homage what they receive by way of protection. This is what I have wished for in my own country, for I can only conceive of liberty, apart from licence, as based upon a strong aristocracy. This is a fact which nobody in France understood.[55]

Clearly the lady had taken her lessons in Whiggery to heart. More succinctly, Guizot, a historian of England and at home in London society, identified 'the great evil' in France as the hope expressed by all parties of 'annihilating the others'. As regime followed regime, it was clear that the French were in need of instruction.

The textbook used by Whig instructors was the *Edinburgh Review*. Nearly every issue contained an article on some aspect of French life and culture. Many contained more than one. Interest in France was infinitely more extensive than that shown in any other country. Advice poured out. Politicians, before and after the Revolution, had unwisely preferred 'metaphysical discussions' which were 'utterly void of pertinancy' to sound common sense. Rousseau's influence, for example, had simply been 'pernicious'.[56] Equally, there had been too much equality and not enough fraternity. The French had never been able to work in a common purpose. An unfortunate history and a misdirected Revolution had so divided them, one from another, that mutual understanding was out of the question. Instead, they had recourse to violence. Parliamentarianism depended upon a willingness to live by consensual politics, but in France the habit had grown up of legitimating government by force alone. It was this 'which constitutes the fundamental distinction between the political life of England and the political life of France'.[57] The remedy was obvious. French Whigs should listen to their English cousins.

The point where instruction for France and admiration of its citizens met was in diplomacy. Lafayette was not the first French Whig to offer the opinion that, once he and his kind were in government on both sides of the Channel, a new liberal system could be established in Europe. He remembered Fox telling him so on one of his visits to France.[58] Again and again the same belief was expressed. Sébastiani, while ambassador in London, told Louis Philippe's sister that, 'L'alliance entre la France et l'Angleterre assure la paix du monde. L'ébranler, l'aff-aiblir, c'est tout mettre en question'.[59] For Lord Holland, 'the only true Holy Alliance is England and France'.[60] Whig government in England and Orléanist government in France after 1830 were so obviously allied in outlook and intent that Lord Clarendon could dismiss any notion of war with France as 'unEnglish'.[61] Nor were these merely pious and conventional statements. From 1830 to 1841, the fact that the two greatest powers in the world were governed by friends raised extraordinary possibilities. People who thought otherwise, like Palmerston in England and Thiers in France, found themselves pushing against decades of fellow feeling. When Guizot arrived in London as ambassador in 1840, his instructions carried the sentence: 'Les dispositions du Gouvernement du Roi à l'égard de la Grande Bretagne sont aussi bienveillants, aussi conciliantes qu'à aucune époque.' At his first meeting with Lord Melbourne, he was delighted to hear the same sentiments expressed. The Prime Minister simply remarked, 'il n'y a pour nous rien de bon à faire sans vous'.

Of course, no relationship runs smoothly all the time. There were moments of tension between the two countries, notably in 1831 and 1840, that were so severe that they provoked fears of war. But the playing out of these dramas threw up strange diplomatic practices. In the first, Talleyrand, the French ambassador, was in the habit of dropping in to Holland House once or twice a week. The Belgian and Polish crises were discussed over dinner among friends. Letters from Paris would be shown round as a demonstration of good faith and replies drafted.

Everything was done to reassure each side of the other's good intentions.[62] A dinner table of friends made this possible. In 1840, war was averted on much the same principles. The deliberate leaking of information meant that Guizot was fully aware of discussions held in the English Cabinet, and Holland and Lord John Russell enjoyed the same intelligence from France.[63] At times, cooperation was so close that ambassadors and ministers sat down together to draft the appropriate paragraphs in royal speeches that related to Anglo-French affairs.[64] Throughout the period, the diplomacy of the dinner table and boudoir operated in particular campaigns and projects. After 1830, with Whig and Orléanist governments in place, this type of informal diplomacy rivalled that of official foreign offices.

Not surprisingly, many people thought that there was something unEnglish about Whiggery. They could never really be trusted as good patriots. They boasted about the unique quality of English history and the glories of England's capital city, but half their souls had been sold to foreigners. For many of them France seemed to be a psychological resource. That country supplied all the deficiencies in English life. Eating, drinking and dressing of course came into this category, but so did the arts, conversation and morality. The bedroom and the dining room were French. It added up to what critics of the Whigs called a 'Gallomania'. Such contacts brought many benefits. The Whigs often enjoyed intelligence about European politics that was denied to the British government. Their leadership of London society was to depend to some degree on their bringing of French tastes to England. In all these respects the French connection was empowering, if controversial.

Yet at the heart of the Whig appreciation of France was an insoluble problem. France had no Whig tradition. Its unfortunate history of violence and division made it unlikely that it would ever acquire one. English Whigs never gave up the quest for Frenchmen like themselves. They freely baptized their friends with the title of 'French Whig', and they hoped for a future in which France would be as stable and as sensible as England. But disappointments were everywhere. Bonapartists liked equality but hated liberty. Lafayette would often prefer to sulk rather than do his duty. Even Louis-Philippe eventually muzzled the press and undermined elected governments. In fact, Whig contacts with France underlined just how English their creed was. Only England had

Whigs. Well-intentioned attempts to export the idea came to nothing. Ironically therefore, whenever a Whig wrote or spoke about his admiration for France, he was by implication restating the superiority of his English origins.

6

The March of Mind

The young Whig, or 'Whigling', was subjected to three educational experiences, one formal and two informal. They were instructed in the universities of Glasgow and Edinburgh, confirmed in their beliefs by a regular reading of the *Edinburgh Review*, and polished up in the Whig salons of west London. As a set of experiences it made them distinctive. In calling their Tory opponents 'the stupid party', they meant nothing more than that these men had unfortunately missed out on opportunities that explained and interpreted the contemporary world. To have had contact with Scots thinking was to be up to date, on top of events, even intellectually chic. In the late eighteenth century, Scots professors had established the idea of 'the March of Mind'. They had proved that human society was moving forward. They had invested the word 'progress' with magical powers. It was not so much that they were optimists by nature, but rather that they reported truths that history and allied arts made abundantly clear. As a formula it was absolutely intoxicating. Many Whigs recorded in their memoirs that they entered a kind of intellectual captivity in Scotland in their youth, and had never escaped from it.

Between 1793 and 1815, sending young Whigs on the Grand Tour was largely out of the question. It was simply too dangerous as England and France indulged in almost uninterrupted warfare. Before 1789, the accident of warfare had rarely bothered tourists. Wars were fought between governments and states. Ordinary citizens were free to go about their business without worrying about them. They were even free to express the hope that their government might lose. All this changed with the French Revolution. War was now a matter involving whole peoples. No one doubted that Napoleon was not a gentleman, and these suspicions were confirmed by his introduction of internment for enemy aliens. English communities in Europe were now under direct threat. Where

then could young Whigs be sent? Oxford and Cambridge might be visited for a year or so, but no one pretended that at this period they could
offer much in the way of intellectual stimulation. Only one real possibility remained, and that was to dispatch them to Scotland where, it
appeared, everything that was new and exciting in European thought
had its exponent.

Dominating the universities of Edinburgh and Glasgow were professors who had themselves been pupils of Adam Smith. Young Whigs
could claim to be the intellectual grandchildren of this master. These
same professors were regular contributors to the *Edinburgh Review*. Men
such as John Millar, Dugald Stewart and John Black undertook to form
the minds of a generation. They were confident in what they taught and
unsentimental in how they did it. Millar, for example, 'was a decided
Whig, and did not perhaps bear any great antipathy to the name of a
republican; yet there was never any mind, perhaps, less accessible to the
illusions of that sentimental and ridiculous philanthropy which has led
to the adoption of popular principles. He took a very cool and practical
view of the condition of society; and neither wept over the imaginary
miseries of the lower orders, nor shuddered at the imputed vices of the
higher.'[1] Little humour is recorded in memories of these Scots savants.
Rather they commanded respect and loyalty for the power and clarity of
their minds.

Coming under the influence of these men was a defining experience.
The young Melbourne spent much of 1799–1801 in Glasgow as Millar's
pupil and paying guest. By way of preparation, he read 'Millar on the
English Constitution, Stewart's Philosophy of the Human Mind, Cicero
de Officiis'. On arriving in Scotland, he was commanded to discard the
last title on this list. Millar had a total contempt for ancient writers. For
him, the world seemed to start anew with the works of David Hume and
Adam Smith, and 'their works were to him what the Koran was to the
Mahometans'. Melbourne was immediately put on to *The Wealth of
Nations*. In Millar's home, instruction was rigorous and structured. Melbourne undertook 'a course of study and exercise, of debate, doubt,
contradiction and examination such as I had never witnessed nor been
engaged in before'. His reading lists brought him into contact with the
very latest ideas on history, philosophy and economics. So intense was
the regime that it became a question of where education stopped and

indoctrination began. He recorded that, 'I lost the conceit and prejudices of Eton and Cambridge, but in their place I had adopted the conceit and prejudices of Scotland and Mr Millar'. Only after returning to London was he able to put Scots teaching into perspective and temper it with other views. Then, it might become clear that Mr Millar had not been above silliness. He had, for example, wondered whether a successful Napoleonic invasion of England might not have been a good thing. But, such mental foibles aside, his influence on Melbourne was profound.[2]

Melbourne's brother-in-law, Lord Palmerston, had a very similar experience. Indeed, comparing notes about time spent in Scotland as students must have been standard conversational fare at Whig dinner tables. Palmerston's tutor had been Dugald Stewart, who went on to be another of the stalwarts of the *Edinburgh Review*. His influence was acknowledged with gratitude and respect. From him, Palmerston claimed to have learnt that change was to be managed rather than feared. Although conservative by instinct, he was taught that the correct Whig response to change was to accept it, welcome its possibilities, and moderate its impact. Recalling Stewart's tuition, he came to agree that:

> all countries ... are, and always have been in a state of transition, and it is
> the character and purpose of human nature that all societies should be con
> stantly altering. Were this not so we might still have [been] painted blue like
> the Britons. The province of a wise Government is to keep pace with the
> improved notions of the people; not to insist upon knowing better than
> those they govern, what those they govern wish; neither to chain down soci
> ety to a point, nor hurry it along too fast, to be ever and anon modifying
> institutions to suit them to altered habits, and new wants.[3]

As a statement of how change should be managed, Palmerston had taken his lesson well. As societies developed, public men had to define new situations. It was a heavy responsibility that only well-read men could fulfil. Mercifully, new insights offered by Smith and his kind gave them the tools with which to do their duty.

Scotland served Whiggery well by injecting it with the idea that society was always in movement. Sometimes, Scots teaching was simply described as 'The Movement'. Once this idea had been absorbed, to talk of absolutes in politics, in morality or in anything else became very difficult. Relativism permeated most Whig views. They could always relate a contemporary problem to something that had happened in the past, or to something that might be hoped for in the future. They stood at a point in a linear progression from what had gone before to what would happen next. It was impossible to be too dogmatic, because things had been done differently before and would be done differently again. Scotland allowed Whiggery to recast itself, claiming to see politics as a managed process of change.

Whigs never escaped from their Scots professors. Four times a year, the *Edinburgh Review* arrived in Whig libraries, and, every time a volume was taken down and read, radiating blasts of Scots thinking filled the room. It was the Whig Bible. One of John Doyle's most amusing cartoons caught its impact. Published in October 1830, it was entitled *A Masked Battery*. It showed a battlefield. Whigs have taken up a position behind a huge rock. Their secret weapon has been deployed on top of the same rock. It is a volume of the *Edinburgh*. Whigs smile as the power and light emanating from its open pages bedazzles and befuddles the advancing legions of Toryism led by Wellington and Peel. Started in 1802 as a means of earning a little money and reputation by a group of Scots academics and writers, it rapidly became the Whig testament. By 1805, many of the original contributors had been brought to London under Whig patronage. Their books were published and their careers promoted. As regular guests in Whig houses, they infused official, London Whiggery with a Scots yeast. In 1808, the *Edinburgh* threw off any ambiguity in its opinions and proclaimed its unadulterated Whig allegiance.

No journal was ever more didactic in purpose. As Walter Bagehot observed: 'The modern man must be told what to think – shortly no doubt – but he must be told it. The essay-like criticism of modern times is about the length he likes. The *Edinburgh Review*, which began the system, may be said to be, in this country, the commencement on large topics of suitable views for sensible people.'[4] Whigs had no hesitations in identifying themselves as the sensible people in question, or in crediting Whiggery with 'suitable views'. Of these the most central was still an optimistic appreciation of a society in movement. The philosophizing Scotsman, who knew the price of everything and founded his optimism on that knowledge, became a standard figure in many contemporary novels and plays. Hazlitt's pen-portrait of Francis Jeffrey, the *Review's* editor, was typical:

> Our sprightly Scotsman is not of a desponding and gloomy turn of mind. He argues for the future hopes of mankind from the smallest beginnings, watches the slow, gradual, reluctant growth of liberal views, and smiling sees the aloe of Reform blossom at the end of a hundred years; while the habitual subtlety of his mind makes him perceive decided advantages where vulgar ignorance or passion sees only doubts and difficulty.[5]

When Scots thinking escaped the universities and entered mainstream life through the pages of the *Edinburgh* and the speeches of suitably educated politicians, it changed the intellectual climate for good. By understanding its provenance and processes, change could be manipulated for the best. After seeing the Great Exhibition, Queen Victoria reportedly declared her belief in the idea that man could now do anything. In doing so, Whigs claimed that she was reverting to the lessons of her Whiggish youth.

The forum in which Scots thinking and official politics mingled most productively was the salon. As a form of social life salons were rare in England. Foreign visitors sadly noted on many occasions how aggressively masculine society was in London. The gentlemen's clubs of the West End and pub life everywhere segregated the sexes in a way that foreigners found positively wilful. By contrast, the salon was gender neutral, or even feminine. It certainly demanded the presidency of a formidable female personality. So salon life in England was a pale reflection of that in Paris or Vienna. Where it did exist, it was Whig. Over a seventy-year period, first Georgiana, Duchess of Devonshire, and then Lady Holland presided over the most exciting assemblies in London. Quite deliberately such entertainments were grounded in the diversity of the company that attended them. The Scots academic and his former Whig pupils rubbed shoulders with distinguished foreigners, hapless refugees from the latest failed uprising in Europe, and any young man of talent who was thought to be up and coming.

This salon world had a severely serious purpose and was not for the faint-hearted. Those who were too shy or too ignorant to contribute were well advised to stay away. A performance was expected from each guest. In this company 'beset with Embassadors [sic], Dandies and

Beaux of every class, gay and serious',[6] the competition was frightening. Sir James Mackintosh, it was said, nearly ruined his brilliant career in the law by rehearsing his epigrams for an evening at Holland House rather than mastering his briefs. Others, even more nervous, actually took notes into dinner.[7] Reference has already been made to Lady Melbourne's distaste for what she called 'rough diamonds'. The conventions of the salon provided the answer to her problem. Listening to conversation, and joining in when possible, was a polishing process. To hear Talleyrand reminiscing about the French Revolution or Bonaparte, to follow Macaulay through English history or Francis Horner through the bullion question, confirmed the process, begun in Edinburgh or Glasgow, of turning young Whigs into people of consequence. As one of the Russells recalled:

> It argues no political bias to maintain that, in the earlier part of the nineteenth century, Toryism offered to its neophytes no educational opportunities equal to those which a young Whig enjoyed at Chatsworth and Bowood and Woburn and Holland House. Here the best traditions of the previous century were constantly reinforced by accessions of fresh intellect. The circle was, indeed, an aristocratic Family Party, but it paid a genuine homage to ability and culture. Genius held the key, and there was a *carrière ouverte aux talents.*[8]

In this celebration of intellect, many Whigs were much more than passive observers. Charles James Fox's work on the Greek poet Lycophron stands to this day. He was also an historian of note, as were Lord John Russell and Sir James Mackintosh. The Marquess of Rockingham balanced his addiction to the Turf with his role as a committed Fellow of the Royal Society. Installing a forty-foot telescope on the roof of Wentworth Woodhouse, he took useful measurements about planetary movements and the nature of sun spots. Even the Duchess of Devonshire, when social commitments allowed, had a serious interest in science. She collected chemists and mineralogists in particular, and attended their lectures. In Sir Charles Blagden's diary, entries like the following are not uncommon: 'Spent evening at Duchess of Devonshire's. Much talk about chemistry and mineralogy.' Georgiana, with some justice, declared 'she was quite wild with studies of that nature'.[9] Little wonder that Lady Bessborough could remind a Tory acquaintance that 'whatever else we fail in, we beat you fairly in wit'. It was absurd for

Tories merely 'to *assert* boldly'.[10] Such assertions were no substitute for information and cleverness.

None of this was calculated to make a Whig modest about his own attainments or those of his friends and relations. Their education had introduced them to everything that was up-to-date and sparkling. The social life of their daily round endlessly renewed the challenge. Unfortunate Tories were denied access to this elixir. They were unhappy and fearful because they could not understand the dynamic of change. To be in their company was not an experience to be actively sought. During the Revolutionary Wars, William Windham broke with the Whigs for a time and took up with their Pittite opponents. When he returned to the fold, the Whig savant, Dr Samuel Parr, could not resist teasing him about how relieved he must be to be once again in the company of civilised men:

> Mr Windham and I dined together; he was in high spirits, we had abundance of literary conversation, and he bore with my freedom when I told him that during his connection with Pitt he had been a total stranger to those intellectual repasts which he had been accustomed to enjoy among the Whigs, and for which he could not have lost his very keen appetite and very excellent relish.[11]

Repeatedly unsuccessful in politics, Whigs yet enjoyed the confidence that was founded in an education that assured them of ultimate victory and vindication.

Central to this self-confidence was the belief in the inevitability of progress and improvement. Society inexorably pressed forwards towards something better, something more civilized, something more Whiggish. They called this process 'Progress', 'the Movement', or simply 'the March of Mind'. This notion was the key to all mysteries. Once grasped, it explained everything. The rise and fall of empires, the change from agricultural to industrial economies, and advances in knowledge and toleration all came within its compass. Of course there had been temporary setbacks which had stalled the process, as a result of which the model of the spiral was often preferred to that of the straight line. But the direction of human affairs was determinedly upward. Scots professors had told the Whigs that this was so, and the *Edinburgh* rehearsed the creed at regular intervals.

The language in which the doctrine was enunciated is almost brazen in its uncompromising assertiveness. John Millar told his pupils that:

> There is, however, in man a disposition and capacity for improving his condition, by the exertion of which, he is carried on from one degree of advancement to another; and the similarity of his wants, as well as of the faculties by which those wants are supplied, has everywhere produced a remarkable uniformity in the several steps of his progression ... There is, in human society, a natural progress from ignorance to knowledge, and from rude to civilized manners, the several stages of which are usually accompanied with peculiar laws and manners.[12]

The urge to improve and ameliorate was innate in human nature and therefore unanswerable. The *Edinburgh Review* read its subscribers the same lecture a generation later:

> The affairs of mankind do not revolve in a Circle, but advance in a Spiral; and though they have their periods of obscuration, as well as of brightness, tend steadily, in spite of these alterations, and by means of them, to a sure consummation of glory. There is, we are firmly persuaded, a never-ceasing progress to amelioration; and though each considerable movement is followed by a sensible reaction, the system moves irresistibly onward; and no advance that is made is ever utterly lost.[13]

Official religions offered believers an eternity in heaven. Whiggery literally held out the possibility of a paradise on earth.

Whigs may have discovered and first enunciated these secrets, but they were now available to all men. Europe had taken the lead, but the rest of the world would surely follow. With the expansion of European empires would go the possibility of enlightenment. To modern ears this might sound condescending, but Whigs believed themselves to be generous. When Sir James Mackintosh addressed the following words to the newly-formed Literary Society of Bombay, he meant them to be encouraging:

> The smallest society, brought together by the love of knowledge, is respectable in the eye of Reason; and the feeblest efforts of infant Literature in barren and inhospitable regions are in some respects more interesting than the most elaborate works and the most successful exertions of the human mind. They prove the diffusion, at least, if not the advancement of science; and they afford some sanction to the hope, that knowledge is

destined one day to visit the whole earth, and, in her beneficial progress, to illuminate and humanize the whole race of man. It is therefore, with singular pleasure, that I see a small but respectable body of men assembled here by such a principle.[14]

All cultures were moving in the same direction. Some were simply a little more advanced than others. All would eventually arrive at the same destination.

The evidence for these opinions was overwhelming. Whigs had little personal experience of the Industrial Revolution but they noted its impact. Mass production, steam-powered travel and a healthy consumerism literally transformed lives. It seemed to go hand in hand with growing literacy and awareness. Inevitably there were new problems to be overcome. Crowded cities were homes to crime, brutal working practices and disease. But, for Whigs, these problems would ultimately be solved. To dwell on them was to miss the point. They were merely the unfortunate and temporary by-products of a transforming process that brought incalculable opportunities for betterment. Scientists like Sir Humphry Davey and Sir Charles Blagden were welcomed at Whig tables. These changes in their own generation were to be contrasted with what had gone before. The new science of geology suggested that the biblical account of the earth as approximately six thousand years old was untrue. The human mind had literally to expand to accept the idea that the planet was millions of years old. The equally new discipline of archaeology, focusing on the excavation of Pompeii, Herculaneum and Rome, instigated an interest in the customs and practices of ancient civilizations that could be so usefully compared with those of contemporary society. Progress was proved by demonstrating how nineteenth-century man had moved on from the usages of his ancestors.

More evidence was provided by voyages of discovery. Captain Cook and his like brought to the attention of informed Europeans the cultures of China and Japan, the religions of India and Arabia, and the customs of the Aborigine and the Maori. There is no doubting the interest generated. The pages of the *Edinburgh* were crammed with reviews of travel literature. The missionary, the soldier and the naturalist all provided huge amounts of new material. Their efforts allowed Whig writers to make comparisons between their world and those in other continents. Inevitably, these other worlds could only be inferior or superior. Just as inevitably, they were invariably thought inferior, if travelling hopefully. In two dimensions, the historical and the geographical, Whigs were challenged to give substance to the idea of progress. How did the Roman relate to the Hottentot? How did both relate to the Whig? Was there a reading of the past and the contemporary world that brought them both into association, one with another? Whigs had no doubt that there was such a reading and that they were its exponents.

Basically, human society advanced in clearly defined stages. In his *Essay on the History of the English Government and Constitution* Lord John Russell identified four of these. In trying to explain the process by which cavemen had been transformed into Russells, he offered the following scheme of history. First came 'the state of savage life', in which hunter gatherers moved from place to place in small family or tribal groups. Next came 'the state of imperfect government'. In these societies, men lived and farmed in settled communities and the concept of property held under law was established, but good order could not always be guaranteed. For Russell, such a description fitted most of Europe in the Middle Ages and equally suited many parts of the Turkish Empire in his own time. There followed 'a state of order without liberty'. Here, central government was sufficiently established to sustain law and order, but these benefits depended precariously upon the whim of individual rulers. Russell identified France before 1789 and contemporary regimes in China and Persia as examples of this model of government. Finally, there was the fourth and highest stage of development: 'the union of liberty with order'. At this exalted level, all the blessings of government were generated by the elected representatives of a free people. As Russell concluded, 'the union of liberty with order, then, is the last stage of civilization and the perfection of civil society. It is in proportion as these two qualities are combined that the merit and the value of different governments are to be estimated; the larger portion they have of both, the more adapted they are to diffuse happiness among their subjects.'[15]

Here was progress visibly proved. Every historical study and every traveller's account placed peoples somewhere along a continuum from barbarism to civilization. Scottish teaching was vindicated at every turn.

Some Whigs refined the process even more. Richard Payne Knight wrote a poem entitled *The Progress of Civil Society*, in which man's ascent involved six steps.[16] But the message was always the same. Despite setbacks and relapses the movement was forever upward. True, few countries had yet reached the sunny uplands of Russell's fourth and last stage, but, crucially, thanks to the Whigs' defence of the parliamentary tradition in crisis after crisis, England had. That country pre-eminently enjoyed a political system that linked liberty and order, and Whigs unblushingly claimed this as their party's achievement. It gave them the right to lecture their own countrymen on how to preserve freedom and foreigners on how to achieve it.

For such lectures to be useful, a crucial question had to be asked. What was the factor that allowed a political system to have a government strong enough to guarantee order but not so overwhelming that it threatened liberty? The answer was found in the single word 'property'. Whigs believed passionately that men resisted tyrants in order to defend their property. Equally, the props of liberty, such as Habeas Corpus or trial by jury, were prized as weapons in the same war. If the possibility of property-owning was open to the citizens of a state, there was every chance that a free society would emerge. The correlation between property and liberty was exact. As Sir James Mackintosh observed: 'It will not only be curious, but useful, to trace the history of property from the first loose and transient occupancy of the savage, through all the modifications which it has at different times received, to that comprehensive, subtle, and anxiously minute code of property, which is the last result of the most refined civilization.'[17]

To demonstrate the link between property and liberty, Whigs once again simply looked at their contemporary world. Hunter gatherers had no notion of property and no notion of government. Pastoralists in Asia lived with a system of tribally owned property, by which chiefs and headmen dictated decisions. Even in many agricultural communities, the huge estates of kings, aristocrats and churchmen translated easily into oligarchical politics. Only in countries like England, where a happy history had encouraged the widespread and individual ownership of property, was real liberty possible. Real historical events confirmed the link. Magna Carta was born out of resistance to the idea that property could be taxed at will. Four hundred years later, the Stuarts were resisted to the point of civil war in the same cause. Parliamentary government survived in England because that country's numerous property-owners decided that representative government best guaranteed their holdings. It was in this sense that Macaulay could declare that 'the history of England is emphatically the history of progress'.[18]

England's pre-eminence in the March of Mind was a matter of pride, but the firm expectation was that other countries would one day catch up. Industrialization, mass production and international trade would expand the property-owning base of all countries, with inevitable political consequences of a desirable nature. To understand this point was to be on what Macaulay called 'the right side' of history.[19] It was all made comprehensible by the magical new science which called itself political economy. Its god was Adam Smith and its bible was *The Wealth of Nations*. The claims made for this book were extravagant. Whig writers bathed it in superlatives. One asserted that, 'Some of the most beautiful chapters of the *Wealth of Nations* are not so properly parts of an elementary treatise on political economy, as they are contributions to that science which will one day unfold the general laws of the progress of the human race from rudeness to civilization'.[20] Admittedly not all Whigs actually read the book. Charles James Fox allegedly found it heavy going and gave it up half way through. Equally, Charles Grey preferred to rely on the advice of David Ricardo or Francis Horner, men who knew the book by heart, rather than confront it himself. But every Whig acknowledged its authority, and all of them, directly or by proxy, were keen to incorporate its findings in what they did and said. At Whig dinner parties 'political economy and bullion' could be 'discussed at terrible length'.[21]

By reason of their student days in Scotland, many Whigs were Smith's intellectual grandchildren. They had learnt political economy at one remove from the master himself. It was an intoxicating inheritance, and, even if they had not read or understood every nuance in the argument, two broad lessons were absorbed. First, Smith seemed to have given an economic dimension to the historical and political forces that had hitherto attracted the Whig's attention. Apparently, irresistible economic laws led one man to trade with another for the best possible price, demanded that individuals should seek to better themselves, linked inventions with industrial application, and prompted nations to relate to each other through trade and commerce. All these factors prompted that multiplication of the possibility of property-owning that Whigs so much applauded. Trade and commerce forced men to be liberal. As Mackintosh put it:

> The commercial or monied interest has in all nations of Europe (taken as a body) been less prejudiced, more liberal, and more intelligent than the landed gentry. Their views are enlarged by a wider intercourse with mankind; and hence the important influence of commerce in liberalizing the modern world. We cannot wonder then that this enlightened class ever prove the most ardent in the cause of freedom, and the most zealous for political reform.[22]

It was comforting to learn that the progress reported by the historian and the anthropologist was economically determined. Minor setbacks like being out of office so often and for so long paled into insignificance before these cosmic assertions. Sooner or later the vindication of Whig views was assured.

The second legacy of Smith and his pupils to the Whigs was a respect for figures and statistics. Few Whigs had either the time or inclination to devote themselves to compiling or interpreting data, it is true. Such an occupation was too dry. But they respected 'the talented men' who laboured in these matters and employed them to give factual substance to any debate. Statistics was also an enabling science. Many problems were thrown up in the course of industrialisation, but none that were insurmountable if the appropriate data was assembled. Tories and Romantics bewailed the miseries of life in industrial cities. Whigs brandished statistics to work amelioration. The 'talented men' in their employ could always be looked to for answers.

The power inherent in the study of statistics seemed to be limitless. Sir James Mackintosh urged the intelligent in Bombay to undertake 'the investigation of those facts which are the subjects of political arithmetic and statistics'. They might start with studies of wealth and population distribution. Everything else followed naturally:

> These inquiries have the advantage of being easy and open to all men of good sense. They do not, like antiquarian and philological researches, require great previous erudition and constant references to extensive libraries. They require nothing but a resolution to observe facts attentively, and to relate them accurately: and whoever feels a disposition to ascend from facts to

principles will, in general, find sufficient aid to his understanding in the great work of Dr Smith – the most permanent monument of philosophical genius which our nation has produced in the present age.[23]

Again and again, Whigs arrogated to themselves adjectives like 'sensible'. Grounding their arguments in statistics provided by their 'talented men' allowed them to do so. In contrast Tories argued on the basis of myths and fantasies.

Critics of the Whigs found political economy arid beyond description. Its practitioners were rumoured to be so dry that they cracked as they walked. Romantics found them bloodless and spiritual men found them soulless, and with some of this description Whigs would have to agree. These were not studies which they themselves should follow. They could laugh at Bagehot's joking assertion that, 'No real English gentleman, in his secret soul, was ever sorry for the death of a political economist; he is much more likely to be sorry for his life'. After all, he was a man who 'talks excruciating currency'. But Whigs knew, from their Scots inheritance, that such men were not to be gainsaid. Their theories demonstrated beyond contradiction that the political values held dear by the Whigs would one day triumph. Their statistics suggested answers to problems at which others merely threw up their hands. They were 'useful', even if it was only 'as drying machines are useful'.[24] The Scots professor and the political economist had a rightful place at a Whig table. Their new magic held no threat for traditional Whig values, but rather gave them a powerful new, intellectual validation. In this sense, political economy was rightly seen as the Whigs' 'darling study'.[25]

Empowered by such knowledge, Whigs had to be optimists. But, if a smug self-confidence in the ultimate vindication of all their principles grated on the nerves of Tories, their determined cheerfulness about nearly everything irritated even more. Tories saw the First Reform Bill as a disastrous opening up of politics to mob rule. Whigs sponsored the Bill as a sensible attempt to accommodate more property-owners within the franchise. Dickens, Harrison Ainsworth and Bulwer Lytton wrote novels detailing the appalling conditions in which many Englishmen lived. Whigs preferred to point to endless examples of betterment. Anything that was socially askew could be straightened. If proof were needed, Whigs might point to the discoveries of the scientists and engineers who also sat at Whig tables. In addition, they would certainly call into evidence the educational advances which were so marked a feature of their lifetimes. For, unlike political economy, education was a subject in which many Whigs became personally involved. Intelligence and information, like property, encouraged individuals to assert rights and to resist tyranny. The expansion of educational opportunity was therefore a good in itself and another visible proof that progress was indeed on the march.

In the early nineteenth century, there was a vigorous debate about the value and likely consequences of widening educational possibilities. Tories had doubts. For the Duke of Wellington, literacy in the lower orders was synonymous with criminal or radical activity: 'I approve of education, but let it be education connected with a system of discipline. The first object of education should be to teach them not to break the laws of God and man. Now, you teach them to read, and turn them loose into the street to pick pockets.'[26] Whigs could not have disagreed more. For them, the more a man was educated, the more he would see the value of an ordered society and the nonsense of crime. The claims made for the regenerative powers of education were astonishing, and often Romantically phrased. On Victoria's accession to the throne in 1837, Sydney Smith declared:

> First and foremost, I think, the new queen should bend her mind to the very serious consideration of educating the people. They may be turned, I admit, to a good, or a bad purpose; but for several years of his life the child is in your hands, and you may give to that power what bias you please ... When I see the village school, and the tattered scholars, and the aged master or mistress teaching the mechanical art of reading or writing, and thinking that they are teaching that alone, I feel that the aged instructor is protecting life, insuring property, fencing the altar, guarding the throne, giving space and liberty to all the fine powers of man, and lifting him up to his own place in the order of creation.[27]

To fit his actions to his words, Smith was the founder or benefactor of village schools in all the parishes he served.

These views resonated prettily in Whig houses. How else was it possible to explain the astonishing patience of the lower orders as they suffered all the consequences of industrialization and the long French wars. Only widespread literacy could allow them to understand the necessity of these events. Only contact with advanced thinking could give them the confidence to anticipate an end to their suffering in a better world. There was no revolution in England between 1789 and 1848. While nearly every other European country underwent convulsions, the good temper of the working man remained unruffled. Perhaps this could be explained by the fact that, 'education raises up in the poor an admiration for something else besides brute strength and brute courage'.[28] Lord Melbourne lectured his wife along the same lines:

> I know you have a notion, hastily taken up, that instruction and education dispose people to be turbulent and render them difficult to be governed. I am of a contrary opinion; I am quite sure that knowledge and understanding are upon the whole favourable to tranquillity and order. I do not see how it is possible to account for the exemplary patience with which the manufacturers have borne and are at present bearing their severe distress and difficulty except upon the notion of their being better acquainted with the real causes of it.[29]

In other words, through education, the poor would understand that their condition was the result of inexorable, economic forces and not due to the malevolence of a governing elite who deserved a good guillotining.

With such positive views, it was not surprising that Whigs should have been prominent at all levels of the educational process. Sydney Smith fostered village schools and wrote in defence of Robert Raikes and Joseph Lancaster, whose ragged and Sunday schools were offering the chance of education to the lowest in the land. At the other end of the spectrum, Charles Grey was active in the founding of Durham University, while Lord John Russell and Henry Brougham helped to establish University College, London. Brougham was also the inspiration behind a project that carried the grandiloquent and evocative title of the Society for the Diffusion of Useful Knowledge. Penny or halfpenny tracts were to be published, the reading of which would equip the earnest artisan with a basic understanding of the world around him. Implicit in all this activity was the comfortable assumption that, once exposed to education, the poor man would begin to think like a Whig. Whig culture and Whig preferences would simply acquire thousands of new subscribers.

Naturally, syllabuses should reflect these priorities. Once basic literacy and numeracy had been attained, study should be centred on the absorption of the laws of political economy, supplemented by a knowledge of history and the classical world. Everything should have a firmly academic purpose. Whigs therefore looked with some suspicion at the new public schools of the early nineteenth century. Dr Arnold's Rugby seemed to promote non-academic activities to an alarming extent. He also fostered gender definitions associated with 'manliness' that the Whigs found rather curious. Whig concerns on these points came together in their amused attacks on the growing taste for team sports:

> There is a manliness in the athletic exercises of public schools which is as seductive to the imagination as it is wholly unimportant in itself. Of what importance is it in after life whether a boy can play well or ill at cricket; or row a boat with the skill and precision of a waterman? If our young lords and esquires were hereafter to wrestle together in public, or the gentlemen of the Bar to exhibit Olympic games in Hilary Term, the glory attached to these exercises at public schools would be rational and important. But of what use is the body of an athlete, when we have good laws over our heads – or when a pistol, a postchaise, or a porter, can be hired for a few shillings? A gentleman does nothing but ride or walk; and yet such a ridiculous stress is laid upon the manliness of the exercises customary at public school – exercises in which the greatest blockheads commonly excel the most – which often render habits of idleness inveterate – and often leads to foolish expense and dissipation at a more advanced period of life.[30]

According to Lady Stafford, even playing tennis only led on to 'gaming, Idleness and bad Company'.[31] Dr Arnold's system was condemned as a throwback to a time when citizens had to be trained to be warriors. Whigs wanted an educational system that equipped citizens to be voters.

In sum, the central feature of a Whig intelligence was the acceptance of change. This could only be an invaluable asset, for few generations before that born around 1770 had been subjected to greater upheavals. To be born into an agricultural society with fixed values, to witness the overturning of all political assumptions in the French Revolution and to die in a world of steam-driven machinery was demanding of the intellect and the spirit. For many the effort was too great. Many Tories feared change and gave way to pessimistic prophesying. They could regard any amendment to the constitution, any reassessment of morality, as the

onset of the apocalypse. Whigs thought differently. A distinctive education had, they believed, made them masters of the situation. Tories
seemed overwhelmed by events; Whigs claimed to direct them. History
and political economy taught them about the inevitability of change and
explained its mechanisms. Comparing the England of their day with
other communities around the world or with the English past, it was
obvious that man's ascent from barbarism to civilization was unstop-
pable. In *Crotchet Castle*, Thomas Peacock created the memorable
character of a Tory who gave it as his opinion that progress simply
meant that educated criminals would steal your spoons more scientifically. Whigs, by contrast, believed that 'the March of Mind' would allow
everyone to own their own spoons, thereby making criminal endeavour
redundant.

7

Unbelievers

In February 1844, Lord Radnor was confronted with a serious problem. The widowed Lady Holland was proving a demanding house guest. She had long outstayed her welcome and yet showed no signs of leaving. In order 'to get rid of her', Radnor could only think of two stratagems: he could literally unroof the house or confront her with religion. He decided on the second of these possibilities as the cheaper and more expedient. He announced accordingly that family prayers would be held. To his dismay and astonishment, Lady Holland declared that she would attend them. What happened next was described by another guest:

> She was highly pleased (very gracious, Lady Morley said, because she knew they longed to get rid of her), and said she would go down for prayers. Whether she was ill I do not know, but it seems she had to be carried downstairs, and wrapped herself up in cloaks, etc. In the midst she called out for more cloaks, which were brought to her. When she went up to the drawing room again, she said to Lord Radnor (he having finished with the Lord's Prayer): I like that very much, that last prayer you read. I approve of it, it is a very nice one – pray, whose is it?[1]

Radnor's scheme had failed. His guest had dealt with religion by interrupting its services with demands for more wrappings, and by expressing a real or feigned ignorance of the Lord's Prayer. She had turned threat into comedy.

In principle, however, Radnor had been on the right track. It was generally held that to offer religion to a Whig was the equivalent of offering garlic to a vampire. They were thought to be temperamentally incapable of understanding anything spiritual, being too full of what Thomas Carlyle called 'dead Edinburgh Whiggism, scepticism, and materialism'.[2] They were not so much against religion as oblivious to it. Even anticlericalism was beyond them, for that too demanded a certain fire and energy. Some Whigs indeed openly pleaded guilty to the charge of being outside religious experience. For, empirically, religion seemed to have such dire effects on the people who practised it. Most creeds seemed to frown on colour, inconsequence and dalliance, all the things that made life agreeable. Religious people were always 'so dreadfully in earnest'.[3] By contrast, Edinburgh provided its pupils with an explanation of how life was to be lived that allowed for gaiety. On their death-beds, few Whigs were surrounded by priests, or were much occupied with the mechanics of repentance. Last words were heard by close friends and family. Those allegedly uttered by Charles James Fox, 'Don't cry, my dear Liz, it don't signify', sounded all too plausible.

The blank in Whig thinking about matters religious interested and puzzled contemporaries. Some, like Walter Bagehot, concluded that it was almost genetically determined, less a case of a rejection of religion than an innate imperviousness to its appeal. In his view, Whigs suffered from

> a want of imagination, of impulsive enthusiasm, of shrinking fear ... Glance over the whole of history, as the classical world stood beside the Jewish; as Horace beside St Paul; like the heavy ark and the buoyant waves, so are men in contrast with one another. You cannot imagine a classical Isaiah; you cannot fancy a Whig St Dominic; there is no such thing as a Liberal Augustine. The deep sea of mysticism lies opposed to some natures; in some moods it is a sublime wonder; in others an 'impious ocean', – they will never put forth on it at any time.[4]

Whigs had cold natures, by this account, that could never be warmed by belief. One writer in *Blackwood's Magazine* even suggested, teasingly, that Whig constitutions were so cold, that gout was unknown in their circles:

> I don't think Whigs ever have the gout – they sometimes get a twinge of rheumatism which they mistake for it, but Whigs have not genuine gout; the cold juices of their system do not generate it ... I believe Sir Francis Burdett has genuine gout sometimes, but he is a misguided English gentleman, and no Whig, as he has expressly declared. To say the truth, I am glad that the Whigs do not get gout, as I would not that they should share even a complaint in common with his Majesty King George the Fourth, whom God long preserve.[5]

Not surprisingly, Whig clergymen were few and far between. When in office, filling vacancies in the Church was always a problem. In 1837, for example, Lord Ebrington was asked by a desperate Cabinet Minister if he had a 'list of the few Devonshire parsons who are Whigs and to whom *small* livings would be acceptable?'[6]

The public behaviour of Whigs seemed to more than confirm the diagnosis offered by their opponents. Never regular church-goers, they nevertheless found themselves in holy places from time to time in the fulfilment of state duties. On these occasions their performances failed to please. Typically, Lord Melbourne found the coronation of Queen Victoria a terrible bore. Disraeli noted that he carried the Sword of State rather in the manner of a butcher. Even more shocking was his tendency to disappear from time to time, in order to refresh himself with wine and sandwiches, which he had ordered to be laid out on the altar in St Edward's Chapel.[7] Equally surprising were the public pronouncements of Richard Watson. As a Whig bishop, he was something of a collector's item in himself. His confession of faith was also singular: 'Now my mind was wholly unbiased; I had no prejudice against, no predilection for the Church of England; but a sincere regard for the *Church of Christ*, and an insuperable objection to every degree of dogmatical intolerance.'[8] Even judged by the standards of modern Anglicanism, such a creed might be thought rather loose. In his own generation, the Church of England had the right to expect something a little more forceful.

Further, the greatest Whig salon of the early nineteenth century, Holland House, made no secret of its dismissal of religion. Its owners, Lord and Lady Holland, never went near a church. Lady Holland, in particular, was so unhopeful of life after death that any intimations of her own mortality terrified her. The very word 'death' was taboo in her presence. For the same reason, she always left performances of *Hamlet* before the funeral scenes were played. Lord Carlisle had difficulty in rejecting her request that he demolish the Mausoleum in the grounds of Castle Howard. Apparently, the sight of it from her window made her 'too sad'.[9] Equally distinctive was the figure of John Allen, the house's librarian. A Scot by birth and education, he acquired the nickname of 'Lady Holland's Atheist'. Becoming increasingly eccentric and caustic, he could be seen walking around the West End, 'constantly repeating "No first cause, No first cause", by way of keeping himself up to his system'.[10] The dogmatism of Allen and his employers on the subject

of religion could be turned into humour. Once, on being caught up in
a house fire, Allen, 'hearing the crackling of the flames, and smelling the
smoke and seeing Lady Holland, conceived he had slipt off in the night
to a very serious place at a very high Temperature: he attempted to
recollect a prayer, but entirely failed and was fairly pulled out of bed by
Lady Holland and the maids'.[11]

Predictably, clergymen and divines were not to be found at Whig
tables. 'The only one of the class' who did drink Whig toasts on a regular basis was Sydney Smith, in himself something of a rarity. He was
a dutiful parish priest and a convinced Christian. But he was also
Scots-educated, a noted contributor to the *Edinburgh* and endowed with
a magnificent wit. He represented religion in its most polished and
amusing form. Even John Allen could look forward to evenings when
'Sydney is to entertain us with a sermon'.[12] Indeed, he and Smith
became sparring partners in conversation, to the amusement and edification of other diners. In their mouths, religion ceased to be dull and
threatening:

> At the Hollands there was a motley company of lawyers, statesmen, critics
> and divines – Sydney Smith, the only one of the latter class, in high glee
> attacking Mr Ward and Allen, telling them that the best way to keep a merry
> Xmas was to roast a Scotch Atheist as the most intolerant and arrogant of all
> two legged animals. Allen did not look pleas'd, but kept clapping his hands
> together till his fingers crack'd (a great trick of his). S.S. called out, 'See!
> there's one beginning to crackle already.'[13]

Such levity and high spirits turned Smith into a Whig pet. He became
their token clergyman. Revelling in their company, he paid the
price of forgoing all prospect of serious promotion within the
Church. The episcopal bench could not accommodate men such as
this. His Whig credentials looked too incongruous in a man of his
profession.

Given the wide gulf that existed between Whiggery and all forms of
official religion, any suggestion that the latter should influence family
life was met with something close to panic. In particular, it was almost
inconceivable that Whigs could be converts. In 1828, the sixth Duke of
Bedford was struggling with the consequences of his son, Wriothesley,
taking an interest in Methodism:

He has a weak mind, and is too easily led by designing people, less honest and upright than himself. Among them I reckon the Evangelicals, the Calvinistick Methodists, and all the class of the over righteous, who assume to themselves a superior sanctity and contempt for the doctrines of others, like the Pharisee in the Scriptures. These are an increasing and very dangerous sect. Wrio. has recently written to Eliza, which makes me unhappy. It is a rhapsody about 'grace' etc etc and full of the Methodistical cant, though not so in his view of it ... He tells her that she must not hide the talent entrusted to her under a bushel, but must enlighten the whole house by it, thus constituting her a Missionary to my whole family. Poor girl, all this bewilders her head.[14]

The idea that Woburn Abbey should be illuminated by Methodist enlightenment rather than gas jets was preposterous. In the same year, the fifth Earl of Darnley was confronted by an Evangelical daughter-in-law. He found it salutary to read her a lecture on pleasure:

> As to your quotations from Scripture, 'Set your affections on things above' etc 'Love not the world' etc So say I – but I must still maintain that between setting affections on and loving and using moderately and occasionally, as recreation from more serious matters, there is a wide and important difference, and I know not how this can be better exemplified than by the illustration ... in the difference between drinking a glass or two of wine and getting drunk.[15]

A committed Christian, particularly one with Evangelical promptings, was a thorn in any Whig family. Maximum irritation was the result. Such people could never keep their views to themselves or respect other opinions. Their behaviour was condemned as boorish and fundamentally impolite.

Inevitably, few Whigs believed that religion should be the principal regulator of private morality. For them, the Ten Commandments were not to be accepted *en bloc*, but were to be seen as a kind of menu, from which choices could be made. To allow any creed to influence social life was a matter for teasing in affected speech. Harriet Granville was more amused than shocked when William and Frederick Lamb, returning home very late and 'very drunk', warned her lispingly 'of the danger of a young womans believing in religion and pwacticing morality'.[16] Perhaps the most tiresome person to invade Whig society was the reformed

rake who had taken up religion late in life. Lady Caroline Lamb feared
that Madame de Genlis, the former mistress of Talleyrand and Louis
Philippe among others, had taken this path. Certainly, her later novels
suggested a worrying falling off towards morality:

> I think the methodistical stile [sic] it is written in and the whole of her refl-
> ections very dull, I am sure she is turned *dévote* and like all those who are in
> their youth free thinkers and free livers, the sort of religion they take to in
> their age is, I think, a very unpleasant sort, that of putting everything to faith,
> to enthusiasm, to immediate and particular interferences of Providence.[17]

It was much better to keep the demands of religion and the demands of
cutting a figure in good society quite separate.

Predictably, Whigs found themselves at odds with the increasing
religiosity of the early nineteenth century. Lady Holland's position as a
divorcée had always given her a particular interest in these matters,
but her letters give voice to increasing irritation at religious prohibitions. Strict observation of the sabbath day, for example, excited
indignation:

> Here we are going wild about the better observance of the Sabbath. It is pro-
> posed to shut up the Parks, and put barriers across the streets to prevent the
> passage of carriages. You would be astonished at the numbers of people who
> are inclined to give ear to this proposition. It is strange that people should
> meddle with the opinions and conduct of others upon religious matters; but
> so it has been and ever will be.[18]

Not someone who accepted reverses passively, she insisted that her husband should use his influence in Cabinet to secure her a personal
dispensation from the new law. Since churchmen also tended to espouse
temperance, marital fidelity and harsh laws against gambling, it was
clear to Whigs that their influence in daily life should be carefully
monitored.

Theology was unsurprisingly absent from Whig syllabuses. There was
simply no point in discussing what must forever be inscrutable. Whigs
lived through the heated debates which accompanied the growth of
Methodism, the Evangelical Revival and the Oxford Movement as bored
spectators. In Lord Byron's view, points of theology were either brutal,
or incapable of solution, or both:

> A *material* resurrection seems strange and even absurd except for purposes

of punishment – and all punishment which is to *revenge* rather than *correct* must be *morally wrong* – and *when* the *World is at an end* – what moral or warning purpose *can* eternal tortures answer? – human passions have probably disfigured the divine doctrines here – but the whole thing is inscrutable. It is useless to tell one *not* to *reason* but to *believe* – you might as well tell a man not to wake but *sleep*.[19]

The main purpose of religious creeds was, according to Whig historians, to justify men in slaughtering their fellows. Every doctrinal dispute easily transmuted into massacre and persecution. As a Whig petitioner to the House of Commons in 1772 put it: 'No Doctrines so obscure, but what in some Diet or Council have been subtilized and sublimed, by scholastic Sophistry, into hallowed Mysteries; none so unedifying and indifferent, but what the over-weening Wisdom of some intolerant Enthusiast has imposed as *Credenda,* necessary to eternal Salvation.'[20] Too often, in the Whig view, religions claimed an exclusivity of truth that inevitably led them to persecute those who differed in opinion.

Nowhere was this more evident than in the missionary activity that preoccupied so many of their contemporaries. Whigs detested missionaries, and the pages of the *Edinburgh* are full of sallies at their expense. In the first place, it was simply impertinent for one religious system to impose itself on another. Whig reviewers were quite clear that some other creeds were the equals of Christianity in terms of insight and philosophical complexity. The societies they supported therefore had a rationale which should not be undermined. Sydney Smith, though a clergyman, denounced missionary activity in India, and asserted that it would contribute to the loss of British influence in the subcontinent:

> We see not the slightest prospect of success; – we see much danger in making the attempt; – and we doubt if the conversion of the Hindoos would ever be more than nominal. If it is a duty of general benevolence to convert the Heathen, it is less a duty to convert the Hindoos than any other people, because they are already highly civilized, and because you must infallibly subject them to infamy and present degradation.[21]

Richard Watson agreed. He did 'not expect much success in propagating Christianity by missionaries ... but I do expect much from the extension of science and commerce'.[22] In other words, other cultures might possibly adopt the religious system of the West after being led to appreciate its humane improvements. If missionaries really had to follow their trade, they should not teach doctrine but rather demonstrate the best in medicine, commerce and education. A convert or two might be the reward, but such souls would be saved out of gratitude rather than fear.

Personally distant from any religious influences in their daily lives, and with such strong views on how far faith should be allowed to regulate society generally, Whigs held equivocal opinions on the value of religion as a whole. They were clear that their own conduct should remain unsupervised. But they were less certain of their fellow men. As long as most people were uneducated and unenlightened, restraining their behaviour with a mild dose of religion may not have been a bad thing. At least Christianity taught obedience and resignation to the lower orders. This might be thought valuable in times of French revolutionaries and Chartists. Lord John Russell was being practical rather than cynical in saying, 'Take away religion, and, in the minds of most men, you take away the obligation to restrain their passions – to speak truth – to respect the rights and feelings of others'.[23] In his view, 'most men' were not yet able to do without religion. They had not yet learnt to regulate their conduct by self-imposed discipline. Until they could they were dangerous.

Atheism might therefore be talked about and joked about in Whig salons but it was not for public consumption. The atheist, if freed from the restraints of religion without adopting the disciplines of enlightened thinking, was as disruptive a phenomenon as the fanatic. Francis Jeffrey offered the readers of the *Edinburgh* a direct analogy between the two:

> He who thinks himself a favourite with the Deity, is apt to be as careless about his behaviour, as he who does not believe at all in his existence: both think themselves alike entitled to dispense with the vulgar rules of morality; and both are alike destitute of the curb and guidance of a sober and rational religion. Submission to lawful activity is indisputably the maxim of Christianity; and they who destroy our faith in that religion, take away one security for our submission, and facilitate the subversion of governments. This is a great truth, the authority of which is not impaired by the rebellions that priests have instigated, or the disorders that fanatics have raised.[24]

As education became more and more widespread, religious systems would in turn become less and less convincing and less and less necessary. Until that moment arrived, freethinking in Whig circles had to go hand in hand with a nod towards religious observances in public places.

What was wanted was what Jeffery referred to as 'a sober and rational religion'. It would be a creed which was state-supported but which was disinclined to persecute. It would moderate men's behaviour without banning pleasure. Above all, it would allow dissenting opinions, as long as such opinions were couched in respectful language. Such a Church had existed in the early eighteenth century, when, according to Lord John Russell, Anglicanism had been 'moderate and tranquil, advanced to the full extent of a reasonable age, persecuted no one, and was respected by all'.[25] Religion should be taken as a dry sherry before meals rather than gulped down in pints of hot toddy. Whigs might dispense with religion altogether, but other people should heed its prescriptions. Worn lightly, it could possibly bring them benefits. As Richard Payne Knight rhapsodized:

> Religion's lights, when loose and undefined,
> Expand the heart, and elevate the mind;
> Brighten the fancy, and the spirits raise,
> Exalt the artist's touch, and poet's lays;
> With smiling hope the brow of anguish cheer,
> And dry up melancholy's silent tear;
> Bring down from heaven bright visions of delight,
> And pour their glories on the fading sight;
> Blunt the keen pangs of sorrow in distress,
> And ebbing life's last gasping struggles bless.
> But, in dogmatic definitions bound,
> They only serve to puzzle and confound;
> To awe the timid, and the weak enslave,
> And make the fool subservient to the knave.[26]

According to Whigs, their times demanded a gentle creed that restrained the excesses of uneducated men without hectoring or falling back on menaces.

Only one religious option came anywhere near meeting these requirements. Anglicanism, if only by default, secured Whig approval, even though they never entered its churches and made fun of its doctrines. Compared to all other systems, it seemed to take less delight in burning its competitors. Once again, the study of history and the observation of contemporary societies seemed to prove the point. Islam was philosophically of interest, but, as Henry Brougham pointed out, it seemed to be so grounded in a 'hatred of other sects' that 'we should not be surprised to find scarcely one freethinker in the whole of the Turkish population'.[27] The Koran was 'a farrago of absurdities ... and gossiping stories'.[28] Hinduism was not really any better. Brahmin society, admittedly, enjoyed a culture that was refined and highly literary, but their religion also seemed to condemn too many people 'to poverty and wretchedness'. Neither religion fostered ideas that were compatible 'with the existence of a prosperous or flourishing country'.[29] The answer was not to offer these people Christianity instead, but rather to introduce them to secular ways of thinking.

For few Christian sects carried Whig approval either. Roman Catholicism was particularly distasteful. Grand Tourists endlessly commented on its baleful effects. Lady Bessborough could not understand the rejoicing which accompanied the disappearance of a young girl into a convent. In her view, this could only be 'a very melancholy occasion'.[30] When in Rome in 1825, the fourth Lord Holland found the antics of the Pope perfectly ridiculous: 'He has among other liberal proceedings published an edict against vaccination which is strictly forbidden as being an impious impediment to the will of Heaven. His edict against ladies' dresses was really worthy of Tartuffe.'[31] Whig tourists were even more unflattering about Catholic services. George Bridgeman experienced them for the first time in Palermo, in 1813, and reported to his mother as follows:

> I am now come to that part of your letter in which you ask my opinion of the Roman Catholic churches and services. There are certainly several things that inspire more awe than ours, but the heavy, gaudy, tasteless ornaments of them, together with the absurd monkey-like actions and motions of their priests, chanting or reciting like parrots, while their thoughts are employed in anything but devotion, never excite in me any feelings but those of derision or disgust.[32]

Catholicism and its equivalents in Asia depended too much on ritual, dietary prohibitions, the downgrading of women and a suspicion of all improvement.

When Whigs were confronted by the problem of explaining

Catholicism's great success historically, they could not believe that its attraction lay in the truths it offered. Rather, it seemed to suit peoples which had not taken many steps along the March of Mind. Sydney Smith accounted for the conversion of so many people in Sri Lanka by referring to that island's 'rude inhabitants'.[33] Whigs were clear that, once peoples became more enlightened, the power of Catholicism would rapidly diminish. The correlation between progress and rationalism was exact. As John Millar lectured his pupils:

> Independent of accidental circumstances, it was to be expected that those countries, which made the quickest progress in trade and manufactures, would be the first to dispute and reject the papal authority. The improvement of arts, and the consequent diffusion of knowledge, contributed, on the one hand, to dispel the mist of superstition, and, on the other, to place the bulk of the people in situations which inspired them with sentiments of liberty. That principle, in short, which is to be regarded as the general cause of the reformation, produced the most powerful effects in those countries where it existed the soonest, and met with the greatest encouragement.[34]

Knowledge and commerce would be the solvents of Catholic influence.

With all these imperfections, however, Catholicism did not occupy the lowest place in Whig esteem. That dubious honour was reserved for the Methodists. In even their most critical mood, Whigs had to acknowledge that Catholicism understood order and hierarchy, and that it had an intellectual tradition within its communion of real quality. Methodism had none of these things. Rather, Wesley and his followers seemed to rely only on inspiration and charismatic enthusiasm. No word was more despised in Whig conversation than 'enthusiasm'. It conjured up horrific images of men who put inspiration before reason, who always carried arguments to extremes and who regarded moderation as a curse. By contrast, Whigs revered the memory of an early eighteenth-century bishop who had had it proudly recorded on his memorial that he had taught the word of God for forty years without enthusiasm. As Methodism steadily grew in numbers throughout the late eighteenth and early nineteenth century, Whigs felt fully justified in making it a special object of attention. Indeed, attacking Methodism was a confirmed Whig hobby, something in the nature of a special pastime.

Sydney Smith was the acknowledged general in this campaign. He lambasted Methodism for allowing emotion to triumph over reason, for subordinating science to revelation, and for the impertinence of suggesting to ordinary people that they could develop moral and religious systems without reference to their social superiors. And then Methodism made everyone so intolerably gloomy. According to Smith, Methodists

> hate pleasure and amusements; no theatre, no cards, no dancing, no punchinello, no dancing dogs, no blind fiddlers; all the amusements of the rich and of the poor must disappear, wherever these gloomy people get a footing. It is not the abuse of pleasure which they attack but pleasure itself, however much it is guarded by good sense and moderation ... Ennui, wretchedness, melancholy, groans and sighs are the offerings which these unhappy men make to the Deity, who has covered the earth with gay colours, and scented it with rich perfumes; and shown us, by the plan and order of his works, that he had given man something better than a bare existence and scattered over his creation a thousand superfluous joys, which are totally unnecessary to the mere support of life ... The Methodists are always desirous of making men more religious, than it is possible, from the constitution of human nature, to make them ... there is not a mad-house in England, where a considerable part of the patients have not been driven to insanity by the extravagance of these people. We cannot enter such places without seeing a number of honest artisans, covered with blankets, and calling themselves angels, apostles, who, if they had remained contented with the instruction of men of learning and education, would still have been sound members of their own trade, sober christians, and useful members of society.[35]

Methodism was nothing more than a wicked manipulation of gullible people, and the more dangerous because it rejected all notions of hierarchy.

In a similar vein, Lord John Russell, writing a history of Europe in the eighteenth century, saw Methodism as the one major blot on an otherwise improving landscape. Irritation at their behaviour overcame his usual reticence in language. He accused Wesley himself of being 'bold enough to believe that miracles were worked in behalf of his religion and himself'. He thought that George Whitefield was mentally unbalanced, being someone who 'ardently longed for martyrdom'. As for the sect as a whole, 'Those who were favoured with the direct, full and individual communication with the Almighty, were, of course, full of hope'.[36]

Increasingly, Methodists became intolerant of all those who held different opinions, and this, according to Whig writers, was to be expected.
All religious systems that claimed a special or an exclusive access to truth
were bound to follow the same path. It was inevitable and depressing.
Precisely at the moment when science and discovery offered such possibilities, thousands of people retreated into the darkness of
Methodistical enthusiasm.

At home and abroad, therefore, Whigs were confronted by unpleasant religious systems, which peddled myth and poverty, and which
offered their adherents a trip to the asylum. None came near to the sort
of religion that Whigs wanted: a system which would gently regulate
religious instincts without persecution or coercion, and which, above
all, could tolerate dissent. This was a point of enormous importance.
Whigs were virtually unanimous in promoting the cause of religious toleration. For some it was the defining point of Whiggery. In 1833, Joseph
Jekyll, having lived long enough to see slaves emancipated and religious
dissenters liberated, told his sister that his life's work had been achieved.
Now he could sing a personal *Nunc Dimittis*: 'For thirty three years, I
gave hopeless votes for Reform, Catholics, Dissenters, and black men,
but all has been accomplished, and I may now sing the song of Simeon,
and be let depart in peace.'[37] Critics of the Whigs made the same association between them and religious toleration. *Fraser's Magazine* saw
Holland House as a 'temple of Baal', promoting everything that took
place in 'the meeting-house, the mass-house, and the pot-house'.[38]

As has been indicated, the Whig search for a religious system that
allowed toleration would be long and arduous. A survey of world religions rather suggested that these creeds gloried in and fed on the wish
to persecute. Observing the Europe of the early nineteenth century,
Sydney Smith only found 'A panting to burn B; B fuming to roast C;
C miserable that he cannot reduce D to ashes; and D consigning to
eternal perdition the first three letters of the alphabet'.[39] Certain Anglican traditions seemed to offer the only hope of more reasonable
behaviour. But even that Church contained within it 'three classes of
fanatics', namely 'the Arminian and Calvinistic methodists and the
evangelical clergymen', all of whom represented 'one general conspir-
acy against common sense'.[40] Clearly the battle would be hard fought.
Non-Anglicans faced implacable enemies. Yet Anglicanism also had a

milder face. Some of its servants were prepared to admit that, perhaps, they did not enjoy a monopoly of the truth. If they could prevail, England might set an example in toleration that would educate the whole world. For over fifty years, Whigs fought a parliamentary campaign to that end.

The basic problem lay in the Test Acts. These had been passed in the 1670s with the express purpose of giving Anglicanism a privileged position within the state. Only its adherents could hold public office as Justice of the Peace or Member of Parliament. Only they could hold commissions in the army or attend Oxford and Cambridge. Roman Catholics and Nonconformists were required to worship in private if they worshipped at all. The justification for these punitive measures was simply that Anglicanism was the only option that was politically safe. In the sixteenth century, Catholicism was linked in the public mind with the absolutist kings of Spain and their endless attempts to invade England. At the other end of the spectrum, Oliver Cromwell had used troops to destroy a Parliament, because his Nonconformist God had told him to. Most seventeenth-century people of any importance agreed that Anglicanism was the only parliamentary religion. That quality was one of the things that made it so thoroughly and unequivocally English. The persecution of non-Anglicans was vital to the safety of the parliamentary tradition. One hundred years later, in the 1770s, it was this idea, so engrained in the public mind, that the Whigs had to attack.

It was an uphill task. Whigs were endlessly astonished by the extent to which adults could allow themselves to be frightened by religious bogeymen. As late as 1829, when Catholics were finally released from their disabilities, the development quite literally made people ill. Lady Darnley gleefully reported to her son that the Tory Duchess of Rutland had taken to her bed, prostrate 'with alarm about Bloody Mary, Guy Faux and the Duke of Norfolk'.[41] On the same point, Whigs noted that the name of Oliver Cromwell, under the soubriquet of 'Old Noll', was paraded at every election to terrify electors. Quite clearly the horrors of the seventeenth century had not gone away. There could be no prospect of toleration until these mists had been dissipated, and it was to this task that Whigs, as historians and polemicists, turned.

Central to their campaign was the argument that, even if Catholicism and Nonconformity had been real political threats in the seventeenth century, they had ceased to be so by 1800. Whigs found it incredible that English voters could still be afraid of the Pope and Oliver Cromwell in a world of steam engines. They pointed out, with patience and a certain wry amusement, that these religions had become so unthreatening that the Test Acts had not actually been enforced for many years. From the 1730s, an annual indemnity Bill released Nonconformists from their penalties for the next twelve months. In moments of crisis, Roman Catholics were drafted in as temporary JPs. Oxford and Cambridge maintained their Anglican purity, but in many other respects the Test Acts had simply ceased to operate. In the Whig view, it was silly and hypocritical to keep these laws on a statute book when fewer and fewer people had any interest in enforcing them. As Sydney Smith observed in 1807:

> I never met a parson in my life who did not consider the Corporation and Test Acts as the great bulwarks of the church; and yet it is now just sixty-four years since bills of indemnity to destroy their penal effects, or, in other words, to repeal them, have been passed annually as a matter of course ... These bulwarks, without which no clergyman thinks he could sleep with his accustomed soundness, have actually not been in existence since any man now living has taken holy orders.[42]

To fear the political power of Rome any longer was absurd. According to Smith, it would be more rational to fear Gog and Magog.[43]

In fact, Whig historians insisted that it was not just a question of non-Anglicans representing no threat; in every crisis of the late seventeenth and eighteenth centuries, they had been positively helpful. When the Stuarts had invaded the country in 1715 and 1745, backed by French soldiers and French priests, English Catholics had gone out of the way to express loyalty. The Nonconformists had been equally patriotic. On what Richard Watson described as 'trying occasions', they had 'shewn their attachment to the house of Brunswick and the principles of the revolution [1688]; and I should think myself guilty of calumny, if I should say that they had in any degree abandoned either their attachment or their principles, or were disposed to join the invaders of their country'.[44] The performance of both groups had been so impeccable that, in Watson's opinion, the only thing that could drive them into treasonous practices was their continuing to be persecuted. History proved to the Whigs that the uselessness of the Test Acts was demonstrated in their being repeatedly ignored. Contemporary society must be made to face this fact.

Armed with arguments such as these, and personally free of religious affiliations, Whig politicians were prominent, over three generations, in campaigns to secure full toleration for all sects. Their activity was observed at all levels. Once a year, for example, St Albans Tavern in the Strand would be the venue for a dinner attended by London's leading Nonconformists. The guest of honour would be one of the most renowned Whig leaders. Charles Fox fulfilled this duty in his day, as did Lord Holland, the Duke of Bedford and many others. At the end of the meal, speeches would be given which mingled thanks for an agreeable evening with promises to raise the question of toleration in the next parliamentary session. Roman Catholic functions were also occasionally so honoured. And since such proceedings were mirrored in towns up and down the country, the Whigs were very publicly associated with religious Dissenters. As one grateful Catholic put it, their patronage was 'of essential service to the cause'.[45] Promises made at dinners were then regularly translated into parliamentary motions, article-writing and acts of benevolence. Anglicans simply had to be convinced that their beliefs were not at risk, and that no Catholic incendiary lurked in the cellars below the Houses of Parliament.

The Whig contribution to the cause of seeing full religious toleration was so considerable that they fully expected the beneficiaries of such toleration to support their politics whenever opportunity offered. It would have been the height of ingratitude for Catholics and Dissenters to do anything else. Lord Holland was outraged to hear a rumour that certain Nonconformists were proposing to abandon Lord John Russell in his candidature at Bedford. The town was within hailing distance of Woburn Abbey. Considerations of property-owning alone entitled the Russells to great respect and influence. Their involvement with campaigns for toleration redoubled their claims to loyalty. Given all these factors, Holland had no compunction about lecturing Bedford's Nonconformists on their duty:

I am told that a large body of Methodists have not only taken offence and misconstrued a passage in Lord John Russell's book but are active and virulent in their canvass against him at Bedford. Such hostility from any party distinguished by peculiar tenets in religion against the man who has broken the shackles to which *all men sincerely religious* were exposed by the principle of the test acts, seems to me, I own, equally discreditable and impudent. It would be ungracious to prefer a candidate who professed the same principles as themselves in religion, to one who has politically served them so essentially in a town where his connections and name give him so fair and so natural an interest; but to prefer to the very person who repealed the test and corporation acts, who presided at your meetings once or twice, and who with very eminent talents and attainments has uniformly devoted them to the cause of religious liberty ... another gentleman who however respectable he may be has given the publick no proof of his political principles ... is surely preposterous and unjust in the extreme ... I hope and trust that your friends and all kindred sects will exert themselves to mitigate such ill-judged hostility.[46]

Mercifully such incidents were few. Normally, Whigs and their religious protégés kept in step. But, as Holland's outpouring on paper in long and badly-punctuated sentences indicates, his party demanded gratitude for their efforts, and were indignant when it was compromised.

Of course, people who had little or no personal religion themselves found it easy to espouse toleration. It cost them very little. That said, the Whigs still performed an essential service. Their contacts with Catholics and Nonconformists gave those groups the firm hope that the political establishment was not uniformly against them. Excluded from public life and educational opportunities by the Test Acts, it would have been easy for them to conclude that they had no choice but to challenge the system. A flirtation with Jacobitism or Revolution would have seemed plausible. The fact that no such flirtations took place must in part be due to the experience of seeing Toleration Bills being brought before Parliament on an almost annual basis. Such initiatives offered the hope that their exclusion from so much of national life could be ended without a revolution or a change of dynasty. Whigs, marching along a high road towards Progress, had a completely different mindset from those people who attended Mass or listened to long, hell-fire sermons in unadorned chapels. But the very lack of a personal involvement in any religion made them the patrons of all religions. Whigs would be decried as atheists, agnostics and immoralists, and these were charges to which they often pleaded guilty. Their defence was that, if religious people insisted in pursuing persecution and exclusivity, a little secularism in a nation's politics might not come amiss.

8

History and Politics

Whig politics rested on the simple proposition that property was king. Its acquisition and the rights inherent in its ownership prompted men to support free government. Its pre-eminence was fundamental to any attempt by men to live together as a political community. As Lord John Russell succinctly observed: 'The government of the states of modern Europe ... rests on property; the love of enjoying, the fear of losing an estate, is the main principle of action with all who have an estate to keep of lose.'[1] By comparison, the natural rights talked of by Tom Paine and Mary Wollstonecraft, inherent in man at birth, were not to be regarded. No rights can be exercised outside a political community, and the *Edinburgh Review* sternly lectured its readers on why such communities were formed in the first place:

> Men first desire subsistence – property – and some sort of security for both. Till they have attained these for themselves, they have no leisure to think of the rights of others, or of their own rights, to think, to speak, or to act in matters of less immediate concernment. Till then, they can scarcely be said to have attained the qualifications of political agents ... With property, however, and the means of acquiring it, come the feeling of these rights, and the capacity and habit of reasoning which leads irresistibly, and by a very short process, to their full development.[2]

The ownership of property was so obviously the principal buttress of a free constitution, that, when Whigs were denounced as subversives and radicals, Charles Greville simply exclaimed: 'All false, for nobody's policy is subversive who has so much to lose, and the Whigs comprise the great mass of property.'[3]

Inevitably, Whigs would have looked with suspicion on modern notions of human rights. For individuals, or groups of individuals, to pursue their narrow interests, without reference to the common good or the security of the stabilising power of property-ownership, would have seemed an invitation to chaos. Equally, as their disdain for 'the talented man' has shown, mere ability should not challenge the claims of property. Edmund Burke believed that such a challenge had been a contributing factor in producing the great disaster of the French Revolution. In his *Reflections* on that event, he observed that: 'Nothing is a due and adequate representation of a state, that does not represent its ability, as well as its property. But, as ability is a vigorous and active principle, and as property is sluggish, inert, and timid, it never can be safe from the invasions of ability, unless it be, out of all proportion, predominant in the representation.'[4] Whigs had no doubt that men had evolved from the savage state to form civil societies solely to establish the possibility of property-ownership and, once established, to safeguard it with the rule of law.

It followed that the exercise of the franchise and public life in general should be restricted to those with property. Democratic alternatives were absurd. Property-ownership alone qualified a man for full citizenship. The arguments for this proposition were so obvious to Whigs that they could almost be taken as read in any decision reached by that party. First, property gave its owner a real interest in the stability and security of a country, for, if either were jeopardised, he had much to lose. To use the contemporary expression, such a man had 'a stake in the country'. Given a vote, he would use it wisely. By contrast, the unpropertied had literally nothing to lose. If enfranchised, they were at liberty to follow any whim or caprice. Secondly, Whigs believed that property-ownership opened up the possibilities of acquiring the leisure to take politics seriously, and the education necessary to interpret politics rationally. Thirdly, property gave a man 'an independence'. No one could be bribed or bullied whose own income was substantial and secure. Taking all these factors into consideration, Henry Brougham had no doubt that, 'a body of men, independent in their fortunes, and bearing a part in public affairs, seems quite essential to the maintenance of civil liberty'.[5]

When Whigs approached the tricky question of Parliamentary Reform therefore, their aim was always to enfranchise more property-owners and to make their voice heard at ever greater volume. There was never any genuflection towards the democratic notion that one man's opinion was the equal of his fellow's. It was nonsensical to suggest such a thing. How could artisans and labourers, with little or no education or leisure, hope to form opinions on the management of the economy or foreign affairs of a kind to compel attention? Unanchored by concerns about property, what would prevent such people being caught by spurious arguments peddled by political mountebanks? The March of Progress would of course mean that more and more individuals would gradually acquire property and, with it, the virtues necessary for a role in public life. But their enfranchisement had to be on Whig, rather than democratic, terms. As a writer in *The Times* put it: 'Property, which bespeaks, first the means of obtaining education; next, a stake in the maintenance of law and order; and lastly independence of ordinary temptations, may be far from a universal or unvarying test of character; but as a test at once general and tangible there is none so good.'[6]

On top of all this, the political magic worked by property-ownership had had one positive and demonstrable consequence. It led men to resist any tyranny that threatened their holdings. History proved that it prompted men to defend liberty. Parliamentary government and the laws it made defended property. Liberties such as Habeas Corpus and trial by jury were devices to the same end. In the seventeenth century, would-be tyrants like Charles I and James II had been checked and defeated by men of great property. Not for nothing did the historian Sir James Mackintosh consider the right to own and inherit an estate 'the bulwark against tyranny'.[7] In his view, and that of others, it was precisely this willingness of property-owners to act that provided the singularity of English history. The early establishment of the property principle created parliamentary government and defended it against all assaults. It was England's good luck and good fortune that this should have been so.

Naturally, such theories put tremendous pressure on property-owners. They enjoyed the privileges of assured incomes and educated lives, but they also had the responsibilities to serve the state without remuneration, and to be ever watchful about the diminishing of parliamentary power. Such men were called 'the natural aristocracy' of the country. Only a few of them had title and votes in the House of Lords, but all were 'aristocrats' in the sense of owing their country disinterested service. Again, England was distinctive in having such people. A Frenchman, writing in the *Edinburgh*, wistfully noted this fact:

> The *natural* aristocracy of a country cannot be created by laws ... Individuals in affluent circumstances, residing habitually on their estates in the country, and devoting their time without remuneration to the service of their fellow-citizens, in the municipal and provincial administration – on juries – as justices of the peace – supplying the poor with work, and the rich with amusement – affording advice and protection to all in inferior condition – liberal in their private transactions with their neighbours – able and willing to defend the rights of the people on all occasions; – those, and only those, are the *natural aristocracy* of a free country ... Such an aristocracy, far from alarming the pride of the people, affords it a continual gratification.[8]

No doubt this was an idealized and partial description. But enough people behaved like this for some of the time to give it credence at home and abroad.

Naturally, Whigs saw themselves as the exemplars of this thinking. They were aristocrats by nature and by title. They owned property on a huge scale, and they carried commensurate responsibilities. Accordingly, they were taught their roles early in life. When a future Countess of Carlisle was nine years old, she was given a political grammar drawn up by her mother on Aristotelian lines. In it four types of government were identified, 'the Despotick', 'the Monarchical', 'the Aristocratical' and 'the Democratical'. Of these a firm preference was expressed for 'the Aristocratical'. All the others showed a terrible tendency to run into extremes.[9] Monarchs and despots too easily became tyrants. Democrats turned into demagogues and promoted mob rule. The young Countess was instructed that it was the role of aristocrats to keep everything in a pleasant state of balance, somewhere in the parliamentary middle of politics. As Lord John Russell explained, sometimes the wicked designs of kings had to be resisted, sometimes the ill-considered clamourings of the people, sometimes both at the same time: 'The Constitution of England admits, as a leading principle, that the aristocracy prevents any collision between the King and people, resisting every illegal encroachment of the Crown, and every intemperate innovation of the Commons. And even when the King and people have united in projects unfavourable to law and liberty, the aristocracy have been found defending the ancient rights of Englishmen.'[10] Whigs saw themselves as the guardians and trustees of political liberty, which defended their great properties from offence, and, by doing so, made all their compatriots free.

Their behaviour was the more remarkable because, in their view, the English aristocracy had been the only one in Europe to do its duty. Nearly everywhere else, aristocrats had abandoned their balancing function. Most had become so associated with the monarchs and courts of the Ancien Régime that they had become improbable champions of parliamentary procedure. A few had thrown in their lot with revolutionaries after 1789. Both options represented a dereliction of duty and predictably led to disaster. English aristocrats had acted differently. In the great crises that punctuated the progression towards parliamentary government, 1215, 1642 and 1688, they had done all that could be expected of them. Foreign writers humbly acknowledged the singularity of the English Whigs. There was no adjective in French to describe a group of aristocrats who tutored kings and peoples indiscriminately. One writer unhelpfully suggested '*Monarchi-Aristo-Démocratic*'. Unfortunately, there was no Whig tradition in most European states, and, although the Whigs themselves endlessly suggested its value to their friends on the Continent, nothing came of their advice.

For Whigs to appoint themselves as the keepers of the parliamentary covenant greatly irritated their critics. To award themselves a special role and special responsibilities looked like arrogance. But Whigs themselves were completely sincere in making these claims. Property-owning was the basis of all free government. The March of Mind and Progress endlessly brought more new property-owners into being. It was the Whigs' function to make sure that this new property was represented, and to supervise the opening up of political life to more and more people. So sacred was this duty, that any Whigling who showed a desire to avoid it could expect denunciation. The fourth Lord Holland opted for a career in diplomacy rather than Parliament. For this delinquency he suffered a lifetime of abuse from his parents. In their view, Whig responsibilities could only be discharged at the highest levels of Westminster politics. Trustees of English liberties had no other arena.

All of this carried considerable implications for the Whig invocation of the word 'people'. They deployed it over and over again and quite shamelessly. Richard Watson told a Cambridge congregation that 'the

People are not made to swell the dignity of a Legislature, but the Legislature is every where established to promote the interest of the People'.[11] The London Whig Club proudly asserted in the middle of the French Revolution that, 'The Constitution of Great Britain is established on the consent and affection of the People'.[12] Lord John Russell took it for granted that 'the Whigs look towards the People, whose welfare is the end and object of all government'.[13] The people were also awarded the right to rise up and overthrow tyrannical government. According to John Millar, the events of 1688 had been 'glorious' precisely for this reason. In his view, 'it is the height of absurdity to suppose, that, when an illegal and unwarrantable power is usurped, the people have no right to resist the exercise of it by punishing the usurper'.[14] In a similar vein, Sir James Graham assured his Cumberland constituents in the electoral campaign of 1830 that 'the people have an indefeasible right of resistance to kings', and that, 'constitutional kings reign only in virtue of their compact with the people'.[15] Apparently, there was nothing the people could not do.

Members of foreign aristocracies, particularly those who had had unpleasant experiences in the French Revolution, were at once awed and appalled to hear such words issuing so unselfconsciously from Whig mouths. When Madame de Staël met the great Whig lawyer Thomas Erskine at dinner, she could not help being impressed by his claim that he had 'chatted' to every elector in his Westminster constituency. She approvingly noted, 'tant il y a de rapports politiques entre les bourgeois at les hommes du premier rang'.[16] The Duc de Broglie, well known in Whig circles, similarly recognized and applauded this unique, English trait:

L'aristocracie Anglaise honore l'humanité: c'est un imposant phénomène dans le monde et dans l'histoire: associé de tout temps aux intérêts du peuple, elle n'a jamais cessé de revendiquer les droits du moindre citoyen, aussi couragement que les siens.[17]

On the other hand, was it quite wise for Whigs to use language such as this in a period delimited by the French Revolution at one end and the uprisings of 1848 at the other? At times, the Whigs seemed to be dangerously oblivious of how easily their rhetoric could be turned against themselves. Of course the crucial point was deciding who 'the people' actually were. Whigs had clear views on this. But perhaps less sophisticated minds would give values to words and phrases like 'people' and 'popular rights' that might prove embarrassing.

So who were 'the people' in a Whig vocabulary? Who were these paragons for whose benefit all legitimate government existed? To find an answer to these questions, the clear distinction in Whig minds between civic and political rights has to be taken into account. The distinction was a commonplace in their thinking. In short, all citizens enjoyed civic rights. These included Habeas Corpus, trial by jury, the ability to read a free press and equality in matters of taxation. But only propertied individuals, for reasons already outlined, could exercise political rights. Among these were included the right to vote, to hold major public offices and to sit in Parliament. When Whigs talked about 'the people' in the context of civic rights, they referred to everyone. When the same words were used in association with political rights, they meant only people like themselves. Confusion between the two was always possible, not least in the minds of their opponents, but context was everything.

This distinction allowed Whigs to argue without sarcasm or sophistry that government was for the people while government by the people was an absurdity. Their duty was to protect both civic and political rights. Both were equally important, and, with the spread of education and property-owning, both would be experienced by more and more people. During the darkest days of the French Revolution, Whigs like Charles James Fox and Thomas Erskine put their own careers at risk with parliamentary defences of Habeas Corpus and the right to assemble freely. Editors who fell foul of censorship, or Radicals whose intercepted correspondence led them to be charged with treason, could count on Whig support. Thomas Erskine defended Thomas Hardy, the Radical leader, free of charge. Fox offered himself as a character witness in the trial of the Irish patriot, Arthur O'Connor. These public appearances did the Whigs no service. Accusations of conniving with traitors inevitably followed. But the Whigs saw themselves as merely doing their duty. The civic rights of Hardy and O'Connor had been affronted by government, and men who claimed the title of aristocrats had to act. This was to vindicate their kind. To have done nothing would have suggested a degeneration into 'a mere Aristocracy'.[18]

If obligations were fulfilled, there could be no question of an English revolution. The lower orders owed aristocrats gratitude, not resentment. In these turbulent decades, foreign visitors were endlessly startled by the insouciance of the Whigs. Alexis de Tocqueville, who had lost members of his own family on the guillotine, marvelled at their calm. Their confidence in themselves and in their handling of poorer men was astonishing. He was not sure that it was justified:

> Lady Charlemont said to me today: 'One should not judge our situation by the fears that are expressed; since I have been in this world, I have heard it said each year that we are going to have a revolution, and at the end of the year we always found ourselves in the same place.' ... I have quoted Lady Charlemont's words because I have heard the same from many *Whigs*. They seem characteristic of their Party. For a century and a half the Whigs have played with the constitution; they believe that the game can continue, but the machine is worn and should be handled with discretion. They have talked of equality and freedom at a time when the people had a vague instinct, not a clear, practical idea of these two things ... After all the Whigs are only a fragment of the aristocratic party; they have long used democracy as a tool, but the tool has become stronger than the hand that guides it.[19]

These are wise and interesting words, but words of a Frenchman and the heir to unfortunate political experiences. Lady Charlemont's lofty remarks rang truer.

For England had no revolution, and Whigs were quite certain that this happy outcome was in some measure due to their own efforts. Whig contacts with the people and a vigorous defence of their rights guaranteed order. Whigs presided at dinners and presented petitions to Parliament as part of campaigns for reform and change over a wide area. Every reformer could ride his hobby-horse in the sure knowledge that someone in the Whig establishment would be helpful and sympathetic. When new forms of radicalism cropped up, Whigs almost invariably went out to meet it, mould it, and give it parliamentary form. Some Radicals inevitably suspected that aristocratic offers of help were mere humbug, but it was hard to sustain this view all the time. After all, Whig efforts kept Radicals out of prison and gave their ideas a parliamentary hearing. Even if characterized as a kind of political charity, very much *de haut en bas*, it had concrete effects. There was no parallel to this activity in Europe. Continental aristocrats simply followed different traditions. They suffered revolutions but the English did not, and the Whigs could not believe this was a coincidence.

In fact, to bore on about the dangers from below was, in the Whig view, to misunderstand the direction from which the real threat to liberty came. The mob could be violent and destructive but offered no real challenge to the structures of the state. Kings, on the other hand, who already exercised great powers under the prerogative, were dangerous if they wanted yet more. Whigs convinced themselves that George III and his sons had the serious intention of undermining parliamentary government. Autocrats in their other role as Electors of Hanover, they were accused of wishing to rule in the same manner in England. The great, political crises of the period turned on this point. In 1765–66, 1783–84 and 1834–35, parliamentary authority was challenged by kings, often successfully. In the Whig view, the Stuart tyrants of the seventeenth century had again taken human form and had to be resisted. Most of the time, this was a minority view within the nation, which confirmed the Whigs as a minority party. In the age of the French Revolution, most people found it odd to argue that a king was more threatening than a mob. The Whigs never really succeeded in convincing their countrymen on this point, though, in convincing themselves, they developed arguments of some interest.

The case went as follows. Charles I and James II had literally menaced Parliament with troops. After 1688, such a gross tactic was no longer plausible. Accordingly, George III adopted a more subtle scheme. Parliament was not to be forcibly dissolved but rather infiltrated. In the first half of the eighteenth century, numbers in the House of Lords had been static or slightly falling, but, after 1760, they rose steadily and alarmingly. All royal nominations, they seemed to overwhelm men with long-established titles. The King was packing the House with his minions, some of whom had the distressing surnames of Smith and Robinson. Whigs had no doubt that this was part of a deliberate strategy. Lady Spencer shared her 'Whig lamentations' on this point with a friend:

> Our genuine old English aristocracy is fast and soon driving out of doors to make way for new names, new wealth, new habits and new notions. A sad and unworthy change! and which I must ever attribute to Mr Pitt's long administration. His whole object was to raise commercial men and to lower

landowners and old families; and he had time and opportunity afforded him
to accomplish that vile object.[20]

By 1789, Whigs believed that the House of Lords had been so corrupted
by royal nominees that it could no longer fulfil its constitutional duty
of checking the executive. The King was free from interference from that
quarter.

With the Lords neutered, all attention turned to the Commons, but
here again the King had been at work. The Crown was the largest dis-
penser of patronage in the eighteenth century. It could determine
success or failure in the professions, offer employment and titles, relieve
with pensions or sinecures. Every one of these activities bought men's
loyalties. Working for the Crown or hoping to work for the Crown
decided voting behaviour. These placemen appeared more and more
regularly in the Commons and in ever greater numbers. As men of independent means, Whigs were of course free of these temptations. They
had no need to take the king's shilling. The ownership of great property
guaranteed their integrity. But they were usually outvoted in the Commons and that was sinister. Such votes demonstrated that values based
on property-ownership had been replaced by subservience to the
Crown. In 1777 and 1797, Whigs actually seceded from Parliament for a
time, hoping that their absence would point up the ineffectiveness of the
Commons. In their lifetime, royal nomination and intrigue had
destroyed Parliament more effectively than Charles I could ever have
imagined. The Whig analysis was genuinely apocalyptic.

Nor did this hydra of royal influence restrict its activities to Westminster. Its tentacles reached out into the electorate as a whole. In the
extended wars against France between 1793 and 1815, bureaucracy mush-
roomed, and every new bureaucrat was a royal employee. Every new
colony acquired demanded an establishment and every new tax required
collectors. When the House of Commons passed a resolution in 1780,
asserting that the influence of the Crown had increased, was increasing
and ought to be diminished, it was, according to Whigs, merely stating
the obvious. The figures were frightening. The power of the Crown and
its ministers had grown 'to an extent heretofore unknown'.[21] Perhaps
every second or third person was in some way beholden to it. Sydney
Smith certainly thought so: 'Our establishments are so enormous, and
so utterly disproportioned to our population, that every second or third

man you meet in society gains something from the public; my brother the commissioner – my nephew the police justice – purveyor of small beer to the army in Ireland – clerk of the month – yeoman to the left hand – these are the obstacles which common sense and justice have now to overcome.'[22] Smith of course turned everything into humour, but his point could not have been more grave.

With more science, Francis Jeffrey undertook a calculation in the pages of the *Edinburgh* in 1808 that came to the same conclusion. Perhaps a third of the electorate was in the pocket of the executive:

> Government ... has the disposal of nearly fifteen millions *per annum*, and the power of nominating to two or three hundred thousand posts or places of emolument; – the whole population of the country amounting to less than five millions of grown men. The consequence is, that, beyond the rank of mere labourers, there is scarcely one man out of three who does not hold or hope for some appointment or promotion from Government, and is not consequently disposed to go all *honest* lengths in recommending himself to its favour. This is, it must be admitted, a situation which justifies some alarm for the liberties of the people, and ... accounts sufficiently for that habit of presuming in favour of all exertions of authority, and against all popular discontent or commotion which is so remarkably the characteristic of the present generation.[23]

In other words, threats from mobs and revolutionary principles paled into insignificance beside the relentless advance of royal-led, government influence. It was a gangrene that had rotted the proper functions of Lords and Commons, and was now seeping into the electorate as a whole. Writing fifteen years later, Lord John Russell echoed Jeffrey's analysis, and expressed 'the hope that as the influence of the crown is so greatly and so dangerously extended, it may be met by a new and determined spirit in the people'.[24] It was the Whig duty to excite that spirit.

This autocratic assault on parliamentary life became incarnate in the person of William Pitt and his heirs. For Whigs, Pittism meant, if it meant anything at all, the wilful promotion of royal interests. Pittites had talent but they lacked every other qualification for high office, notoriously great properties. If the rights of property were being properly respected, such men should hope for nothing more than junior office or a moderate position in the bureaucracy. The fact that they were nominated as Prime Ministers proved that the rights of property were not being respected. Their careers began and ended with royal nomination. Accordingly, Pitt delighted 'in trying to humble ... *Noble Families*'.[25] Without the independence that a private income conferred, he could never stand up to George III, but rather was his puppet. The Duchess of Devonshire was clear that 'Mr Pitt's fault as an Englishman and statesman was that he came into place against the constitution and supported himself in place by exercising the power of the throne'.[26] If he and his master George III were to succeed, 'he will have brought about an event that he himself as well as ev'ry Englishman will repent ever after, for if the K. and the H. of Lords conquer the H. of C. he will destroy the consequence of that house and make the government quite absolute'.[27] So Pitt became the butt of vicious Whig satire as 'the Bottomless Pitt' or 'the Pitt of Hell'.[28]

And behind the mannequins lurked their masters, Hanoverian kings who were all mad, bad and dangerous to know. The charitable view of George III was that he had been misled into despotic ways by his tutor, the Earl of Bute, and his mother, 'a German Princess' who 'devised her notions of the rights and immunities of a sovereign from the petty despotic court in which she had been herself brought up'.[29] So thought the Earl of Albemarle. With poisonous politics being daily dripped into his ears, George was too weak-minded to resist them. Whig cartoonists labelled him 'David Simple of Noodle Hall'.[30] When Richard Fitzpatrick was invited to contribute something to Lady Charlotte Campbell's commonplace book, he penned a verse about the King that the lady found 'very ill natured but clever':

> In Merry Old Times it was always the Thing,
> To pension a fool, for pleasing the King:
> But George with Oeconomy wishing to rule
> Writes in himself both the king and the fool.[31]

Few Whigs were prepared to be so charitable. Most believed that George's political wickedness was thought out and ruthless. At a dinner in King's Lynn, Thomas Coke objected to dining beneath a portrait of his monarch, whom he damned as 'the worst man that ever sat on a throne, George III, that bloody King!'[32] Intemperate language such as this was a commonplace in Whig circles. Charles James Fox likened the King to Satan. Extreme words were necessary to express the fear that

Whigs harboured about George III and what they took to be his intentions in government.

George IV started life well. He danced and vomited in Whig houses, sharing mistresses with grandees and calling Charles James Fox his greatest friend. After violence overtook the French Revolution, however, he reverted to family type. In 1810, 1812 and 1827 his personal veto blocked a Whig return to power. Like his father, he seemed to prefer the political company of Pittites. He did nothing to resurrect the powers of Parliament. Finally, grandiloquent views of himself and his royal powers tipped over into madness. In the last year of his life, he regaled startled courtiers with tales of riding several winners at Goodwood races.[33] As for his brother, William IV, Charles Greville thought him only 'a mountebank, but he bids fair to be a maniac'.[34] His tendency to sing naval songs of a ripe quality at official banquets was just tolerable, but his absent-minded tendency to wander out of Buckingham Palace into central London alone to be mobbed by his subjects was alarming. Hastily assembled search parties had to be mobilised.[35] In 1834, like his father a generation earlier, William thought he had the right to dismiss a ministry that had the confidence of the Commons, just because he found it personally distasteful. From a Whig perspective, the Hanoverians were a depressing and dangerous family.

None of these princes had any real appreciation of constitutional practices. They seemed to have brought too much of Germany over in their luggage. As Lord Holland observed, they, 'like all princes, especially Germans, were lofty and arbitrary' in their 'notions of Government'.[36] None of them could be safely entrusted with the guardianship of English liberties, and that fact made them the Whigs' enemies. No prisoners were to be taken in this war. The savagery in Walter Savage Landor's assessment of the Hanoverians expressed the mood of many Whig writers:

> George the First was always reckoned
> Vile, but viler George the Second;
> And what mortal ever heard
> Any good of George the Third?
> When from Earth the Fourth descended,
> God be praised, the Georges ended.[37]

The Whigs themselves had installed the Hanoverians on the throne in

1714 to ward off the even greater threat of the Stuarts, but it seemed that they had never absorbed Whig teaching or acknowledged the English affection for Parliament.

So what was to be done with these kings? Clearly, unremitting warfare had to be waged, though much of it seemingly took the form of retreating. New weapons were required urgently, and the most potent of these was to firm up the concept of party. Traditionally, party activity had been spoken of with suspicion. The word suggested a group of men acting in concert to force themselves into government, with the object of legislating in their own narrow interests rather than for the common good. After 1760, Whigs increasingly argued that squeamishness about party had to be overcome. Indeed, only a disciplined party had any chance of challenging the Crown. It was, wrote Lord John Russell, 'the duty of the lovers of their country to counteract system by system, and numbers by numbers'. In his view, 'men of noble minds' had become aware that acting together in parties constituted 'the workshop of national liberty'. Only 'mock philosophers, sentimental women, and effeminate men' continued to damn party life as self-interest in disguise.[38] For over forty years until his death in 1828, William Adam, as general manager, gave Whiggery an organized face. Regular subscriptions, the employment of full-time agents in some constituencies, the subsidizing of candidates, and the purchase of newspapers all came within his remit. In 1760, such activities would have been widely condemned as devices to thwart the legitimate exercise of the royal prerogative. By 1830, Whigs regarded them as the only way of keeping that same prerogative under control. Congenital individualists though they were, Whigs were forced to accept the discipline of party, because their political survival depended on it.

The second new weapon was the promotion of Parliamentary Reform. Its attraction was slowly revealed along the way. This cause was not taken up for theoretical reasons, but rather for the practical benefits it could bring. Quite simply, if the Crown had neutered the House of Commons by filling it with its own nominees, a cleansing of that House became a matter of priority. Parliamentary Reform would allow the Commons to face down kings. In speeches and articles, Whig leaders were quite open about their intentions. In 1811, Francis Jeffrey told the readers of the *Edinburgh* that 'we desire to see the Parliament reformed, chiefly, if not entirely, that a barrier may be raised against the overgrown power of the Crown'.[39] Nine years later, Thomas Erskine gave his Westminster constituents the same message: 'The prevailing sentiment amongst men whose influences are more likely that any thing I know, to bring about change in the representation, is *this*: – That the alteration should not be such as to change *the character of Parliament*; but that such an extension should be enacted as would create a fair, just, and constantly operative balance against the increased influence of the crown.'[40]

The same priorities were enunciated in the debates of 1831 and 1832, which ended in the passing of the first Reform Bill. Whigs never spoke in favour of democratic ideas, and certainly did not see the measure as a first step towards a democratic future. The Bill was rather the answer to the old problem of Crown influence, with which they had been wrestling since the accession of George III. By increasing the number of voters from 14 per cent to 18 per cent of the adult male population, they would enfranchise just enough new property to keep the executive in check. No one could accuse them of being democrats on the basis of such a tiny adjustment. The Bill would reaffirm the primacy of values based on property-owning. As the Prime Minister, Charles Grey, assured the Commons, he had no intention of introducing any new principle into the constitution. It was a question of restoring the balance within the old constitution.

Yet even more sustaining than party cohesion and an increasing taste for Reform was the power of history. Whiggery was historically rooted. In the long years of opposition between 1760 and 1830, Whigs wrote history as a vindication and a point of catharsis. It was the most congenial of subjects. Charles James Fox, Lord John Russell, Sir James Mackintosh and Thomas Macaulay were just a few of the party's historians. Inevitably, every contemporary situation was put into an historical context. For, if Whigs of this generation had to fight would-be tyrants, they were acutely aware that this had all happened before. At all times and in all countries, they identified a manichean struggle in progress. On one side were those who fostered representative government and basic liberties. On the other were despots and autocrats. For this reason they were happy to claim Socrates as the first Whig, and to put him in a pantheon alongside Aristides and Germanicus. Whig history was a matter of heroes and villains. As Russell put it, 'two opposite pretensions have naturally given rise to contest and calamity'.[41] The embattled Whig of 1800 could not be alone, for he stood in an apostolic succession of martyrs and warriors. It was a question of fulfilling a duty in one's own generation which had been discharged by like-minded men in earlier centuries.

A study of English history made this point most convincingly. The Whig account is a penny-dreadful story with virtue wrestling with wickedness, cliff-hanging crises and the ultimate triumph of good. Anglo-Saxon England was described as a state in which the representative principle had been firmly entrenched. Unfortunately, William the Conqueror, a natural despot, destroyed much of this good work at the Conquest. He could not, however, destroy the free spirit of the English. They fought back with Magna Carta and a revived parliamentary tradition. The struggle was long and hard, and there were many reverses, but by 1620 it was a matter of pride that only in England did a Parliament survive. The Spanish Cortes met for the last time in 1598 and the French Estates General fell silent after 1614. Lord John Russell saw the century between 1450 and 1550 as 'the aera of the downfall of freedom' in Europe.[42] England mercifully took a different path, marking a diversion from continental politics that has never been corrected.

It was the seventeenth century, however, that would prove the real testing ground, as Stuart kings challenged Parliament legally and militarily. Gallons of Whig ink were expended on describing these events. In book after book, historians explained that, consonant with Whig theory, men of great property defended the liberties of Parliament against Charles I and James II. An Earl of Bedford had been one of the earliest commanders of the parliamentary forces in 1642. A generation later, another Russell, a Cavendish and a Keppel were among the seven men, who invited William of Orange to come over to England. By calling the Glorious Revolution 'that modern Magna Carta',[43] Whigs neatly gave historical context to these events. The barons of 1215 and the Whigs of 1688 were warriors in the same battle. It was 'Glorious' because it was bloodless, and it was bloodless because it was 'not effected by an indignant and enraged multitude, but was slowly prepared by the most virtuous and best informed amongst the higher and enlightened classes of people, who took prudent and effectual steps for securing its success without bloodshed ... These were the Whigs of England at the Revolution.'[44]

Whigs could never say or write enough about the events of 1688. Out of them came for the first time legal guarantees of Parliament's role in law-making, an independent judiciary, and freedom from arbitrary acts of governments. No wonder that Lord John Russell, who had an ancestor at the centre of politics in 1688, could describe the Revolution of that year as 'the perfection of boldness and of prudence'.[45] Crucially, these great benefits had been secured by Whig aristocrats doing their duty. Lord Albemarle, another direct descendent of the heroes of 1688, observed in 1852 with pride rather than complacency that:

> It need hardly be stated that it was to a small body of wealthy landed proprietors that the country is indebted for the Revolution of 1688: that it was *for* the people, and not by the people, that the great measure was accomplished: that both at the time, and afterwards, the nation at large were passive spectators of the struggles made and making on their behalf.[46]

Less partisan historians would have to point out that Tories too were intimately involved in these glorious contests, but such caveats were not for Whigs. The fact that England had developed unique institutions and freedoms was attributable entirely to Whig efforts over long centuries. The thegns who gave King Alfred good counsel, the barons who taught King John and King Henry III how to behave, and the courtiers who encouraged Henry VIII and Elizabeth to use Parliament were all Whigs. So were the men of 1688. So were Charles James Fox and Charles Grey.

Grafting the development of English institutions onto family trees gave Whigs self-importance, confidence in their values and the hope of ultimate success. History was a weapon to be wielded against George III. In the long years of political opposition, it was reassuring to control the past, just as it was pleasant to lead social life. Inevitably perhaps they developed an intense veneration for their ancestors. Lord John Russell, writing the biography of a kinsman who had been beheaded by Charles II, observed that 'It should indeed be the endeavour of men who have inherited liberty from their ancestors, to transmit the possession unimpaired to their descendents'.[47] An intelligent observer noted that, whenever a Whig wanted to justify an action or opinion, he merely observed that some great Whig in the past had done something similar or said something similar.[48] History became a point of reference from which there was no appeal. Framed portraits of grandfathers and great-grandfathers covered the walls of Whig houses, reminding the living that there was much work still to be done.

Ancestor-worship shaded painlessly into hagiography and ritual. The names of men who had been persecuted or executed by tyrannical kings, such as John Hampden or Algernon Sydney, could not be evoked enough. Indeed, extraordinary steps were taken to link the living with the dead. Thomas Erskine named his eldest son Hampden, as 'an honest remembrance of his high renown in the great cause of liberty'.[49] When Charles Grey retired from politics in 1834, Samuel Rogers used poetry to put his career into historical context:

> Grey, thou hast served, and well, thy sacred cause
> That Hampden, Sydney, died for. Thou hast served
> Scorning all thought of self, from first to last
> Among the foremost in that glorious field.[50]

Few Tories had ancestors worth mentioning. Indeed Whig wits doubted that they had any at all. So Tories were reduced to turning Whig claims on the past into satire. The *Etonian* of 1822 purported to give an account of the upbringing of a Whig child:

> Instead of the common food with which the love of the marvellous, so early evinced by children, is usually served – such as the astonishing exploits of Jack the Giant Killer, or the adventures of Tom Thumb –; Little Frank was supplied with political caricatures and electioneering ballads. His laced baby-cap was made in the shape of that of liberty; and whenever he was admitted to the family dessert, to have half a glass of wine on Papa's knee, he was first required to lisp out the patriotic toast of 'the cause for which Hampden bled on the field and Sydney perished on the scaffold', long before he could possibly understand the import of the sentence.[51]

Such Tory jokes raised smiles, but also seemed to concede that the past belonged to the Whigs.

The speed with which the Whigs turned history into profitable myth, and the ease with which they could beatify their heroes, may be seen in the cult of Charles James Fox. After his death in 1806, he almost achieved iconic status. His names were showered on Whig babies at christenings throughout the first half of the nineteenth century. With less reverence but still respectfully, Gainsborough named his favourite dog 'Fox'. The Nollekens bust of the hero stood in Whig halls and drawing-rooms, proclaiming the political allegiance of the house to all and sundry. On assuming his duties as Prince Regent in 1811, the Prince of Wales delayed his first ministerial audience for an hour, so that he and all his ministers could contemplate the bust. Since the ministers in question had nearly all been sworn enemies of Fox, it must have been an uncomfortable sixty minutes. Even more ritualistic were the Fox Dinners held up and down the country on Fox's birthday. The guest speaker would be someone who had known the great man. His trials and tribulations in the defence of liberty would be retailed to new generations. Tears not infrequently flowed. Needless to say, the equivocations which had marked his political career, and the doubtful quality of his private life, were not mentioned. Myth-making always makes the rough smooth. The evening would conclude with standard toasts that linked Fox's name with the heroic battles of the past and with the issues that preoccupied the current generation. To invoke his name was a final argument. The last of these dinners was held in Brooks's Club in 1907.

Whole families laboured under the obligations imposed by history. The Russell family, for example, had played a prominent part in politics since the sixteenth century. Indeed their performance had been so well received that Sydney Smith shamelessly declared that 'the manufacture of Russells is a public and important concern'.[52] One Earl of Bedford had defended Parliament against Charles I; another Russell lost his head for trying to force that King's son into parliamentary ways; yet a third was one of the major players in 1688. Little wonder that, when Lord John Russell took to writing history, he should find it 'very gratifying' to be recording the exploits of his own family.[53] Pride in family was a quintessentially Whig characteristic and Russell had it in abundance. As late as 1918, G. W. E. Russell started yet another history book by reflecting that, 'I trace my paternal ancestry to a Russell who entered the House of Commons at the General Election of 1441, and since 1538 some of us have always sat in one or other of the two Houses of Parliament; so I may be fairly said to have the Parliamentary tradition in my blood'.[54] The use of the word 'us' is evocative. When depressed by political reverses, the same man wished 'we could imitate the courage of our ancestors. They were not ready to lay their liberties at the feet of the

Crown upon every vain and imaginary alarm.'[55] Perhaps no political party ever drew more comfort from the past or felt more personally linked to history.

Ties of blood created even more obligations if some of that blood had been spilt in the defence of liberty. Whiggery nurtured and fed on a cult of martyrs. Some like John Hampden had died in battles against a would-be tyrant. Some like Algernon Sydney and William, Lord Russell had been executed. It was imperative that the cause of parliamentarianism for which they had suffered should ultimately triumph. By 1800, Whigs were no longer murdered, but there were still sacrifices to be made. Fear of the French Revolution kept the Whigs out of power for a generation. A contemporary joke made the point that,

> Nought's constant in the human race
> Except the Whigs not getting into place.[56]

Fox enjoyed only five years in power in a parliamentary career that ran from 1769 to 1806. Charles Grey had spent forty-three years in opposition before becoming Prime Minister in 1830. Many talented men are virtually unknown to history because their careers were spent entirely in the wilderness. Professional men suffered too. Whig doctors found it hard to recruit patients. Whig barristers were denied briefs. Michaelangelo Taylor was disinherited. With some justification, such men called themselves 'Fox's Martyrs', and this phraseology linked their misery to the suffering of those who had gone before.

The martyr theme could at times degenerate into something close to self-pity. Whigs often felt beleaguered and unappreciated. Tories to the Right and Radicals to the Left denigrated their sufferings and achievements, and too often convinced a majority of their countrymen. As Francis Jeffrey put it:

> The great body of the nation appears to us to be divided into two violent and most pernicious factions; – the courtiers, who are almost for arbitrary power, – and the democrats, who are almost for revolution and republicanism. Between these stand a small, but most respectable band, – the friends of liberty and order – the old constitutional Whigs of England, – with the best talents and the best intentions, but without power or popularity, – calumniated and suspected by both parties.[57]

The chill in the world around them for so much of the time led the

Whigs to enclose themselves still more firmly within their own circles of acquaintance. There, the tales of martyrs and ancestral heroism could animate and console.

So overpowering was this sense of being personally linked to a glorious past that the Whigs transmuted history into stone, plaster and terracotta. The building or renovation of a great Whig house had to have an historical dimension. Busts, panels, and portraits were everywhere. As Whigs moved about the grounds or drifted from one room to another, they were endlessly reminded of their origins and of the obligations that history placed upon them. At Holkham, Thomas Coke panelled his hall with scenes from the Whig past. One showed King John signing Magna Carta. The faces of the barons surrounding him were those of the Whig cabinet of 1830. At Wentworth Woodhouse, the Mausoleum erected to the memory of Lord Rockingham contained a lifesize statue of the Marquess by Nollekens, 'surrounded by busts of *the Patriots* who were most intimately connected with him'.[58] A long walk in the gardens at Chatsworth acted as a history lesson in stone, as passers-by first encountered Aristides, Socrates and Cicero, then Cromwell, and finally Charles James Fox and the fifth Duke of Devonshire. Grandest of all was the sixth Duke of Bedford's Temple of Worthies at Woburn Abbey. This exhibited a bust of Fox flanked by representations of his friends. The fifth and sixth Dukes of Bedford were side by side with the Elder and Younger Brutus. A pediment by Flaxman depicted Liberty and a frieze by Westmacott the march of Progress. It was open to the public on Mondays. A perceptive visitor was expected to make the necessary linkages; Whiggery and its Roman past; Whiggery and its sacrifices; Whiggery and its glorious future.

Of course, it was very easy for critics of the Whigs to make fun of ancestor-worship. They brutally pointed out that most Whig families had no ancestry at all before 1500. It was simply outrageous to claim descent from Roman senators or medieval barons. The Spencers, the Cavendishes and many more had made their fortunes in the wool trade and in the destruction of the monasteries. Great Whig houses often stood on land taken from monks. Ironically, much of their success in the sixteenth century was attributable to royal patronage. It was almost blasphemous for Whigs to claim that they had always opposed kings. Rather they were merely ungrateful. In 1831, *Fraser's Magazine* produced a spoof version of *Macbeth* with Lord John Russell in the title role. In order to determine his course of action, he seeks the advice of 'three witches, supposed to be Spirits of the ancestors of some noble families of the present day'.[59] By way of answering his enquiry, the witches summon up the ghosts of notorious rebels and demagogues, including Tiberius Gracchus, Catiline, Bonaparte and Cromwell. Russell then turns into Cromwell. According to Tory propaganda such as this, Whigs had no claim to the approval of history. Their titles were of relatively recent origin. They had shown no disapproval of royal behaviour when self-interest was in question. And not so long ago they had been tradesmen.

It was all too easy to satirize the Whigs for their exclusivity in claiming history for their party. Their reading of the past was idiosyncratic and partial. The flaws in their heroes were miraculously smoothed away while their virtues were magnified. Yet all this was slightly to miss the point. For at least Whiggery addressed itself to the major problems in politics. How should the people at large be brought into a relationship with the institutions of government? Would representative systems be wise to retain some aristocratic values and perceptions? What lessons, if any, did the past offer for the guidance of future generations? Whig answers to these questions could not please everyone. The emphasis on property-owning, the dismissal of democratic claims, and the warnings about the growth of executive power all repelled as well as attracted. Yet the Whig case had a certain internal cohesion. They had learnt from harsh experience how fragile liberties were. Kings had clearly threatened them for centuries, and perhaps demagogues were about to do so. Since real democracy in most states is considerably less than one hundred years old, perhaps the jury is still out on the validity of the Whig agenda.

9

Enemies

Whiggery was distinctive, exclusive and enjoyable. For all these reasons it was cordially loathed by Radicals, Tories and many in the population at large. The ownership of vast estates made the Whigs an inevitable feature of the political landscape, but it did not make their pretensions any more acceptable. To claim to be cleverer than other men makes most people feel stupid. To sustain social exclusivity makes others feel unwanted. And to assert that Whigs alone had secured the parliamentary tradition in England was open to all sorts of correction. To their opponents all these claims were nothing more than attempts to disguise the fact that the Whigs were a self-seeking faction wanting power for entirely selfish ends. David Robinson, one of the best Tory propagandists, took this line again and again in the pages of *Blackwood's Magazine*:

> The Whigs ... have laboured to pull down every monarchy in Europe to replace it with a form of government that gave despotic power to faction. Can this be called friendship for liberty? While they have attacked the despotism of monarchs, they have constantly defended the despotic deeds of republican and revolutionary rulers. Has this been fighting for liberty? They have regularly supported those who laboured to make mankind irreligious, vicious, licentious, disorderly, and turbulent – no one will say this had been friendship for liberty.[1]

Catalogues of Whig failings were not hard to compile. Irritatingly, they rarely breached the walls of their self-satisfaction.

Whether it was fair to use the pejorative noun 'faction' in describing Whigs may be a matter for debate, but most people agreed that Whiggery at most times was a minority interest. The siege psychology of the Whigs themselves proved the point. To win power and to form governments they could not rely on their own resources. They were simply too few. Allies had to be found from other parts of the political spectrum. Coalitions were the Whigs' natural habitat. According to their critics, this gave Whiggery a mongrel quality, in that they were apparently happy to cohabit with any other coterie of politicians. In 1783, for example, they had joined Lord North in a coalition, having spent the previous decade or so vilifying the man and his works. In 1807, they neatly executed the same *volte-face* in the case of Lord Grenville. The Reform Ministry of 1830 was a veritable harlequinade of political traditions, stretching from ex-Ultra Tories like the Duke of Richmond to the Radicalism of Henry Brougham. Whigs appeared to be natural coalitionists and were utterly without discrimination in their choice of partners.

Of course coalition politics always entailed compromises about specific policies. Critics could not take seriously Whig claims to be a party of principles when they indulged so freely in political miscegenation. In fact their behaviour was distinctly sluttish. David Robinson affected to pity Whiggery on this count:

> That man, be he the most rigid of Tories, must have a heart formed of very strange materials, who can now look at Whiggism, and not compassionate its wretchedness. The blooming damsel who shone forth in so much fascinating loveliness in 1688, sacrificed her virtue to the French Revolution; and her subsequent adventures and present condition prove that she had drunk the cup of misery which seduction offers, even to the very dregs. She felt successively the blandishments of Buonaparte, of the Radicals, of the Liberals, of the Carbonari, of the Benthamites, of any dirty body, and she is now sunk so low as to be rejected by all.[2]

Given the nature of the private life of Whigs, to use such provocative sexual imagery was a particularly effective way of establishing their lack of political principle. In Tory eyes, these unfortunates, always a minority within the political nation, simply could not afford the price of integrity, and this fact made them all the more dangerous.

It was not, however, just a question of how Whigs shuffled to overcome their minority status among the English. There was a larger concern about whether they were English at all. They seemed to be foreign to all notions of patriotism. More often than not, they would be found in wartime speaking and writing on behalf of the enemy. In 1777, at the height of the American War of Independence, the Whigs adopted buff and blue as the Whig Party's colours. Thereafter, 'the Buff and Blue' became a tribal toast. They were apparently unconcerned that the same colours were worn by Washington's soldiers. Whigs strutted around the West End in insurgent uniforms in the hope of irritating George III. Their hope was realized. But many of their countrymen rightly wondered where their real loyalties lay. After 1789, they praised the French Revolution at its beginning, and then tried to explain away its violence under Robespierre. They adopted the haircuts of the Jacobins and the collars of the Directory. Later still, their equivocation about Bonaparte was noted, as was their determination after 1830 to think of France as England's natural ally, when all history and common sense suggested the opposite.

Critics believed that all the evidence proved that the Whigs lacked patriotism and team spirit. In every contest in which British troops were involved, Whigs could be relied on to say nice things about the enemy. Their behaviour was so mystifying that Tory writers accused them of espionage and treason. In 1798, a contributor to the *Anti-Jacobin*, reflecting on why Whigs and others should read and subsidize newspapers that regularly excused French policies, concluded that, 'Members of the *Whig Club* and the *Corresponding Society* have need of them; *these* to convey intelligence to France, and *those* to register their drunken toasts, and still more drunken speeches'[3] When Fox's nephew, Lord Edward Fitzgerald, connived with the French to raise a great insurrection in Ireland against British rule in 1798, the Whig party as a whole was tarred with suspicion. Too often they found the company of foreigners too congenial. As a result, Tories often spoke of their opponents as being unEnglish, as standing apart from the nation as a whole.

This aloofness was also a pronounced feature of their relations with their compatriots. Every aspect of the Whig system seemed designed to keep the English at arm's length. Their complacent insistence on exclusivity was maddening. In 1826, *Blackwood's* published a very effective exposé of Whig elitism. It took the form of a letter supposedly written by 'an Old Member of the Lower House', a penitent Whig who had seen the error of his ways:

Having enumerated a few specific measures, which I reluctantly supported, I wish to remind you of some general practices, which I conceived to be highly prejudicial to the interest of our party. One was an arrogation by a certain style, and still more by a certain manner in which we indulged, of superiority, not in principle only but also in talent, of a reputation of which men are still more jealous. Our exaggerated praise of all, even of the lawyers, physicians, poets, and artists, who professed themselves Whigs, was felt an unfair depreciation of all who did not, and as a circuitous mode of charging the latter with dullness or dishonesty ... We have indeed managed so, that the name of *Whig*, to all but those who assume it, suggests the idea of a pert, self-sufficient being, filled with Pharasaical conceit, equally gratified with notice, which he ascribes to admiration, or with neglect, which he imputes to fear; and complacently chuckling, even at his exclusion from influence, because it reminds him of the comparative worthlessness of those to whose jealousy it is owing.[4]

As the last sentence of this quotation suggests, Whig arrogance made them irritatingly invulnerable. If Whigs were denied office, it merely proved that the system was wrong and needed changing. Opposition was therefore as much a vindication of Whiggery as being in government. Tories looked in vain for a chink or two in this well-fashioned armour.

People who were not born into Whiggery, or who could not accept the terms on which its wages were paid, knew that they would always be outsiders, in a kind of chill, watching its rituals. Tories and Radicals despised Whigs, but the fact that they returned again and again to comment on their exclusivity may suggest itching envy. Apparently, every Whig defeat reinforced their confidence. Every new arrival in a Whig family was hailed as a messiah. Every writer, orator and drudge was a prodigy. Tory writers satirized the phenomenon but had no way of undermining it:

> Inconceivable is the cackle and row on the birth of a Whigling: – When he gives his first squeal, there is an expression of boisterous merriment – of robustious jollification – When he first cocks his youthful eye with a knowing leer at any remarkable object, there is a clapping of hands, and shouts of Maenadic glorification: – When he accents his first syllables of the vernacular, the amazed listeners exclaim, 'Behold a wonder!'[5]

Clubs which bar the great majority of the population from all hope of entry are the most fascinating and the most resented. Antipathies casting long shadows are set up. In the second half of the twentieth century, one of W. H. Auden's alleged reasons for setting up home outside Vienna was that 'no Whig landlord, the landscape vaunts, ever empired on Austrian ground'.[6] Whig exclusivity provoked all sorts of men to bridle: Tories and Radicals, patriots and kings, moralists and all those with religious sensibilities.

Some objections to Whiggery were, however, more party specific. Tory writers in particular widened the attack and sought out the heart of the matter. In their view, Whig self-confidence was built on that party's belief in Progress and the March of Mind. Whig historians assured their patrons that irresistible trends in society guaranteed a rose-coloured Whig future. Tories disagreed and knew that, if alternative readings could be established, much of the Whig castle would come tumbling down. Tory historians wrote of the past as a matter of chance and accident as much as of design or purpose. Barbarians won as often as the philosophers. Any civilized society living under law was itself a kind of miracle that needed careful tending not violent change. In the Tory view, Whig hopes for extending educational opportunity were also absurdly optimistic. It was possible that the newly-enlightened would accept the cultural values of Woburn Abbey and Chatsworth, but it was just as likely that they would want to pull them down. Far too much of Whiggery was built on theorizing rather than commonsense. According to Tories, Whig confidence was based on the adoption of a blinkered set of doctrines, put together in the damp ivory towers of Edinburgh and Glasgow, and a refusal to listen to objections.

Thomas Love Peacock well understood these two positions and turned them into humour. In *Crotchet Castle*, two of Mr Crotchet's guests lock horns over dinner; The Rev. Dr Folliott for the Tories and Mr MacQuedy [QED] for the Whigs:

Dr Folliott   Well Mr MacQuedy, it is now some weeks since we have met: how goes on the march of mind?

Mr MacQuedy   Nay, sir: I think you may see that with your own eyes.

Dr Folliott   Sir, I have seen it, much to my discomfiture. It has marched into my rick-yard, and set my stacks on fire, with chemical materials, most scientifically compounded. It has marched up to the door of my vicarage, a hundred and fifty strong; ordered me to surrender half my tithes; consumed all the provisions I had provided for my audit feast, and drunk up my old October. It has marched in through my back parlour shutters, and out again with my silver spoons

in the dead of night. The policeman, who was sent down
to examine, says that my house has been broken open on
the most scientific principles. All this comes of education.

Mr MacQuedy   I rather think it comes of poverty.

Dr Folliott   No, sir. Robbery perhaps comes out of poverty, but
scientific principles of robbery come out from education.

At this point the dinner party is interrupted by an incursion of the lower
orders. When order is restored, Dr Folliott remarks, 'Ho! Ho! Here is a
piece of the dark ages we did not bargain for. Here is the Jacquerie. Here
is the march of mind with a witness.'[7]

In fact, Tories believed that Whig confidence in the future was built
on sand. Human nature was dark and brutal as well as rational and
sweet. No amount of education could change that. The terrors of the
French Revolution, the widespread admiration for Bonaparte's tyranny,
and the violence that infected so many people's lives all proved the
point. Whigs believed without qualification or doubt. Awkward
moments in history or unpleasant moments in contemporary politics
gave them no pause. According to Tories, this was not intellect at work,
but rather a new creed that allowed no dissent. It was ironical that
Whigs who claimed to be free of all religion and priestcraft should have
entangled themselves with new and inflexible dogmas. For some reason
they continued to advance theories as truth which should be only theories. Quite rightly the electorate rejected this fundamentalism over and
over again, preferring a little more practicality in its politics.

So why did intelligent Whigs persist in this strange behaviour? Perhaps, Tories speculated, it was a question of temperament. Whig blood
perhaps contained compounds that compelled its owners to look with
sour faces on anything that worked or worked well, and to suffer from
an endless itch to change something somewhere. They obviously put no
store in the notion that any custom or practice that had performed a
useful function moderately well should be left alone. Rather, Whigs
seemed to have an inner compunction to rearrange the constitutional
furniture. So great was their will to initiate change, that even their
vaunted respect for the work of history and ancestors had to be viewed
with suspicion: 'Their maxim has ever been, "Whatever is, is wrong".
They believe that even their own ancestors were fools, more firmly even

than they believe the Gospel. "The wisdom of our ancestors" is their standing jest, in order to reconcile men to their changes and patchwork.' They appeared to be consumed by an 'inordinate thirst for change'.[8] It was something embedded deep in the innards of Whiggery, something visceral. Some men simply never see value in what is, or marvel that, given the vagaries of human nature, anything works at all. For Whigs, change and reform were total arguments in themselves.

As a result, Whiggery was a positive menace in politics. Its periods in office, mercifully brief, were all disturbance and tumult. Tory writers conjured up gothic images of Whigs plotting disorder:

> I think I see a Whig before me at his evening recreation. He has left his wife and children, and gone into his dimly-lighted study. A bad fire of damp coals chokes up the grate, and he is dismissing his servant with a growl, who has just placed a bottle of sour claret on the table. He sits down to read the last Number of the *Edinburgh Review* and his face begins to work with what at first appears twitches of sharp pain, but which you ultimately discover to be Whig smiles; then as he reads some ribald jest at all that is most estimable, most venerated, and most sacred in his country, a shrill laugh breaks from him, something like a shriek.[9]

The Whig itch to change something contributed mightily to their image of being an unEnglish party, in that they seemed to hold in contempt institutions and practices that had served the country well for centuries.

Of course they were assumed to be secret republicans. Their attacks on George III and his sons were not responses to misbehaviour on the part of some kings but preludes to an assault on the institution of monarchy itself. Lord John Russell reputedly confessed on one occasion that 'we must come to American institutions, that will be the end of it'.[10] When the Grey Ministry had finished reordering the composition of the House of Commons in 1832, he and his successors naturally went on to threaten the universities, municipal corporations and the House of Lords. No aspect of the institutional life of the country was safe from their depredations. In 1831, J. W. Croker, a leading Tory intellectual, seriously believed that the Lords would be destroyed in his lifetime. His only consolation in considering this fact was that Earl Grey would be reduced to 'Citizen Grey'.[11] The young Disraeli practically established his career as a polemicist by describing how far the Whig party stood apart from real English concerns:

> The Whigs are an anti-national party. In order to accomplish their object of establishing an oligarchical republic, and of concentrating the government of the state in the hands of a few great families, the Whigs are compelled to declare war against all those great national institutions, the power and influence of which present obstacles to the fulfilment of their purpose. It is these institutions which make us a nation.[12]

At election after election, the point was hammered home. Whigs, the friends of foreigners and sponsors of rebels, could not be trusted with English institutions. They had a preference for change that was genetically determined. For this reason Tories often called Satan the first Whig. He, like them, just had to challenge legitimate authority. For his pains he was quite rightly thrown out of heaven. Just as properly, Whigs were usually denied access to government. The whirlwind of change of the early 1830s was therefore denounced by Tories as satanic:

> Then Satan walk'd forth in the name of Reform,
> To demand an illumination,
> To honour the Whigs – and throughout the land
> Incendiaries ran with the blazing brand,
> For a general conflagration.[13]

To sustain this image, Tory cartoons often showed Whig leaders being ejected from paradise or tumbling from the heavens. In these same productions Whig leaders would find themselves endowed with cloven hooves, horns and long scaly tails. Their very public dismissal of all religion only made the caricature more plausible.

Congenital subversives have no need of principle. Indeed, for Tories, to use the words 'Whig' and 'principle' in the same sentence would have been absurd. Only one word could be allowed the Whigs and that was discreditable. They wished to achieve power on any terms and establish government by a few great families: 'The pseudo-Whigs of modern times incline to neither side, but are guided in all their public actions by one sole desire – that on centring all power of the state in the hands of their own party.'[14] Their aim was to establish oligarchy on the ruins of parliamentarianism. Venice was their model for government. Here, a doge and a handful of families lorded it over the state. Disraeli specifically denounced the Whigs as 'Venetian magnificoes'.[15] It was hard to believe that men of such wealth could be arguing so loudly for reform unless they harboured some secret agenda. Other reformers were therefore cautious about how they handled Whig offers of help. In the election of 1784, the leading proponent of Parliamentary Reform, Christopher Wyvill, voted against Fox, fearing that he wished to turn 'our limited Monarchy into a mere Aristocratical Republic'.[16]

Tories were sure that the evidence for this manipulation of the political system towards oligarchy was overwhelming. As the details of the first Reform Bill emerged, small boroughs controlled by Whig patrons were not among those considered ripe for disfranchisement. The Members for Lord Lansdowne's borough of Calne mysteriously survived and no one questioned the Duke of Marlborough's right to nominate the two Members for Woodstock. In short, the Reform Bill was nothing more than a Whig device to pack the House of Commons with docile supporters. And they treated the House of Lords in the same way. Whenever they were in power, new peerages rained down on their clientele. Tories pointed out that, between 1780 and 1823, only one hundred and fifty-three new peers had taken their seats in the Lords, whereas the Whigs promoted sixty of their friends between 1830 and 1838 alone. Only royal resistance had prevented them from creating even more. Tories considered it the height of impudence for Whigs to claim that the Crown was packing the benches of the Lords and Commons, when they themselves were intent on doing the self-same thing.[17] Lacking all principle save that of winning power, Whigs would ally themselves with any group or faction to achieve this end. Once in power, Whigs began the construction of oligarchy. Their claim to be defenders of parliamentarianism was nothing but a pose.

Tories were equally clear about what Whigs wanted from office. Their much-vaunted pride in family simply translated into providing for their relations at the public expense. No cousin was to be left without a job or a promotion, no aunt without a pension. As a rhymester of 1820 put it:

> And as they onward walk'd, they fix'd their faces,
> On certain fleeting things which they called places,

Pensions, and *patronage* and sinecures,
And whatever else the mind allures.[18]

It was absolutely astonishing to critics like Bulwer Lytton that Whigs should complain about money being diverted into the pockets of members of the Royal Family, when they themselves were masters of the art:

> Compare at this moment, that which your Premier does for his family, with that which his royal master can do for his own. Heavens! What a storm was raised when the king's son obtained the appointment of the Tower! Was he not compelled to resign that petty command – so great was the popular clamour – so silent the ministerial eloquence? But my Lord Grey! what son – what brother – what nephew – what cousin – what remote and unconjectured relative in the Genesis of the Greys, has not fastened his limpet to the rock of the national expenditure.[19]

Oligarchy naturally turned into corruption. Governments not kept regularly under parliamentary scrutiny go that way. But the shameless quality of Whig behaviour in this regard was breathtaking. The Tory Lady Salisbury sarcastically reported a passage from Grey's retirement speech in which he asserted that 'no Minister had ever made himself less liable' to charges of providing for his relations. She then noted that, at the end of the speech, 'his brother, the Bishop of Hereford, cried'.[20]

The exploitation of patronage possibilities was seen to be so central to the Whig system that Tories claimed there was no other policy to be found in Whig government. When Whigs were not accused of wishing to change everything, they were just as often damned for inactivity:

> Your liberal is the worst man of business in the world: it is true, he seems busy, but it is in making speeches, and devising plans and complicated refinements upon what works well enough already, while the more arduous and important concerns of the State are frequently neglected, because they afford no opportunity of display, or for shewing off the advantages of the new and improved system. To make amends, however, for the little he does, he is always ready to talk, or, if you choose, to write an essay.[21]

In sum, Whigs were theorists if they were anything. With no sense of priorities, they dabbled disastrously in the reform of institutions that already worked well, while ignoring issues that really needed attention.

The personification of these twin deficiencies was Lord Melbourne. How such a man could be Prime Minister for seven years was a mystery. Highly intelligent and well read, he found the actual business of government a bore. He saw nothing incongruous in receiving a delegation of Chartists while reclining on a chaise longue wearing a flowered dressing gown. Disraeli accused him of being determined 'to lounge away the glory of an empire'. Melbourne's administration was a parody of a government: 'When I recall to my bewildered memory the perplexing circumstance that William Lamb is Prime Minister of England, it seems to me that I recollect with labour the crowning incident of a grotesque dream.'[22]

When the Whigs went out of office in 1841, after a decade of holding power, Tory images, current for fifty years, had been more than confirmed in their own minds. In those ten years, every institution that defined the national character had been threatened or undermined. Only their incapacity for business slowed them down in the work of demolition:

> They're the dog in the manger, the drone in the hive,
> They're powerless for wrong or for right, sir;
> They can't do the ill they would gladly contrive,
> And won't do the good that they might, sir.[23]

Against all experience, in the same period, they had decided that the French were England's natural allies after all, to be wooed and cosseted in spite of anything Palmerston might say. Randomly destructive and uniformly wrong-headed, they blundered on, each disappointment dissolved in some new subvention from the public purse. Corruption was a speciality. Finally, what made all this infinitely less palatable was the language Whigs employed to cover up their inadequacies. They talked of themselves as principled reformers come to smooth away all dangers to the parliamentary system. In fact, they were an oligarchy, almost carnal in its grasping after the spoils of office. By temperament and outlook they were natural oligarchs who despised most of their compatriots and sought to do them down.

Worst of all, Tories were quite clear that Whigs stupidly encouraged all kinds of extremism. In order to win elections they blithely formed alliances with Radicals. More often than not, they relied on these men's votes to stay in power. Without thinking about the possible consequences, they instructed the people at large about their rights. Periods of agitation and turbulence often preceded the formation of Whig governments and followed their course. Provoking crisis was thought to be a Whig speciality. According to John Wilson Croker, the riots of 1831 answered a 'signal of Lord John Russell's penny trumpet'.[24] Quoting a famous remark by William Wilberforce that, 'when in *opposition*', Whigs 'wished for just so much public calamity as should bring them into power', Croker completed the equation by asserting that, 'on the same principle, the Whigs in *government* wish for just so much popular agitation – to call it by the softest name – as may keep them in office'. They seemed completely oblivious of the fact that to give a mob a sense of its own power was 'a perilous experiment'.[25] When agricultural labourers rioted on Lord Holland's estates in 1830, Tories could not decide whether his surprise or irritation was the most galling. After all, it should have been obvious to anyone that, if men's eyes are opened by education and talk of rights, they would henceforth be able to see.

This was irresponsibility on a grand scale. Examples of its unfortunate consequences abounded, and their obsession with Parliamentary Reform was the most serious of these. For fifty years before 1830, Whigs told poor and rich alike that the cleansing of Parliament would be the beginning of a new and better world in which misery would be unknown:

> With the effrontery of the mountebank, Whiggism had always one object, its fee, and one remedy. Its wonder-working specific was sufficient for every disease: if the calamity came from heaven, or from earth, a failing harvest, or an unlucky expedition, a distemper among cattle, or a panic in the funds, the quack was always ready, panacea in hand; Parliamentary reform was to cure all things.[26]

Of course such promises could not be kept. Whigs were simply raising expectations that they had no chance of fulfilling. They offered a world where 'pauperism was to be no more in the land; prosperity was to be universal, and all men were to be equally wealthy and wise'.[27] For Tories, such language was as inaccurate as Thomas Jefferson's assertion that all men were created equal, when plainly they were not. It was also as dangerous as the action of French Revolutionaries offering their countrymen a Declaration of the Rights of Man. These were dream worlds in which men wandered for a time, before the frustration of their hopes led them to construct guillotines.

Of course, Whigs deluded themselves that they could control the ebb and flow of Radicalism. Their money and intellect would give them the option of directing calls for change whenever they chose to exercise it. They seemed to have no notion that, sooner or later, the democracy would produce its own leaders and articulate its own demands, or that, once this happened, Whiggery itself would be cast aside. The way in which smiling Whigs set out to cut their own throats astounded Tories. As a Liverpool businessman put it: 'The childish way in which Whigs say they can give a large impetus to democratic tendencies and stop them whenever they choose makes me long to whip them like foolish little boys.'[28] Tories viewed the prospect of a democratic future as dark, uncertain and threatening. The Whigs' belief that everything could be changed while their own authority remained intact made that party a danger to themselves and to the country at large.

Tory concerns on this point would have been immeasurably increased had they known just how fragile the Whig influence on Radicals was. True, on the great issues of Parliamentary Reform, religious toleration and the abolition of slavery, the parties marched in step under Whig generalship. But if Whigs expected gratitude for this work it was not forthcoming. For many Radical leaders the real work of reform could only go forward once the Whigs had been brushed aside. J. A. Roebuck frankly informed Alexis de Tocqueville that, 'reform would never go boldly forward until the Whigs had been pushed back among the Tories, since, after all, they were but a modified offshoot of the Tories'.[29] William Hazlitt was even more severe. Tories and Whigs were like 'Tweedledum and Tweedledee', with 'a modern Whig' being nothing 'but the fag-end of a Tory'. In his view, 'the distinction between a great Whig and Tory lord is laughable'. They were two 'coaches, that raise a great dust and spatter one another with mud, but both travel the same road and arrive at the same destination'. Perhaps Whigs were even worse than Tories, because they offered the people friendship only in order to frustrate the full implementation of their just demands. Whigs, Hazlitt concluded, were 'an impertinence'.[30]

Equally, many Radicals resented the Whig claim that by history and instinct they had some special rapport with the people at large. Instead, they only saw insensitive condescension. In a memorable phrase, Hazlitt described Radicals as being treated as low-born suitors to aristocratic virgins. One false move and Whigs had an attack of the vapours. They relapsed 'into convulsions if any low fellow offers to lend a helping hand'.[31] There could be no long-term alliance with people such as these. Radicals should rather look forward to a time when both Tory and Whig had become extinct. As Joseph Parkes colourfully put it: 'The Tories are burked, no resurrection for them. The Whigs will of course raise their bidding with the People's growing power and demands. By concessions spurred on by the People they will be burked soon.'[32] To 'burke' of course was to smother, since the notorious William Burke employed this means of dispatching his victims before selling their bodies for dissection. It promised the Whigs a gruesome end.

With views such as these being publicly expressed, Whig claims to be leading regiments of grateful Radicals and controlling their demands could appear rather hollow. John Stuart Mill observed that Whigs 'were accepted by the Reformers as leaders, because they offered themselves, and because there was nobody else'.[33] This unflattering assessment echoed his father's conviction that, unless pressed very hard and watched very carefully, Whigs would contribute nothing but hot air:

> Vague phrases, though of no service to the people, are admirably suited to the purpose of the Whigs; which is, to please the people, just as far as is consistent with not alarming the aristocracy. A well-turned rhetorical sentence asserting popular supremacy, is expected to be grateful to the ears of many among the people ... But if they require anything tangible – if they ask what are they to get by this boasted sovereignty, it calls them radicals and democrats, who wish for the annihilation of property, and the subversion of the social order.[34]

For much of the 1830s, Whig governments were kept in power by Radical votes in the House of Commons. Even the most sceptical Radical had to think twice about turning out the Whigs, if the only consequence was a return to Tory government. Yet the relationship was always tense and based on mutual suspicion. Radicals regularly threatened to withdraw their support for Whig government. Whigs in turn sometimes offered concessions and sometimes called their bluff. Melbourne and his friends found the business of managing Radicals wearing.

Not surprisingly, Whigs often complained in private about the 'beastly disgusting ungrateful' behaviour of Radicals.[35] Too many of them refused the comfortable role of protégé. And this was unfortunate because Whigs and Radicals needed each other badly. Radicals needed Whig experience and parliamentary influence, while Whigs had for generations admitted their dependence on the electorate at large:

> If the Whigs are not supported by the people, they can have no support; and therefore, if the people are seduced away from them, they must go after them and bring them back; and are no more to be excused for leaving them to be corrupted by demagogues, than they would be for leaving them to be oppressed by tyrants.[36]

The mutual benefits of the alliance should have been obvious to both parties. True, Whigs had developed the bossy habit of taking Radical projects and 'moulding and moderating them to general political Purposes', but this was simply to give them a greater chance of success. When Thomas Erskine redrafted addresses emerging from meetings at Copenhagen House free of charge, Radicals should have been grateful not querulous.[37] Whigs could not understand that their instinctive desire to take over all protest movements might be resented. Radicals felt that they could only stop themselves being smothered by keeping Whigs at arm's length.

Again and again, in the late eighteenth and early nineteenth centuries, Whigs, in a rather pained voice, assured audiences that their interest in change was sincere and intellectually well founded. Sir James Mackintosh, among many others, tried to convince Radicals of this fact:

> A country in which the masses are become powerful by their intelligence and by their wealth, while they are exasperated by exclusion from political rights, never can be in a safe condition. I hold it to be one of the most invariable axioms of legislation, to bind to the constitution, by the participation of legal privilege, all persons who have risen in wealth, – in intelligence, – in any of the legitimate sources of ascendancy. I would do now what our forefathers, though rudely, aimed at doing, by calling into the national councils every rising element in the body politic.[38]

Everything in Whig history seemed to make this truth self-evident, but Radicals could not always agree. Too often the Whigs promised the earth and then gave virtually nothing. The leaders of both parties would speak of the necessity of an alliance, and yet real fellow-feeling proved elusive. So Whigs complained about Radical ingratitude, and Radicals returned the compliment.

In fact, many Radicals felt that they had more than enough proof at hand to demonstrate how limited Whig goodwill actually was. In private conversation and in print, Whigs repeatedly poured cold water on the idea of an extended role for the people in politics. Charles Grey admitted to Horne Tooke that he would choose despotism over anarchy.[39] John Millar 'laughed at the dreams of perfectability, and looked with profound contempt upon all those puerile schemes of equality that threatened to subvert the distinctions of property, or to degrade the natural aristocracy of virtues and talents'.[40] As for the very idea of universal suffrage, Byron dismissed it as the 'Aristocracy of blackguards'.[41] In more measured tones, Lord John Russell thought that the trouble with awarding everyone a vote was that it would give 'the whole power to the highest and the lowest, to money and the multitude'.[42] Classically educated Whigs knew enough of the history of Greece and Rome to understand that democracies undid aristocratic regimes and then undid themselves. But Radicals, appalled that a Reform Bill which increased the electorate by only four per cent could be called 'great', saw only temporising and hypocrisy.

Whig reactions to popular activity proved the point. Whenever the people at large took action on their own account, without the guidance of their social superiors, Whigs reacted defensively. In 1819, Charles Grey and his friends deeply deplored the use of troops against those attending a public meeting at Peterloo, but, having stated that squarely, they went on to criticize Radicals for employing tactics that gave government the excuse to use violence: 'this indeed is one of the most mischievous effects of the proceedings of the Radicals, that by abusing popular privileges they establish precedents for abridging them'.[43] In the same vein, Dr Arnold was for Reform in 1832, but he found the rioting that accompanied the campaign very unattractive. For working people to take to violence was wrong in itself, and it was politically counterproductive. His recommendation for dealing with it again drew on classical sources: 'as for the rioting, the old Roman way of dealing with *that* is always the right one: flog the rank and file, and fling the leaders from the Tarpeian Rock'.[44] Whig governments in the 1830s brought in punitive legislation against 'the social evil' of trade unionism, while their coercive responses to Irish grievances seemed to out-Tory the Tories.[45] In the face of evidence such as this, what right had Whigs to look for or expect Radical support?

The Whigs themselves of course took a different view. For them, violence represented a failure by established authorities to do their duty. As Home Secretary in 1831 and 1832, Lord Melbourne was inundated with appeals from mayors and justices for troops to be sent to their particular areas to deal with disturbances. His reply was always the same, namely that the appearance of soldiers would only make matters worse, and that gentlemen in the area should do what was required. Whigs always believed that violence expressed a failure at the top of society. Mobs themselves had no thoughts or programmes worth mentioning. It was therefore highly irresponsible for Radicals to invoke violence or lend it countenance. It failed to impress Whigs, and it simply frightened Tories into ever more obstinate resilience to all reform. Obviously Radicals would achieve more if they followed parliamentary paths under Whig guidance.

Few Whigs actually came face to face with violence. West End squares and great estates were rarely threatened. When they were confronted by it, their response was resolute. Believing that mobs had no sense of purpose that was not provided from above, there was nothing to fear. In 1830, Thomas Coke was seventy-seven years old. He was also proud to be a justice of the peace for his division of Norfolk. On hearing that agricultural labourers were on the rampage in his jurisdiction, he took the obvious steps:

As Coke approached Burnham, he saw ahead a large gang of ruffianly working men armed with bludgeons and crowbars. He thereupon, turning to his postillions, ordered them to keep at a little distance and not to drive up unless he gave the signal. Next, riding alone up to the rioters, he drew rein in their pathway, and demanded peremptorily how they *dared* disturb the country in such a disgraceful manner? The men, astounded at his sudden appearance and address, hesitated, and were lost. Before they had time to collect their scattered wits, Coke got off his horse, calmly seized two of their ringleaders by the collar, and, all the while rating them soundly for their conduct, signed for his carriage to drive up. So completely was the mob paralysed by this bold move, that they actually suffered four of their party to

be placed in the coach and driven to Walsingham gaol ... This was the last
time Coke was ever on horseback.[46]

Whig *sang froid* in the face of violence merely added to Radical irritation. Men like Melbourne and Coke refused to take mob action
seriously, while, at the same time, they offered reformers of all kinds
assistance just so long as they behaved themselves. It was a form of tute-
lage that many Radicals found hard to bear.

The result of these experiences was to inject into the psychology of
Whiggery a sense of being under siege. To the right and to the left were
parties which regarded them as unEnglish, corrupt and duplicitous.
Tories could not believe that men of such wealth could really be interested in changes that would undermine their own position. So their
motives had to be cynical and opportunistic. Radicals agreed. Indeed the
Tory and Radical critique of Whiggery shared many common themes.
It made it easier for men like Benjamin Disraeli and Bulwer Lytton to
be Radicals in their youth and Tories in old age, without ever coming
near Whiggery. Quite simply, Whigs were a menace to themselves and
to their country. Tories saw them engaged in the childish demolition of
national institutions, and Radicals accused them of playing fast and
loose with vital reforms. On either diagnosis Whigs were dangerous
people.

Whigs heard these views but were largely unmoved by them. Sometimes they complained about not being understood or sufficiently
appreciated. More often than not they averted their eyes. They knew
that they were a minority within the nation and always would be. But
they knew too that history had given them a special mission, that wealth
had given them undeniable standing, and that their comprehension of
the secrets of Progress would lead to an ultimate vindication. Those who
responded to the subterranean rhythms of society could afford to be a
little blasé about events on the surface. Whiggery claimed an inner logic
and coherence that made it possible to dismiss the Tory as unwise and
the Radical as precipitate.

Disappearance

Whiggery is no more. As an adjective, the word Whig has joined the other labels that once adequately defined men's fears and hopes but do so no longer. Their extinction came quickly. For five decades after 1832, the Whigs maintained a distinct, if ever diminishing, presence in British politics. Then, in 1885–86, those who fought under this banner differed so violently about the question of Home Rule for Ireland that schism became unavoidable. Some sought an accommodation with Gladstonian Liberalism, many were gradually absorbed into the Tory party, and a few abandoned politics altogether. Thereafter, for a generation or two, the word Whig was used to describe a temperament rather than a party creed. Today it is rarely employed at all. Dukes of Devonshire have been members of twentieth-century Cabinets. Harold Macmillan spoke of Whigs with affection, but then he was married to a Cavendish. Roy Jenkins would entertain lunch parties with claims to be the only remaining Whig in politics. Harrogate has elected two Whigs to its council in living memory. But collectively these examples add up to very little. They do not even decently mask the fact of Whiggery's sudden demise. Wentworth Woodhouse stands silent and empty, the Earl of Carlisle no longer lives in Castle Howard, and the democracy tours Woburn Abbey on Bank Holiday excursions. Symbolically, in 2004, the great wealth of the Duke of Westminster was overtaken by that of a Russian businessman who owns Chelsea football club.

Tories always predicted that the Whigs would cut their own throats. Without seeming to sense the danger to their own position, the latter blithely encouraged the opening up of politics to new social groups, voicing their rights and championing their causes. They seemed to be unaware that the exclusivity that characterised so much of their social and artistic life could only be maintained by a political system that operated on similarly restrictive lines. To Tories, Whigs strongly resembled those liberal members of the French aristocracy, such as Talleyrand and Lafayette, who, in the early stages of the French Revolution, had thrown in their lot with those advocating great change. Like their French friends, the Whigs were simply consigning themselves to oblivion. They had no one to blame but themselves. A more charitable judgement would suggest that Whigs acted on two assumptions, which, though entirely plausible in their generation, have both been proved by the passage of time to have been disastrously misguided.

First, they took the view that participation in politics would always be a matter of property-holding and education. It was inconceivable that the opinion of the poorest and most ignorant would be given equal standing with that of the richest and most educated. It simply made no sense. The move towards democracy could therefore be welcomed, because it would always be a matter of admitting more and more property-owners into the system. The Reform Bill of 1832 could be called 'a final measure', because, having established clear property qualifications for exercising the franchise, it was merely a question of sitting back and waiting until everyone attained them. All the voters in future democracies, in other words, would be people like them. Astonishingly, this belief had a certain currency. Two more Reform Bills in 1867 and 1884 still produced a situation in which, in national elections, only 60 per cent of men and no women voted. Plural voting based on property-holding and education indeed remained a part of the British system until 1948.

Two world wars destroyed the Whig programme. There was suddenly no possibility of a gentle drift towards democracy, with more and more people becoming electors on Whig terms. The miseries and sufferings of war could only be contained, explained and rewarded by the admission of everyone to a voice in the political process. Equality had to be taken seriously after people had shared the dangers of the trenches or the blitz. Now a voice was a voice, whether its owner had an educated accent or not. The exclusivity and sense of caste that had given Whiggery such self-confidence was not exactly attacked and defeated; rather it simply evaporated. As a result, the democracy which established itself was not the democracy that the Whigs had foreseen. It was rather the democracy that the Tories of 1832 had feared. Watching the embarrassment of the Whigs, Thomas Carlyle had little sympathy. For him, Whig extinction was a consequence of 'democracy, the gradual uprise and rule in all things of roaring million-headed unreflecting, darkly suffering, darkly sinning "Demos", come to call its old superiors to account at its maddest of tribunals'.[1]

The second unfulfilled premiss of Whiggery concerned education. They believed absolutely in its power to transform the bulk of mankind into people like themselves. Give primary and secondary education to all and everyone would then accept Whig values in culture and politics. Since the culture of working people held nothing of substance or interest, it was the job of the educator to offer something better. It was inconceivable to Whigs that, once that offer was made, it should not be universally accepted. Again there was a certain life in this argument. Before the First World War, the libraries of Working Men's Clubs suggest a readership that was eager to have a taste of the high culture that the Whigs represented. There were many Judes, obscure and not so obscure. Charity scholarships and then grammar schools, circulating libraries and the penny lecturer all allowed access to the books and ideas that had once been the prerogative of gentlemen. For Whigs this was how it should be. The terms of the political debate would be unchanged, because newcomers would make the same classical references, and deploy the same normative values, of former elites. For a time all seemed to be going to plan.

But then came developments that no Whig could have foreseen. Working people acquired great purchasing power. A mass media and the principles of the open market gave men the means and opportunity of tapping into it. The democracy was to be flattered and cosseted. Working people were now told that their culture had a validity of its own, and that the accents in which it was expressed were entirely acceptable. They had no need to ape any of the tastes or mannerisms of their former masters. Distinctions based on dress, education or lifestyle melted away. Any kind of exclusivity became suspect. The sense of caste that lay at the heart of Whiggery had become intolerable. It is a fair guess that Lord John Russell would have been unimpressed by the tabloid press and much that passes for popular instruction and education, but he would now be unable to criticise it simply because he was who he was. Deference is no longer automatically accorded on the basis of an inbred or educated superiority. The very word 'elite' has undergone a major redefinition.

Until the 1960s it meant something good and meritocratic. Now it suggests something sinister and exclusive. In short the very vocabulary of democracy militates against Whig propositions. Against the thrust of Whig prophecies, democracies have developed cultural references that owe little or nothing to the past.

So the onset of democracy was more devastating for the Whigs than for the Tories. The latter had always distrusted the people, so, if things turned out badly, no one should be surprised. But Whigs had hoped for so much and all their hopes had been confounded. Tories identified a basic tension in Whig thinking; namely that the party insisted on going along in a current that was carrying them onto the rocks:

> Aristocratic feelings ... in the Whigs ... created an anomaly, and involved, if ever traced fairly up to their source, two contradictory and hostile principles. A proud and exclusive temper, a demeanour somewhat haughty and reserved, a devotion to the interests of particular families, a great deference to the accident of birth, were scarcely reconcilable with that extreme attachment to the spirit and the practice of the democratic parts of our government which they so loudly proclaimed.[2]

In mid nineteenth-century Cabinets, Whigs rubbed shoulders with Radicals and tried hard to find their company congenial. More often than not they were snubbed for their pains. Embarrassments naturally resulted, and Anthony Trollope enjoyed exposing them in his political novels. He described in *Phineas Finn* 'as gallant a phalanx of Whig peers as ever were got together to fight against the instincts of their own order in compliance with the instincts of those below them'.[3] Watching Whigs squirm in the embrace of Radicals consoled Tories a little, but it did nothing to repair the damage they caused.

It became increasingly uncomfortable, even ridiculous, for great aristocrats to pursue the logic of progress as far as mass politics. Whigs were increasingly forced into employing double standards. They argued for progress in public and for caution in private:

> Enter the cabinets or drawing-rooms of these grandees, you hear nothing but the most haughty and conservative language. The necessity of taking steps to arrest the evil, the imminent danger to the holders of property from the progress of radicalism, the need for a cordial union among all the better classes to resist the spoliation springing from their inferiors, is universally talked of ... But listen to these Whig aristocrats on the hustings, or at public

meetings; you will hear nothing but the necessity of yielding to public opinion, the growing importance and vast intelligence of the people, the
irresistible weight of their voice, the paramount sway which they have
acquired in the Constitution.[4]

By the late nineteenth century there was no language that could carry
the Whigs through all situations. Rather, different vocabularies had to
be used to suit the context. The public and private faces of Whiggery
wore different masks. Their true feelings were disturbingly at odds with
their historical and intellectual self-identification.

So Whiggery died unmourned by either Tory or Radical. The first
thought that they had received their just desserts and the latter showed
no gratitude. Yet Britain's march towards full democracy was slower
than in any other European country and more moderated. The journey
was accomplished without violence, and even with a certain good
humour. Industrialization and its political consequences was a managed
affair. Sharp class confrontations were avoided. All these things meant
that, when full democracy finally came, it was a peaceable and stable
phenomenon. Few countries on the Continent could claim as much. It
must be the Whigs' ultimate defence that matters turned out as successfully as they did because their own efforts were unsparing. To have
a section of the ruling elite that was happy to accommodate and moderate change, rather than merely resisting it, was invaluable.
Back-slapping between Whigs and Radicals in London taverns meant
that reform never became a simple matter of class. Some people in
Parliament were always encouraging to the reformer. If only France or
Germany had known Whiggery, European history might have been very
different. To be a Whig was to have a temperament that placed a pre-
mium on keeping up and being sensible. Toryism was accused of being
deficient on both counts. Allegedly the late Duke of Devonshire and a
companion were once caught in a downpour in St James's. It was
suggested that the two men might take refuge in the Carlton Club, the
Tory Holy of Holies. The Duke declined the offer, indicating that a
wetting was to be preferred to Tory company. A little further on he
found shelter in Brooks's.

Notes

Notes to Chapter 1: The Whigs

1. *Anti-Jacobin*, 26 March 1798, 157.
2. L. Jennings, *The Correspondence and Diaries of the Late Rt Hon. John Wilson Croker* (London, 1884), i, 401.
3. *Fraser's Magazine*, i, 4, February 1830.
4. Princess Lieven to A. Benckendorff, 20 May 1827, L. Robinson, *Letters of Dorothea, Princess Lieven* (London, 1902), 98.
5. Palmerston's personal sense of distance from the Whig tradition was marked. For example, in the following quotation, the use of 'their' instead of 'our' speaks volumes: 'The Whigs wish Althorp to lead as likely to keep their party from straying', Palmerston to Mrs Sulivan, 18 November 1830, *The Letters of the Third Viscount Palmerston to Laurence and Elizabeth Sulivan*, Camden Series, xxiii.
6. A. Bell, *Sydney Smith* (Oxford, 1980), 153.
7. *Blackwood's Magazine*, vii, 138, February 1833.
8. *Fraser's Magazine*, v, 455, May 1832.
9. J. W. Croker to H. Brougham, 14 March 1839, Jennings, *The Correspondence and Diaries of the Late Rt Hon. John Wilson Croker*, ii, 353.
10. Lord Minto to Lord Lansdowne, 6 January 1830, K. Bourne, *Palmerston: The Early Years* (London, 1982), 305.
11. *National Review*, October 1855, 262.
12. A. de Tocqueville, *Journeys to England and Ireland* (London, 1958), 85.
13. *Blackwood's Magazine*, xvi, 544, November 1824.
14. R. Watson to Lord Rockingham, 25 November 1775, R. Watson, *Anecdotes of the Life of Richard Watson, Bishop of Llandaff* (London, 1817), 57.
15. Lady C. Colville, *A Crowded Life* (London, 1963), 33.
16. This attribution could be challenged. Murray was actually Byron's publisher.
17. G. W. E. Russell, *A Pocketful of Sixpences* (London, 1908), 95.

18. E. B. Lytton, *England and the English* (London, 1833), i, 71–72.
19. *Etonian* (London, 1822), i, 12.
20. A. M. W. Stirling, *Coke of Norfolk and his Friends* (London, 1912), 266–67.
21. Ibid., 203.

Notes to Chapter 2: Circles of Acquaintance

1. M. D. George, *Hogarth to Cruikshank: Social Change in Graphic Satire* (London, 1967), 163; L. Marchand, *Byron's Letters and Journals* (London, 1973–81), v, 14; E. Burke, *Remarks on the Policy of the Allies* (London, 1887), 423.
2. J. Austen, *Persuasion*, chap. 18.
3. G. Bosville to J. Spencer [1770], A. M. W. Stirling, *Annals of a Yorkshire House* (London, 1911), i, 318–19.
4. J. Hale, *The Italian Journal of Samuel Rogers* (London, 1856), 28.
5. Sir J. Walsh, *Chapters of Contemporary History* (London, 1836), 59.
6. *Fraser's Magazine*, ix, 15, January 1834.
7. Duchess of Devonshire to Lady E. Foster, 6 January 1784, Lord Bessborough, *Georgiana, Duchess of Devonshire* (London, 1955), 69.
8. D. Wilkinson, *The Duke of Portland* (London, 2003), 26.
9. Figures such as these would translate into the expenditure of many millions today.
10. Anon., *Government without Whigs* (London, 1830), 15.
11. Duke of Bedford to Lord J. Russell, 27 March 1811, R. Russell, *The Early Correspondence of Lord John Russell* (London 1913), 155–56.
12. A. Trollope, *Phineas Finn*, chap. 2.
13. Lord William Russell to Lady Russell, July 1839, G. Blakiston, *Lord William Russell and his Wife* (London, 1972), 423.
14. Anon., *Letter on the Late Duke of Bedford* (London, 1839), 3. There were, however, eighty-five enamels in the Windsor series and only twenty-five in Bedford's.
15. A. Trollope, *Doctor Thorne*, chap. 15.
16. Lady Bessborough to G. Leveson Gower, 29 January 1796, Lady Granville, *Lord Granville Leveson Gower* (London, 1916), i, 119–20.
17. Ibid., 14 February and 22 June 1805, ibid., ii, 7 and 17.
18. Anon., *Political Miscellanies* (London, 1787).
19. Lady Spencer to T. W. Coke, 8 January 1827, A. M. W. Stirling, *Coke of Norfolk and his Friends* (London, 1912), 501.
20. Anon., *Political Miscellanies*, 56–57.
21. Ibid., 79.

22. E. B. Lytton to A. de Tocqueville, 1833, George, *Hogarth to Cruikshank*, 169.
23. V. Foster, *The Two Duchesses* (London, 1972), 201.
24. J. Gore, *Charles Gore* (London, 1932), 47–48.
25. Stirling, *Annals of a Yorkshire House*, ii, 322.
26. O. Smith, *The Politics of Language, 1791–1819* (Oxford, 1984), 14.
27. G. Leveson Gower, *Hary-O: The Letters of Lady Harriet Cavendish* (London, 1940), 12; F. Leveson Gower, *The Letters of Harriet, Countess Granville* (London, 1894), i, 112 and 248; Lady Airlie, *In Whig Society* (London, 1921), 30.
28. Lady Bessborough to Granville Leveson Gower, 21 September [1805], Lady Granville, *Lord Granville Leveson Gower*, ii, 114.
29. Duchess of Devonshire to Lady Melbourne, 1802, Lady Airlie, *In Whig Society*, 29.
30. Lord W. Russell to Lady Russell, 1816, Blakiston, *Lord William Russell and his Wife*, 12.
31. Diary of the Second Marchioness of Salisbury, 15 November 1833, C. Oman, *The Gascoigne Heiress* (London, 1968), 95.
32. Stirling, *Coke of Norfolk and his Friends*, 586–87.
33. R. Watson, *Anecdotes of the Life of Richard Watson, Bishop of Llandaff* (London, 1817), 49.
34. *Blackwood's Magazine*, April 1819, v, 89.
35. *Fraser's Magazine*, January 1838, x, 51.
36. F. Haskell, *Rediscoveries in Art* (Oxford, 1976), 23.
37. Flaxman was not greatly interested in politics himself, but it may not be a coincidence that the only political works in his library were volumes of the Whig holy book, the *Edinburgh Review*. Anon., *Catalogue of the Small but Valuable Library of Books of John Flaxman* (London, 1828).
38. Haskell, *Rediscoveries in Art*, 15.
39. Marchand, *Byron's Letters and Journals*, viii, 200.
40. *Edinburgh Review*, vii, 2, October 1805.
41. S. Smith to Lady Dacre, 1837, G. Lyster, *A Family Chronicle* (London, 1908), 144.
42. *Edinburgh Review*, ii, 174–76, April 1803.
43. E. Burke, *Reflections on the Revolution in France* (London, 1790), 60.
44. J. Clive, *Scotch Reviewers* (London, 1957), 162.
45. *Edinburgh Review*, i, 66, October 1802. See also J. Greig, *Francis Jeffrey of the Edinburgh Review* (London, 1848), 180.
46. L. G. Mitchell, *Holland House* (London, 1980), 193.
47. Ibid., 180.
48. Greig, *Francis Jeffrey of the Edinburgh Review*, 225.

49. *Edinburgh Review*, xii, 35, April 1808.

50. Lady Bessborough to Granville Leveson Gower, 27 August [1808], Lady Granville, *Lord Granville Leveson Gower*, ii, 323.

51. Lord R. S. Gower, *Records and Reminiscences* (London, 1903), 126.

52. Leigh Hunt to Lady Holland, 2 August ?, Biltmore MSS, xiv, 78; see also T. Campbell to Lord Holland, 20 April 1837, ibid., xiv, 75.

53. W. E. S. Thomas, *The Philosophic Radicals* (Oxford, 1979), 53.

54. *Quarterly Review*, lv, 477, February 1836.

55. *Blackwood's Magazine*, xxiv, 101, July 1828.

56. *Quarterly Review*, lv, 477, February 1836.

57. *Westminster Review*, xlvii, 293, July 1836.

58. Burke, *Reflections on the Revolution in France*, 139–40.

59. G. W. E. Russell, *Prime Ministers and Some Others* (London, 1918), 123.

60. Hale, *The Italian Journal of Samuel Rogers*, 40–41.

61. Marchand, *Byron's Letters and Journals*, ix, 57.

62. A. Bell, *Sydney Smith* (Oxford, 1980), 133.

63. Sir J. Mackintosh, *The Miscellaneous Works of the Rt Hon. Sir James Mackintosh* (London, 1846), i, 456.

64. H. Mackey, *Wit and Whiggery* (Washington, 1979), 180.

65. A. Trollope, *Barchester Towers*, chap. 33.

66. D. Coleridge, *The Poems of William Mackworth Praed* (London, 1864), ii, 204–6.

Notes to Chapter 3: London

1. A. Bell, *Sydney Smith* (Oxford, 1980), 199 and 188.

2. G. Rudé, *Hanoverian London* (London, 1971), chap. 1.

3. N. McKendrick, *The Birth of a Consumer Society* (London, 1982), 21–22. By contrast only 2.5 per cent of the French population lived in Paris in 1750.

4. R. Quinault, *Historical Journal*, xxii, 1979, 148.

5. Ibid.

6. S. Foote, *The Lyar*, Act I, Scene I.

7. T. Cooper, *A Reply to Mr Burke's Invective against Mr Cooper and Mr Watt* (Manchester, 1792), 22.

8. P. G. Bouché, *Sexuality in Eighteenth Century Britain* (Manchester, 1982), 134.

9. H. Stokes, *The Devonshire House Circle* (London, 1917), 94–96.

10. Lord Bessborough, *Georgiana, Duchess of Devonshire* (London, 1955), 56.

11. Lady Brownlow, *The Eve of Victorianism* (London, 1940), 91.

12. W. Combe, *Letter to Her Grace the Duchess of Devonshire* (London, 1777), 10.

13. Ibid., 7. See also W. Combe, *The First Day of April: or The Temple of Folly* (London, 1777).

14. C. Pigott, *The Jockey Club* (London, 1792); *The Female Jockey Club* (London, 1794); *The Whig Club* (London, 1794).

15. L. G. Mitchell, *Charles James Fox* (Oxford, 1991), 94–95.

16. Lady Bessborough to G. Leveson Gower, 1 November 1811, Lady Granville, *Lord Granville Leveson Gower* (London, 1916), ii, 412.

17. Lady H. Granville to Lady G. Morpeth, 1810, F. Leveson Gower, *The Letters of Harriet, Countess Granville* (London, 1894), i, 1–3.

18. L. Stone, *The Family, Sex and Marriage* (London, 1977), 271.

19. Lord J. Russell, *Essays and Sketches of Life and Character* (London, 1820), 189.

20. Lady H. Granville to Lady C. Morpeth, 6 October 1811, F. Leveson Gower, *The Letters of Harriet, Countess Granville*, i, 22.

21. Ibid., 26 October 1805, G. Leveson Gower, *Hary-O: The Letters of Lady Harriet Cavendish* (London, 1940), 130.

22. Ibid., June 1817, F. Leveson Gower, *The Letters of Harriet, Countess Granville*, i, 101.

23. M. Cox, *The Life and Times of the Twelfth Earl of Derby* (London, 1974), 136–37.

24. R. Payne Knight, *The Progress of Civil Society* (London, 1796), 55.

25. F. Reynolds, *Life*, Act I, Scene I.

26. C. J. Fox, *A History of the Early Part of the Reign of James the Second* (London, 1808), 64–65.

27. Duchess of Devonshire to Lady Spencer, February 1786, Lord Bessborough, *Georgiana, Duchess of Devonshire*, 103–4.

28. Cox, *The Life and Times of the Twelfth Earl of Derby*, 56.

29. Duchess of Devonshire to Lady Spencer, 9 September 1790, Lord Bessborough, *Georgiana, Duchess of Devonshire*, 175.

30. Diary of Lord Hatherton, 17 March 1836, Staffordshire Record Office, Hatherton MSS, D260/M/F/5/26/12.

31. D. Howell-Jones, *Lord Melbourne's Susan* (Woking, 1928), 8.

32. Stokes, *The Devonshire House Circle*, 135–36.

33. Wellington's brother asserted that 'Arthur's Father was Mr – Gardener', Hatherton Journal, March 1837, Staffordshire Record Office, Hatherton MSS, D260/M/F/26/13.

34. J. J. Sack, *The Grenvillites* (Chicago, 1979), 127.

35. L. Marchand, *Byron's Letters and Journals* (London, 1973–81), ix, 14–15.

36. Ibid., iv 327.
37. J. Jekyll to Mr Jekyll, 30 April 1775, A. Bourke, *Correspondence of Mr Joseph Jekyll* (London, 1894), 28.
38. J. Miller, *The Caricatures of James Gillray* (London, 1824–6), 50–51.
39. Lady Stafford to Granville Leveson Gower, 22 February 1791, Lady Granville, *Lord Granville Leveson Gower*, i, 33.
40. Lord John Russell, *Memorials and Correspondence of Charles James Fox* (London, 1853–57), i, 91–92.
41. Lord Bessborough, *Georgiana, Duchess of Devonshire*, 24.
42. ? to Lady C. Bury [1815], A. F. Stewart, *The Diary of a Lady-in-Waiting* (London, 1908), i, 410–11.
43. G. Reid, *A Descriptive Catalogue of the Works of George Cruikshank* (London, 1871), i, 2, and M. D. George, *Hogarth to Cruikshank: Social Change in Graphic Satire* (London, 1967), 61.
44. Stone, *The Family, Sex and Marriage*, 529.
45. Lady Bessborough to Granville Leveson Gower, June [1805], Lady Granville, *Lord Granville Leveson Gower*, ii, 79.
46. Lady Stafford to Granville Leveson Gower, 7 August 1788, ibid., i, 10.
47. Ibid.
48. Anon., *Political Miscellanies* (London, 1787), 98.
49. N. McKendrick, *The Birth of a Consumer Society* (London, 1982), 39.
50. Ibid., 55.
51. Ibid., 82, and C. W. Cunningham, *Handbook of Costume in the Eighteenth Century* (London, 1957), 360.
52. *Fraser's Magazine*, xv, 235, February 1837.
53. Ibid.
54. S. Smith, *Works* (Philadelphia, 1853), 289.
55. For example, Anon., *An Answer to the Jockey Club* (London, n.d.).
56. *Dictionary of National Biography*, vol. xvi.
57. Diary of John Hobhouse, 2 March 1839, BL, Add. MS 56560, fol. 87.
58. Anon., *Political Miscellanies*, 21.
59. Mitchell, *Charles James Fox*, 175.

Notes to Chapter 4: The Country

1. J. Jekyll to Lady G. Stanley, 16 December 1824, A. Bourke, *The Correspondence of Joseph Jekyll* (London, 1894), 147.
2. A. F. Stewart, *The Diary of a Lady-in-Waiting* (London, 1908), ii, 24.
3. Journal of Lady Sophia Fitzgerald, 1 March 1793, G. Campbell, *Edward and Pamela Fitzgerald* (London, 1904), 83.

4. J. Jekyll to Lady G. Stanley, 5 November 1823, Bourke, *The Correspondence of Joseph Jekyll*, 134–35.

5. W. H. Lyttelton to Lady S. Lyttelton, 15 September 1820, H. Wyndham, *Correspondence of Sarah Spencer, Lady Lyttelton* (London, 1912), 226.

6. A. Bell, *Sydney Smith* (Oxford, 1980), 122.

7. S. Smith to Lady Holland, 7 January 1813 and 4 October 1823, P. Nowell Smith, *The Letters of Sydney Smith* (Oxford, 1953), i, 232.

8. A. M. W. Stirling, *Coke of Norfolk and his Friends* (London, 1912), 350 and 398.

9. W. Hooker, *Letter on the Late Duke of Bedford* (Glasgow, 1840), 3.

10. Lord J. Russell to Duke of Bedford, 19 November 1809, Ann Arbor, Russell MSS, Box 1.

11. R. Stewart, *Henry Brougham* (London, 1985), 29.

12. Lady H. Granville to Duchess of Devonshire, 4 January 1813, F. Leveson Gower, *The Letters of Harriet, Countess Granville* (London, 1894), i, 46.

13. L. G. Mitchell, *Holland House* (London, 1980), 173.

14. P. Munsche, *Gentlemen and Poachers* (London, 1981), 86.

15. C. Oman, *The Gascoigne Heiress* (London, 1968), 68.

16. Lady H. Granville to Duchess of Devonshire, 2 February 1822, F. Leveson Gower, *The Letters of Harriet, Countess Granville*, i, 223.

17. Lady Sarah Lyttelton to Lord Robert Spencer, 28 December 1808, H. Wyndham, *Correspondence of Sarah Spencer, Lady Lyttelton* (London, 1912), 56.

18. Lady H. Granville to Lady G. Morpeth, August 1810, and Lady H. Granville to Duchess of Devonshire, 30 July 1820, F. Leveson Gower, *The Letters of Harriet, Countess Granville*, i, 7, 153.

19. Lady H. Granville to Lady G. Morpeth, October 1811, ibid., i, 26–27.

20. Lady Bessborough to Granville Leveson Gower [May 1797], Lady Granville, *Lord Granville Leveson Gower* (London, 1916), i, 148.

21. *A Trip to Scarborough*, Act II, Scene I.

22. J. Tobin, *The Faro Table*, Act I, Scene II.

23. R. B. Sheridan, *The School for Scandal*, Epilogue.

24. F. Reynolds, *Cheap Living*, Act I, Scene I.

25. J. Burgoyne, *The Dramatic and Poetical Works of the Late Lieutenant-General J. Burgoyne* (London, 1808), 21.

26. H. Stokes, *The Devonshire House Circle* (London, 1917), 115–16.

27. Lady H. Granville to Lady G. Morpeth, F. Leveson Gower, *The Letters of Harriet, Countess Granville*, i, 23.

28. Lady Bessborough to Granville Leveson Gower [1794], Lady Granville, *Lord Granville Leveson Gower*, i, 98–99.

29. Bell, *Sydney Smith*, 150.

30. L. Stone, *An Open Elite* (Oxford, 1984), 253 and 255.
31. Lady H. Granville to Lady G. Morpeth, n.d., G. Leveson Gower, *Hary-O: The Letters of Lady Harriet Cavendish* (London, 1940), 132–33.
32. Ibid., 23 October 1811, F. Leveson Gower, *The Letters of Harriet, Countess Granville*, i, 25.
33. Ibid., 9 October 1820, ibid., i, 186.
34. C. Hussey, *The Picturesque* (London, 1927), 177–78.
35. Ibid., 183.
36. Ibid., 81.
37. J. Jekyll, *Interesting to Country Gentlemen*, 25 October 1822, Castle Howard MSS. I am most grateful to Dr A. I. M. Duncan for this reference.
38. Lord Holland to Lord J. Russell, 20 January 1829, R. Russell, *The Early Correspondence of Lord John Russell* (London, 1913), i, 829. Lord J. Russell, *An Essay on the History of the English Government and Constitution* (London, 1823), 219–20.
39. A. M. W. Stirling, *Coke of Norfolk and his Friends* (London, 1912), 498.
40. F. Reynolds, *Life*, Act I, Scene I.
41. T. L. Peacock, *Crotchet Castle*, chap. 5.
42. R. Stewart, *Henry Brouhgam* (London, 1985), 172.
43. Bourke, *Correspondence of Mr Joseph Jekyll*, 222.
44. Sir J. Walsh, *Chapters of Contemporary History* (London, 1836), 66–67.
45. Lady Brownlow, *The Eve of Victorianism* (London, 1940), 101.
46. Diary of Lady Salisbury, 11 June 1834, Oman, *The Gascoigne Heiress*, 118.
47. *Fraser's Magazine*, iii, 649, June 1831.
48. Stirling, *Coke of Norfolk and his Friends*, 479.
49. Ibid., 98.
50. Lord Clifton to J. Bligh, 22 September 1830, Lady Cust, *Edward, Fifth Earl of Darnley and Emma Parnell, his Wife* (Leeds, 1913), 349.
51. D. Coleridge, *The Poems of William Mackworth Praed* (London, 1864), ii, 29.

Notes to Chapter 5: The French Connection

1. J. Stonard to R. Heber, 19 August 1794, Bodleian Library, Oxford, Heber MSS, Eng. Lett. d 211, fol. 11.
2. Lavater's *Essay on Physiognomy* (1789) asserted that 'that there is a national physiognomy, as well as a national character, is undeniable'. The French had 'no traits so bold as the English'. The list of subscribers guaranteeing the book's publication includes the names of Charles Fox, the Duke of

Bedford, the Earl of Carlisle, Charles Grey, Lord Holland, Sheridan and many other prominent Whigs.

3. *Quarterly Review*, xxxviii, 158–59, July 1828.

4. J. Boswell, *The Life of Dr Samuel Johnson* (Oxford, 1965), 215.

5. J. E. Austen-Leigh, *A Memoir of Jane Austen* (London, 1870), 14–15.

6. S. Smith to Lord J. Russell, 4 December 1826, R. Russell, *The Early Correspondence of Lord John Russell* (London, 1913), i, 254.

7. Sir J. Mackintosh, *The Miscellaneous Works of Sir James Mackintosh* (London, 1846), iii, 11.

8. Lord J. Russell, *Memoirs of the Affairs of Europe from the Peace of Utrecht* (London, 1824), 161–62.

9. W. Bagehot, *National Review*, October 1855, 265.

10. J. Prest, *Lord John Russell* (London, 1972), 18.

11. *Fraser's Magazine*, vi, 651, December 1832.

12. Talleyrand to Holland [Feb. 1830], BL, Add. MS 51635, fol. 13; Lady Holland to J. Allen, February 1826, ibid., MS 52172, fos 93–94.

13. *Edinburgh Review*, clxxi, 76, January 1847.

14. *Queen Victoria's Journal*, 5 May 1839, Royal Archives, Windsor.

15. Madame de Flahault to Lady Holland, 21 August 1816, BL, Add. MS 51718, fol. 36.

16. Journal of Lady E. Foster, October 1803, D. Stuart, *Dearest Bess* (London, 1955), 113–14.

17. D. Stroud, *Henry Holland: His Life and Architecture* (London, 1966), 61–76.

18. Lady Bessborough to Granville Leveson Gower, 9 October [1805], Lady Granville, *Lord Granville Leveson Gower* (London, 1916), ii, 120.

19. S. Whitbread, *Southill* (London, 1951), 6, and C. Hussey, *English Country Houses: Mid Georgian, 1760–1800* (London, 1955), 212–13.

20. W. Henley, *The Collected Works of William Hazlitt* (London, 1902), 801.

21. Lady H. Granville to Lady G. Morpeth, 7 November 1836, Lady Granville, *Lord Granville Leveson Gower*, ii, 216.

22. *Fraser's Magazine*, ix, 351, March 1834.

23. *Moniteur*, 2 April 1792.

24. *Edinburgh Review*, vi, 138, April 1805.

25. P. W. Clayden, *The Early Life of Samuel Rogers* (London, 1887), 117.

26. R. Watson to Duke of Grafton, 12 October 1791, R. Watson, *Anecdotes of the Life of Richard Watson, Bishop of Llandaff* (London, 1817), 256.

27. *Edinburgh Review*, cx, 559, July 1833.

28. Sir James Mackintosh, *Reasons against the French War of 1793*, in *The Miscellaneous Works of Sir James Mackintosh*, iii, 175.

29. B. Vaughan, *Miscellaneous Observations*, n.d., Bodleian Library, Oxford, Bowood MS 2026, fos 62–63.

30. Lord Holland to Caroline Fox, 30 May 1974, BL, Add. MS 51732, fos 15–16.

31. Sir James Mackintosh, *Reasons against the French War of 1793*, in *The Miscellaneous Works of Sir James Mackintosh*, iii, 182.

32. Lord Holland to Caroline Fox, 19 November 1799, BL, Add. MS 51735, fol. 153; Lady Bessborough to Granville Leveson Gower, 11 October [1807], Lady Granville, *Lord Granville Leveson Gower*, ii, 291; C. J. Fox to D. O'Bryen [16 July 1800], Biltmore, North Carolina, Holland House MSS, ix, 44.

33. *Edinburgh Review*, lx, 303, September 1818.

34. Lord Holland to Caroline Fox, 10 November 1814, BL, Add. MS 51740, fol. 24.

35. H. Bunbury to H. S. Fox, 30 August [1815], Bodleian Library, Oxford, MS Eng. Lett. c 234, fol. 48.

36. Lord Holland to Caroline Fox [April 1814], BL, Add. MS 51939, fos 222–23.

37. Lord Holland's Memorandum [1815], BL, Add. MS 51528, fol. 77.

38. Lord Holland to Caroline Fox [April 1814], BL, Add. MS 51939, fos 222–23.

39. P. W. Clayden, *Samuel Rogers and his Contemporaries* (London, 1889), iii, 187–88.

40. BL, Add. MS 51528, fol. 83, and 51529, fol. 7; Pauline Borghese to Lady Holland, 23 April 1817, BL, Add. MS 51527, fol. 14; Lady Holland to Charles Grey, 25 September 1815, Durham University Library, Grey MSS, box 33.

41. Lady Harriet Cavendish to Lady Spencer, 7 November 1808, G. Leveson Gower, *Hary-O: The Letters of Lady Harriet Cavendish* (London, 1940), 285–86.

42. Lord R. S. Gower, *Records and Reminiscences* (London, 1903), 129.

43. *Parliamentary History*, lxviii, 664–65.

44. Comte de Flahault to J. Allen [18 February 1822] and 16 January 1825, BL, Add. MS 52182, fos 191 and 201; Comte de Flahault to Lady Holland [20 October 1824] and [1825], Add. MS 51717, fos 131 and 141; Madame de Flahault to Lord Grey, 30 July [1830], Durham University Library, Grey MSS, GRE/B15/2/16.

45. Madame de Flahault to Lady Grey, 16 March [1820], Paris, Archives Nationales, 565 AP, 27 4; Madame de Flahault to Lord Grey, 19 November 1819, Durham University Library, Grey MSS, GRE/B15/2/6.

46. Lord Holland to H. E. Holland, 13 August 1830, BL, Add. MS 51751, fol. 30.

47. Ibid., and Duke of Sussex to Lord Holland, July 1830, BL, Add. MS 51524, fol. 24.

48. Comte de Chabot to Lord Holland, 16 August 1830, BL, Add. MS 51524, fol. 199.
49. *Edinburgh Review*, cxii, 491, January 1833.
50. Ibid., 483.
51. Madame de Flahault to Lady Grey, 19 November 1830 and [July 1834], Paris, Archives Nationales, 565 AP 27 7 and 24; Madame de Flahault to Lady Grey, 27 April [1835], BL, Add. MS 51721, fol. 75.
52. Louis Philippe to Lord Holland, 28 May 1837, BL, Add. MS 51524, fos 210–12.
53. G. D. Elliott, *Journal of My Life during the French Revolution* (London, 1859), 146.
54. T. Grenville to Lord Grenville, 15 December 1815, H.M.C. 30 Fortescue X, 408–9.
55. C. Nicoullard, *Memoirs of the Countess de Boigne* (London, 1908), i, 244.
56. *Edinburgh Review*, clxxx, 557, April 1849.
57. *Edinburgh Review*, clxxx, 567–68, April 1849; ibid., i, 11, October 1802.
58. Lafayette to Lord Holland, 20 January 1832, BL, Add. MS 51635, fol. 197.
59. Sébastiani to Mme Adelaide, 3 October 1837, Paris, Bibliothèque Nationale, n.s.f. 12219, fol. 17.
60. Lord Holland to Lord Grey, April 1831, Durham University Library, Grey MSS, box 34.
61. Diary of Lord Clarendon, 5 October 1840, Sir H. Maxwell, *The Life and Letters of the Fourth Earl of Clarendon* (London, 1913), i 211.
62. A. Kriegel, *The Holland House Diaries* (London, 1977), 90.
63. Instructions données à M. Guizot, 19 February 1840, Paris, Quai d'Orsay, Angleterre 654, fos 173–74; Guizot to Thiers, 10 March 1840, Paris, Bibliothèque Nationale, n.a.f. 20610, fol. 25; Guizot to Thiers, 3 April 1840, Paris, Bibliothèque Nationale, 20610, fol. 42.
64. Lord Holland to Lord Grey, 18. January 1834, Durham University Library, Grey MSS, box 34.

Notes to Chapter 6: The March of Mind

1. *Edinburgh Review*, iii, 158, April 1803.
2. I am most grateful to W. E. S. Thomas of Christ Church, Oxford, for allowing me to use his transcript of Melbourne's memoirs.
3. K. Bourne, *Palmerston: The Early Years* (London, 1982), 372.
4. *National Review*, i, 5, 1855.
5. W. Henley, *The Collected Works of William Hazlitt* (London, 1902), iv, 314–15.

6. S. Rogers to Lord Holland, n.d., Biltmore MSS, Holland papers, vol. viii.

7. J. Hale, *The Italian Journal of Samuel Rogers* (London, 1856), 40.

8. G. W. E. Russell, *Prime Ministers and Some Others* (London, 1918), 123–24.

9. Diary of Sir C. Blagden, 31 August and 2 September 1792, *Notes and Records of the Royal Society*, viii, 1951, 76 and 80.

10. Lady Bessborough to Granville Leveson Gower [1798], Countess Granville, *Lord Granville Leveson Gower* (London, 1916), i, 197.

11. Dr S. Parr to T. W. Coke, 1805, A. M. W. Stirling, *Coke of Norfolk and his Friends* (London, 1912), 313–14.

12. W. C. Lehmann, *John Millar of Glasgow*, (London, 1960), 176–78.

13. *Edinburgh Review*, lxxxii, 284–85, January 1824.

14. Sir J. Mackintosh, *The Miscellaneous Works of Sir James Mackintosh* (London, 1846), i, 565.

15. Lord J. Russell, *Essay on the History of the English Government and Constitution* (London, 1823), preface.

16. R. P. Knight, *The Progress of Civil Society* (London, 1796).

17. Sir J. Mackintosh, *Discourse on the Study of the Law of Nations and Nature* (London, 1799), 42.

18. *Edinburgh Review*, lxi, 287, July 1835.

19. Ibid.

20. D. Forbes, 'Scientific Whiggism: Adam Smith and John Millar', *Cambridge Journal*, vii, 2, 1954, 647.

21. Lord Ilchester, *The Journal of Henry Edward Fox, Fourth Lord Holland* (London, 1923), 89.

22. Mackintosh, *The Miscellaneous Works of the Rt Hon. Sir James Mackintosh*, iii, 67.

23. Ibid., i, 572–73.

24. *National Review*, i, 268, 1855.

25. *Etonian* (London, 1822), i, 10.

26. Lady Salisbury's diary, 22 December 1833, C. Oman, *The Gascoigne Heiress* (London, 1968), 100.

27. S. Smith, *Sermon on the Duties of the Queen*, S. Smith, *Works* (Philadelphia, 1853), 422.

28. *Edinburgh Review*, xi, 69, October 1807.

29. Lord Melbourne to Lady Caroline Lamb, 11 April 1827, Lord Bessborough, *Lady Bessborough and her Family Circle* (London, 1940), 288.

30. Smith, *Works*, 87.

31. Lady Stafford to Granville Leveson Gower, 28 October 1791, Lady Granville, *Lord Granville Leveson Gower*, i, 35.

Notes to Chapter 7: Unbelievers

1. G. Lyster, *A Family Chronicle* (London, 1908), 203.

2. J. A. Froude, *Reminiscences of Thomas Carlyle* (New York, 1881), 180.

3. Ibid., 187.

4. *National Review*, i, 283, October 1855.

5. *Blackwood's Magazine*, xxiii, 480, April 1828.

6. Lord Holland to Lord Ebrington, 6 October 1837, Devonshire Record Office, Fortescue MSS, 1262 M/FC92.

7. M. Warner, *Queen Victoria's Sketch Book* (London, 1879), 82.

8. R. Watson, *Anecdotes of the Life of Richard Watson, Bishop of Llandaff* (London, 1817), 39.

9. F. Leveson Gower, *Bygone Years* (London, 1905), 35.

10. Lord Glenbervie's diary, 1 October 1810, F. Bickley, *The Diaries of Sylvester Douglas, Lord Glenbervie* (London, 1928), ii, 71–72.

11. S. Smith to Lady Grey, October 1839, P. Nowell Smith, *The Letters of Sydney Smith* (Oxford, 1953), ii, 693.

12. J. Allen to Lady Holland, 15 September 1822, BL, Add. MS 52175, fol. 101.

13. Lady Bessborough to Granville Leveson Gower, 1 December [1807], Lady Granville, *Lord Granville Leveson Gower* (London, 1916), ii, 313–14.

14. Duke of Bedford to Lord William Russell, 29 December 1828, G. Blakiston, *Lord William Russell and his Wife* (London, 1972), 177.

15. Lady E. Cust, *Edward, Fifth Earl of Darnley, and Emma Parnell, his Wife* (Leeds, 1913), 261.

16. Lady H. Granville to Lady G. Morpeth, 15 January 1803, G. Leveson Gower, *Hary-O: The Letters of Lady Harriet Cavendish* (London, 1940), 44.

17. Lady C. Lamb to Lady Bessborough, 24 April 1808, Lord Bessborough, *Lady Bessborough and her Family Circle* (London, 1940), 168.

18. Lady Holland to H. Fox, 11 March 1834, Lord Ilchester, *Elizabeth, Lady Holland to her Son* (London, 1946), 146.

19. L. Marchand, *Byron's Letters and Journals* (London 1973–81), ix, 45.

20. R. Watson, *A Letter to the Members of the House of Commons by a Christian Whig* (London, 1772), 24.

21. *Edinburgh Review*, xii, 180, April 1808.

22. R. Watson, *Anecdotes of the Life of Richard Watson*, 198.

23. Lord J. Russell, *The Causes of the French Revolution* (London, 1832), 129.

24. *Edinburgh Review*, i, 12, October 1802.

25. Lord John Russell, *Memoirs of the Affairs of Europe from the Peace of Utrecht* (London, 1824), ii, 588.

26. R. P. Knight, *The Progress of Civil Society* (London, 1796), 92–93.

27. *Edinburgh Review*, x, 254, July 1807.

28. Ibid., viii, 41, January 1807.

29. Ibid., iv, 318, July 1804.

30. Lady Bessbrough to Lord Duncannon, n.d., Lord Bessborough, *Lady Bessborough and her Family Circle*, 104–5.

31. H. Fox to J. Allen, 26 February 1825, BL, Add. MS 52175, fol. 117.

32. G. Bridgeman to Lady Bradford, 7 December 1813, G. Bridgeman, *Letters from Portugal, Spain, Sicily and Malta* (London, 1875), 165.

33. *Edinburgh Review*, xii, 88, April 1808.

34. W. C. Lehmann, *John Millar of Glasgow* (London, 1960), 364.

35. H. Mackey, *Wit and Whiggery* (Washington, 1979), 134.

36. Lord John Russell, *Memoirs of the Affairs of Europe from the Peace of Utrecht*, 569, 568, 576.

37. J. Jekyll to Lady Gertrude Stanley, 31 August 1833, A. Bourke, *The Correspondence of Mr Joseph Jekyll* (London 1894), 315–16.

38. *Fraser's Magazine*, xv, 668, May 1837.

39. H. Mackey, *Wit and Wiggery*, 264.

40. *Edinburgh Review*, xi, 341, January 1808.

41. Lady Darnley to J. Bligh, 10 March 1829, Lady Cust, *Edward, Fifth Earl of Darnley, and Emma Parnell, his Wife*, 314.

42. *The Letters of Peter Plymley*, 1807; S. Smith, *Works* (Philadelphia, 1853), 461.

43. Ibid., 478.

44. R. Watson, *An Address to the People of Great Britain* (London, 1798), 17–18.

45. Sir H. Parnell to Lord Holland, n.d., Biltmore, Holland House MSS, vii.

46. Lord Holland to ?, n.d., Biltmore, Holland House MSS, vi, 9.

Notes to Chapter 8: History and Politics

1. Lord J. Russell, *Memoirs of the Affairs of Europe from the Peace of Utrecht* (London, 1824), 63.

2. *Edinburgh Review*, xxxix, 291, January 1824.

3. H. Reeve, *A Journal of the Reigns of King George IV, King William IV, and Queen Victoria by the Late Charles Greville* (London, 1888), i, 159.

4. E. Burke, *Reflections on the Revolution in France* (London, 1790), 48–49.

5. *Edinburgh Review*, lxxxv, 234, November 1825.

6. *The Times*, 17 August 1835.

7. Sir J. Mackintosh, *The Miscellaneous Works of the Rt Hon. Sir James Mackintosh* (London, 1846), iii, 272.

8. *Edinburgh Review*, lxvii, 35, August 1820.

9. I. Leveson Gower, *The Face without a Frown* (London, 1944), 174–75.

10. Lord J. Russell, *A Letter to the Rt Hon. Lord Holland*, (London, 1831), 40–41.

11. R. Watson, *The Principles of the Revolution Vindicated* (Cambridge, 1776), 19–20.

12. *Declaration of the Whig Club* (London, 1795), 2.

13. Lord J. Russell, *An Essay on the History of the English Government and Constitution* (London, 1823), 180–81.

14. W. C. Lehmann, *John Millar of Glasgow* (London, 1960), 352.

15. C. Parker, *The Life and Letters of Sir James Graham* (London, 1907), i, 82.

16. Mme de Staël, *De l'Angleterre* (London, 1907), 58. 'Just how many political contacts there are between the middle classes and men of the highest rank.'

17. *Edinburgh Review*, lxxxvii, 158, June 1826. 'The English aristocracy honours humanity: it is an imposing phenomenon in the world and in history: associating itself at all times with the interests of the people, it has never ceased from demanding rights for the humblest citizen as courageously as it defended its own.'

18. J. Allen to Sir C. Vaughan [1809], All Souls College, Oxford, Vaughan MSS, c 9/3.

19. J. Mayer, *Journeys to England and Ireland* (London, 1958), 80.

20. Lady Spencer to T. W. Coke, 8 January 1827, A. M. W. Stirling, *Coke of Norfolk and his Friends* (London, 1912), 501.

21. *Parliamentary Debates*, xvii, 557, 13 June 1810.

22. S. Smith, *Works* (Philadelphia, 1853), 475.

23. *Edinburgh Review*, xiii, 275, July 1808.

24. Lord J. Russell, *Essay on the History of the English Government and Constitution*, 126–27.

25. Lady C. Strutt to Lady L. Fitzgerald, 2 January 1793, G. Campbell, *Edward and Pamela Fitzgerald* (London, 1904), 80.

26. Duchess of Devonshire to Lord Hartington, 3 January 1806, Lord Bessborough, *Georgiana, Duchess of Devonshire* (London, 1955), 276.

27. Duchess of Devonshire to Lady Spencer, 8 February 1784, ibid., 75.

28. Bodleian Library, Oxford, MS Eng. Misc. e 888, fol. 13.

29. Lord Albemarle, *Memoirs of the Marquess of Rockingham and his Contemporaries* (London, 1852), i, 2–3.

30. M. D. George, *English Political Caricature* (Oxford, 1959), i, 121.

31. Commonplace book of Lady Charlotte and Lady Mary Campbell, Huntingdon Library, MS 33691.

32. Stirling, *Coke of Norfolk and his Friends*, 529.

33. Reeve, *A Journal of the Reigns of King George IV, King William IV, and Queen Victoria by the Late Charles Greville*, i, 204.

34. Ibid., i, 372.

35. Ibid., i, 364.

36. A. D. Kriegel, *The Holland House Diaries* (London, 1977), 349.

37. *The Atlas*, 28 April 1855.

38. Lord J. Russell, *The Life of William Lord Russell* (London, 1820), 63–64, and *An Essay on the History of the English Government and Constitution*, 178–90.

39. *Edinburgh Review*, xvii, 258, February 1811.

40. *A Letter by Thomas Erskine to 'An Elector of Westminster'*, Anon., *The Pamphleteer*, xv, 332.

41. Lord J. Russell, *An Essay on the History of the English Government and Constitution*, 95.

42. Lord J. Russell, *Memoirs of Europe from the Peace of Utrecht*, 21.

43. Anon., *A Short Defence of the Whigs* (London, 1819), 7.

44. Ibid., 4.

45. Lord J. Russell, *An Essay on the History of the English Government and Constitution*, 107.

46. Lord Albemarle, *Memoirs of the Marquess of Rockingham and his Contemporaries*, ii, 92–93.

47. Lord J. Russell, *The Life of William, Lord Russell*, 175.

48. W. Bagehot, *National Review*, i, 264, October 1855.

49. Bodleian Library, Oxford, MS Eng. Misc. e 888, fol. 40.

50. P. W. Clayden, *Samuel Rogers and his Contemporaries* (London, 1889), ii, 101.

51. *Etonian* (1822), i, 9.

52. H. Mackey, *Wit and Whiggery* (Washington, 1979), 25.

53. Lord J. Russell, *The Life of William, Lord Russell*, preface.

54. G. W. E. Russell, *Prime Ministers and Some Others* (London, 1918), 15.

55. Ibid., 21.

56. Sir T. Martin, *Life of Lord Lyndhurst* (London, 1883), 142.

57. *Edinburgh Review*, xv, 504, July 1810.

58. Lady Bessborough to Granville Leveson Gower [1797], Lady Granville, *Lord Granville Leveson Gower* (London, 1916), i 179.

59. *Fraser's Magazine*, iii, 496, May 1831.

Notes to Chapter 9: Enemies

1. *Blackwood's Magazine*, xvi, 543, November 1824.

2. Ibid., 540.

3. *Anti-Jacobin*, xxii, 170, 9 April 1798.

4. *Blackwood's Magazine*, xx, 356, August 1826.

5. *Fraser's Magazine*, v, 587, June 1830.

6. C. Osborne, *W. H. Auden* (London, 1985), 292.

7. T. L. Peacock, *Crotchet Castle*, chap. 17.

8. Anon., *The Dirges of the Whig Administration* (London, 1841), 47–48, 60.

9. *Blackwood's Magazine*, xxiii, 178–79, February 1828.

10. Diary of the Marchioness of Salisbury, 8 March 1835, C. Oman, *The Gascoigne Heiress* (London, 1968), 156.

11. *Quarterly Review*, xlvi, 275, November 1831.

12. B. Disraeli, *Vindication of the English Constitution* (London, 1835), 181.

13. *Blackwood's Magazine*, xxxi, 595, April 1832.

14. Anon., *Government without Whigs* (London, 1830), 5.

15. Disraeli, *Vindication of the English Constitution*, 168.

16. C. Wyvill, *Political Tracts and Papers* (York, 1779–1804), iv, 352.

17. *Blackwood's Magazine*, xliv, 351, September 1838 and *Quarterly Review*, lix, 212, October 1837.

18. Anon., *The Man in the Moon* (London, 1820), 120.

19. E. B. Lytton, *England and the English* (London, 1833), 160–61.

20. Diary of the Marchioness of Salisbury, 9 July 1834, Oman, *The Gascoigne Heiress*, 128.

21. *Blackwood's Magazine*, xxiv, 97, July 1828.

22. B. Disraeli, *The Runnymede Letters* (London, 1936), letter 1.

23. *Blackwood's Magazine*, xli, 783, June 1837.

24. *Quarterly Review*, xlvi, 300, November 1831.

25. Ibid., lxv, 284–85, December 1839.

26. *Blackwood's Magazine*, l, 84, July 1841.

27. Ibid.

28. W. C. Roscoe to R. H. Hutton, 1859, W. C. Roscoe, *Poems and Essays* (London, 1860), lxiv.

29. J. Mayer, *Journeys to England and Ireland* (London, 1958), 84.

30. Preface to *Political Essays*, W. Henley, *The Collected Works of William Hazlitt* (London, 1902), iii, 43–46.

31. Anon., *On the Jealousy and Spleen of Party*, ibid., vii, 376.

32. J. Parkes to F. Place, 2 January 1836, W. E. S. Thomas, *The Philosophic Radicals* (Oxford, 1979), 289.

33. J. Leonhard, *Jahrbuch zur Liberalismus Forschung*, xxxvii, January 1996.

34. *Westminster Review*, i, 506, April 1824.

35. Lord Holland to Caroline Fox, April 1807, BL, Add. MS 51738, fol. 31.

36. *Edinburgh Review*, xiii, 514, January 1810.

37. J. Jekyll to Lord Lansdowne, 14 November 1796, Bodleian Library, Oxford, MS Film 2004, fol. 76.

38. Speech on the Reform Bill, July 1831, Sir J. Mackintosh, *The Miscellaneous Works of Sir James Mackintosh* (London, 1846), iii, 549.

39. P. W. Clayden, *Samuel Rogers and his Contemporaries* (London, 1889), i, 81.

40. *Edinburgh Review*, iii, 158, October 1803.

41. L. Marchand, *Byron's Letters and Journals* (London, 1973–81), viii, 107.

42. Lord J. Russell, *An Essay on the History of the English Government and Constitution* (London, 1823), 338–39.

43. C. Grey to Lord Brougham, 25 August 1819, H. Brougham, *The Life and Times of Lord Brougham* (Edinburgh, 1871), ii, 342–43.

44. J. Chandos, *Boys Together* (Oxford, 1984), 259.

45. C. Grey to Lord Brougham, 4 January 1834, Brougham, *The Life and Times of Lord Brougham*, iii, 322–33.

46. A. M. W. Stirling, *Coke of Norfolk and His Friends* (London, 1912), 539.

Notes to Chapter 10: Disappearance

1. J. A. Froude, *Reminiscences of Thomas Carlyle* (New York, 1881), 199.

2. Sir J. Walsh, *On the Present Balance of Parties in the State* (London, 1832), 10.

3. A. Trollope, *Phineas Finn*, chap. 10.

4. *Blackwood's Magazine*, xxxv, 79, January 1834.

Bibliography

JOURNALS

Anti-Jacobin
Blackwood's Magazine
Edinburgh Review
Etonian
Gazeteer
National Review
New Monthly Magazine
Quarterly Review
Westminster Review

BOOKS

Lady Airlie, *In Whig Society* (London, 1921).

Lord Albemarle, *Fifty Years of My Life* (London, 1876).

—, *Memoirs of the Marquess of Rockingham and his Contemporaries* (London, 1852).

Anon., *A Collection of Odes, Songs and Epigrams against the Whigs alias the Buff and Blue* (London, 1790).

—, *A Letter to the Rt Hon. Thomas Connolly* (Dublin, 1789).

—, *An Answer to the Jockey Club* (London, n.d.).

—, *A Short Defence of the Whigs* (London, 1819).

—, *A Short Essay on Whigs and Tories* (London, 1791).

—, *A Short History of the Opposition* (London, 1779).

—, *Catalogue of the Small but Valuable Library of Books of John Flaxman* (London, 1828).

—, *Chatsworth: A Poem* (London, n.d.).

—, *Confessions of a Whig* (London, 1828).

—, *Criticisms on the Rolliad* (London, 1784).

—, *Declaration of the Whig Club* (London, 1795).

—, *Government without Whigs* (London, 1830).

—, *Lettre d'un Whig anglais à un membre de l'Assemblée Nationale de France* (London, 1791).

—, *Marbles, Bronzes and Fragments at Chatsworth* (London, 1838).

—, *Opposition Mornings* (London, 1779).

—, *Political Miscellanies* (London, 1787).

—, *Reply to Lord Erskine by an Elector of Westminster* (London, 1819).

—, *The Antigallican Club* (London, 1803).

—, *The Dirges of the Whig Administration* (London, 1841).

—, *The Fruits of Whig Legislation* (London, 1837).

—, *The Whigs' Last Shift* (Coventry, 1780).

—, *What Have the Whigs Done?* (London, 1835).

E. Anson, *Mary Hamilton* (London, 1925).

E. Ashley, *The Life and Correspondence of Lord Palmerston* (London, 1879).

J. Austen, *Persuasion.*

J. E. Austen-Leigh, *A Memoir of Jane Austen* (London, 1870).

A. Bell, *Sydney Smith* (Oxford, 1980).

G. Berkeley, *My Life and Recollections* (London, 1865).

Lord Bessborough, *Georgiana, Duchess of Devonshire* (London, 1955).

—, *Lady Bessborough and her Family Circle* (London, 1940).

F. Bickley, *The Diaries of Sylvester Douglas, Lord Glenbervie* (London, 1928).

G. Blakiston, *Lord William Russell and his Wife* (London, 1972).

J. Boswell, *The Life of Dr Samuel Johnson* (Oxford, 1965).

P. G. Bouché, *Sexuality in Eighteenth-Century Britain* (Manchester, 1982).

A. Bourke, *The Correspondence of Mr Joseph Jekyll* (London, 1894).

K. Bourne, *Palmerston: The Early Years* (London, 1982).

G. Bridgeman, *Letters from Portugal, Spain, Sicily and Malta* (London, 1875).

C. L. Brightwell, *Memorials of the Life of Amelia Opie* (London, 1854).

I. Brock, *The Patriots and the Whigs* (London, 1810).

H. Brougham, *The Life and Times of Lord Brougham* (Edinburgh, 1871).

Lady Brownlow, *The Eve of Victorianism* (London, 1940).

Sir F. Burdett, *Speech of Sir F. Burdett at the Crown and Anchor Inn* (London, 1810).

J. Burgoyne, *The Dramatic and Poetical Works of the Late Lieutenant-General J. Burgoyne* (London, 1808).

E. Burke, *A Letter to a Member of the National Assembly* (London, 1791).

—, *Reflections on the Revolution in France* (London, 1790).

Lord Byron, *English Bards and Scotch Reviewers* (London, 1809).

G. Campbell, *Edward and Pamela Fitzgerald* (London, 1904).

G. Cannon, *The Letters of Sir William Jones* (London, 1970).

J. Chandos, *Boys Together* (Oxford, 1984).

P. W. Clayden, *Samuel Rogers and His Contemporaries* (London, 1889).

—, *The Early Life of Samuel Rogers* (London, 1887).

J. Clive, *Scotch Reviewers* (London, 1957).

Lord Cloncurry, *Personal Recollections of the Life and Times of Lord Cloncurry* (Dublin, 1849).

D. Coleridge, *The Poems of William Mackworth Praed* (London, 1864).

Lady C. Colville, *A Crowded Life* (London, 1963).

W. Combe, *A Second Letter to Her Grace the Duchess of Devonshire* (London, 1777).

—, *Letter to Her Grace the Duchess of Devonshire* (London, 1777).

—, *The Diabolid* (London, 1777).

—, *The First of April, or The Triumph of Folly* (London, 1777).

J. Cookson, *The Friends of Peace* (Cambridge, 1982).

T. Cooper, *A Reply to Mr Burke's Invective against Mr Cooper and Mr Watt* (Manchester, 1792).

M. Cox, *The Life and Times of the Twelfth Earl of Derby* (London, 1974).

C. W. Cunnington, *Handbook of Costume in the Eighteenth Century* (London, 1957).

Lady Cust, *Edward, Fifth Earl of Darnley, and Emma Parnell, his Wife* (Leeds, 1913).

J. Dawson, *The Stranger's Guide to Holkham* (Burnham, 1817).

B. Denvir, *The Eighteenth Century: Art, Design and Society* (London, 1983).

W. Derry, *Dr Parr* (Oxford, 1966).

B. Disraeli, *England and France: or A Cure for the Ministerial Gallomania* (London, 1832).

—, *The Crisis Examined* (London, 1834).

—, *The Runnymede Letters* (London, 1936).

—, *The Wit and Wisdom of Benjamin Disraeli* (London, 1881).

—, *Vindication of the English Constitution* (London, 1835).

A. Dyce, *Reminiscences and Table Talk of Samuel Rogers* (London, 1903).

C. Edmonds, *The Poetry of the Anti-Jacobin* (London, 1890).

H. Eeles, *Brooks's, 1764–1964* (London, 1964).

G. D. Elliott, *Journal of My Life during the French Revolution* (London, 1859).

R. Emerson, *English Traits* (Boston, 1856).

T. Erskine, *A Letter by Thomas, Lord Erskine to an Elector of Westminster* (London, 1822).

—, *A Short Defence of the Whigs* (London, 1819).

S. Foote, *Dramatic Works* (London, 1809).

V. Foster, *The Two Duchesses* (London, 1972).

C. J. Fox, *A History of the Early Part of the Reign of James the Second* (London, 1808).

J. A. Froude, *Reminiscences of Thomas Carlyle* (New York, 1881).

M. D. George, *English Political Caricature* (Oxford, 1959).

—, *Hogarth to Cruikshank: Social Change in Graphic Satire* (London, 1967).

M. Glover, *The Life of Sir Robert Wilson* (Oxford, 1977).

J. Gore, *Charles Gore* (London, 1932).

F. Leveson Gower, *Bygone Years* (London, 1905).

—, *The Letters of Harriet, Countess Granville* (London, 1894).

G. Leveson Gower, *Hary-O: The Letters of Lady Harriet Cavendish* (London, 1940).

I. Leveson Gower, *The Face without a Frown* (London, 1944).

Lord R. S. Gower, *Records and Reminiscences* (London, 1903).

Lady Granville, *Lord Granville Leveson Gower* (London, 1916).

J. Grego, *Rowlandson the Caricaturist* (London, 1880).

J. Greig, *Francis Jeffrey of the Edinburgh Review* (London, 1848).

J. Hale, *The Italian Journal of Samuel Rogers* (London, 1856).

N. Hampson, *The Perfidy of Albion* (London, 1998).

F. Haskell, *Rediscoveries in Art* (Oxford, 1976).

W. Henley, *The Collected Works of William Hazlitt* (London, 1902).

E. Herries, *Memoir of J. C. Herries* (London, 1880).

Lord Holland, *Foreign Reminiscences* (London, 1850).

—, *Memoirs of the Whig Party during My Time* (London, 1852–54).

W. Hooker, *Letter on the Late Duke of Bedford* (Glasgow, 1840).

D. Howell-Jones, *Lord Melbourne's Susan* (Woking, 1928).

C. Hussey, *English Country Houses: Mid Georgian, 1760–1800* (London, 1955).

—, *The Picturesque* (London, 1927).

Lord Ilchester, *Elizabeth, Lady Holland to her Son* (London, 1946).

—, *The Journal of Henry Edward Fox, Fourth Lord Holland* (London, 1923).

R. Jenkyns, *The Victorians and Ancient Greece* (London, 1980).

L. Jennings, *The Correspondence and Diaries of the Late Rt Hon. John Wilson Croker* (London, 1884).

R. Ketton-Cremer, *Felbrigg* (London, 1962).

G. Keynes, *Selected Essays of William Hazlitt* (London, 1946).

R. P. Knight, *The Progress of Civil Society* (London, 1796).

A. D. Kriegel, *The Holland House Diaries* (London, 1977).

G. Le Strange, *Correspondence of Princess Lieven and Earl Grey* (London, 1890).

W. C. Lehmann, *John Millar of Glasgow* (London, 1960).

G. Lyster, *A Family Chronicle* (London, 1908).

E. B. Lytton, *A Letter to a Cabinet Minister* (London, 1834).

—, *England and the English* (London, 1833).

—, *Speeches of Edward, Lord Lytton* (Edinburgh, 1874).

N. McKendrick, *The Birth of a Consumer Society* (London, 1982).

T. McLean, *A Key to the Political Sketches of H.B.* (London, 1839).

—, *Cartoons by H.B.* (London, 1823–46).

T. B. Macaulay, *Napoleon and the Restoration of the Bourbons* (London, 1977).

H. Mackey, *Wit and Whiggery* (Washington, 1979).

Sir J. Mackintosh, *A Discourse on the Study of the Law of Nature and Nations* (London, 1799).

—, *The Miscellaneous Works of the Rt Hon. Sir James Mackintosh* (London, 1846).

L. Marchand, *Byron's Letters and Journals* (London, 1973–81).

Sir T. Martin, *Life of Lord Lyndhurst* (London, 1883).

Sir H. Maxwell, *The Life and Letters of the Fourth Earl of Clarendon* (London, 1913).

J. Mayer, *Journeys to England and Ireland* (London, 1958).

J. Miller, *The Caricatures of James Gillray* (London, 1824–26).

L. G. Mitchell, *Charles James Fox* (Oxford, 1991).

—, *Holland House* (London, 1980).

P. Munsche, *Gentlemen and Poachers* (London, 1981).

C. Nicoullard, *Memoirs of the Comtesse de Boigne* (London, 1908).

P. Nowell Smith, *The Letters of Sydney Smith* (Oxford, 1953).

D. O'Bryen, *Utrum Horum?* (London, 1796).

C. Oman, *The Gascoigne Heiress* (London, 1968).

A. Oppé, *Thomas Rowlandson: His Drawings and Writings* (London, 1923).

Lord Palmerston, *The New Whig Guide* (London, 1819).

—, *The Letters of the Third Viscount Palmerston to Laurence and Elizabeh Sulivan*, Camden Series (1972).

V. de Pange, *The Unpublished Correspondence of Mme de Staël and the Duke of Wellington* (London, 1965).

C. Parker, *The Life and Letters of Sir James Graham* (London, 1907).

T. L. Peacock, *Crotchet Castle.*

—, *Headlong Hall.*

—, *Nightmare Abbey.*

C. Pigott, *The Female Jockey Club* (London, 1794).

—, *The Jockey Club* (London, 1792).

—, *The Whig Club* (London, 1794).

J. Prest, *Lord John Russell* (London, 1972).

J. Ranby, *An Inquiry into the Supposed Increase of the Influence of the Crown* (London, 1811).

H. Reeve, *A Journal of the Reigns of King George IV, King William IV and Queen Victoria by the Late Charles Greville* (London, 1888).

G. Reid, *A Descriptive Catalogue of the Works of George Cruikshank* (London, 1871).

F. Reynolds, *Life.*

E. Rickwood, *Radical Squibs and Loyal Ripostes* (Bath, 1971).

L. Robinson, *Letters of Dorothea, Princess Lieven* (London, 1902).

S. Rogers, *Human Life* (London, 1819).

W. C. Roscoe, *Poems and Essays* (London, 1860).

R. Rush, *A Residence at the Court of London* (London, 1987).

G. W. E. Russell, *A Pocketful of Sixpences* (London, 1908).

—, *Prime Ministers and Some Others* (London, 1918).

—, *Social Silhouettes* (London, 1906).

Lord J. Russell, *A Letter to the Rt Hon. Lord Holland* (London, 1831).

—, *An Essay on the History of the English Government and Constitution* (London, 1823).

—, *Don Carlos or Persecution* (London, 1822).

—, *Essays and Sketches of Life and Character* (London, 1820).

—, *Memoirs of the Affairs of Europe from the Peace of Utrecht* (London, 1824).

—, *Memorials and Correspondence of Charles James Fox* (London, 1853–57).

—, *The Causes of the French Revolution* (London, 1832).

—, *The Establishment of the Turks in Europe* (London, 1828).

—, *The Life of William Lord Russell* (London, 1820).

R. Russell, *The Early Correspondence of Lord John Russell* (London 1913).

J. J. Sack, *The Grenvillites* (Chicago, 1979).

H. Sandwith, *A Reply to Lord John Russell's Animadversions on Wesleyan Methodism* (London, 1830).

R. Sharp, *Letters and Essays* (London, 1834).

R. B. Sheridan, *Address to the People* (London, 1803).

—, *The Rivals.*

—, *The School for Scandal.*

A. Smith, *Catalogue of the Sculpture at Woburn Abbey* (London, 1900).

O. Smith, *The Politics of Language, 1791–1819* (Oxford, 1984).

S. Smith, *Works* (Philadelphia, 1853).

T. Spence, *Pig's Meat* (London, 1793).

Mme de Staël, *De l'Angleterre* (London, 1907).

A. F. Steuart, *The Diary of a Lady-in-Waiting* (London, 1908).

R. Stewart, *Henry Brougham* (London, 1985).

A. M. W. Stirling, *Annals of a Yorkshire House* (London, 1911).

—, *Coke of Norfolk and his Friends* (London, 1912).

H. Stokes, *The Devonshire House Circle* (London, 1917).

L. Stone, *An Open Elite* (Oxford, 1984).

—, *The Family, Sex and Marriage* (London, 1977).

Lady Strafford, *Leaves from the Diary of Henry Greville* (London, 1905).

D. Stroud, *Henry Holland: His Life and Architecture* (London, 1966).

D. Stuart, *Dearest Bess* (London, 1955).

W. E. S. Thomas, *The Philosophic Radicals* (Oxford, 1979).

F. Thompson, *A History of Chatsworth* (London, 1949).

A. Trollope, *Barchester Towers*.

—, *Doctor Thorne*.

—, *Phineas Finn*.

Sir J. Walsh, *On the Present Balance of Parties in the State* (London, 1832).

—, *Chapters of Contemporary History* (London, 1836).

M. Warner, *Queen Victoria's Sketch Book* (London, 1979).

R. Watson, *A Letter to the Members of the House of Commons by a Christian Whig* (London, 1772).

—, *An Address to the People of Great Britain* (London, 1798).

—, *Anecdotes of the Life of Richard Watson, Bishop of Llandaff* (London, 1817).

—, *The Priciples of the Revolution Vindicated* (Cambridge, 1776).

S. Whitbread, *Southill* (London, 1951).

D. Wilkinson, *The Duke of Portland* (London, 2003).

T. Wright, *The Works of James Gillray the Caricaturist* (London, 1873).

H. Wyndham, *Correspondence of Sarah Spencer, Lady Lyttelton* (London, 1912).

C. Wyvill, *Political Tracts and Papers* (York, 1779–1804).

Index